Feed Your Child Right

Lynn Alexander
and Yeong Boon Yee

Marshall Cavendish
Editions

This publication contains the opinions and ideas of the authors and is based on their own expertise, knwledge and experiences. The information in this book serves as a general guide. The authors and publisher have used their best efforts in preparing this book and disclaim liability arising directly from the use and application of this book.

Photos by Elements by the Box

© First published 1990 Times Editions Private Limited
© Reprinted 2002 Times Media Private Limited
© Revised 2007 Marshall Cavendish International (Asia) Private Limited

This new edition © 2014

Published by Marshall Cavendish Editions
An imprint of Marshall Cavendish International

Other Marshall Cavendish Offices:
Marshall Cavendish Corporation. 99 White Plains Road, Tarrytown NY 10591-9001, USA • Marshall Cavendish International (Thailand) Co Ltd. 253 Asoke, 12th Flr, Sukhumvit 21 Road, Klongtoey Nua, Wattana, Bangkok 10110, Thailand • Marshall Cavendish (Malaysia) Sdn Bhd, Times Subang, Lot 46, Subang Hi-Tech Industrial Park, Batu Tiga, 40000 Shah Alam, Selangor Darul Ehsan, Malaysia

Marshall Cavendish is a trademark of Times Publishing Limited

National Library Board, Singapore Cataloguing-in-Publication Data

Alexander, Lynn, 1960-
Feed your child right : the first complete nutrition guide for Asian parents / Lynn Alexander and Yeong Boon Yee. – Singapore : Marshall Cavendish Editions, (2014)
pages cm
ISBN : 978-981-4516-24-2 (paperback)

1. Children – Nutrition – Asia. 2. Infants – Nutrition – Asia. 3. Child rearing – Asia. 4. Cooking – Asia.
I. Title. II. Yeong, Boon Yee.

RJ206
649.3 -- dc23   OCN 856031409

Printed in Singapore by Star Standard Industries Pte Ltd

To our husbands
Lionel and Yue Chai

and our children
Jana, Jamie, Jessica, Li Yuin and Li Wei

Contents

Foreword

Many adult diseases often have their origin in infancy and early childhood. It is well known that the quality of foetal growth and development has a profound effect on health during adulthood. Similarly, adult eating habits are often nurtured in early childhood. Healthy eating habits should be cultivated from young so that the child will grow up to be a healthy adult who enjoys eating and knows how and what to eat.

Advances in science and technology have altered many aspects of our life. Over the last four to five decades, there has been marked improvement in social and economic development in this part of the world. Infant mortality has greatly reduced, while malnutrition is becoming less common with more abundant food supply for the population. Most of the childhood infections can either be prevented by vaccination and the provision of clean water, or treated with appropriate antibiotics. However, accompanied by the unprecedented improvement in health care and economic status, there is a parallel increase in disorders such as obesity and diabetes, not just in adults but also in childhood. Changes in our lifestyle such as sedentary living and unhealthy eating habits are likely contributing factors to the increase in these disorders.

It is timely that Lynn Alexander and Yeong Boon Yee have written a book which is devoted solely to the young parents in this part of the world. The book was first published in 1990, has undergone repeated reprinting in the last 16 years, and is still in great demand. Now, they have updated the book for its revised edition.

Although this book is written in very simple language, it is full of scientific knowledge and practical advice. It covers various aspects of infant and childhood nutrition and nutrition during pregnancy. It summarises the current recommendations for infant feeding and is valuable throughout early childhood.

The chapter on breastfeeding is particularly important as it provides a wealth of information on the topic. It is filled with down-to-earth advice on how to succeed in the process and have an enjoyable experience.

It is a joy to read the book as it is written by two extremely experienced practicing nutritionists cum dietitians. Their advice is based on sound scientific knowledge and personal practical experience. Many young mothers will find the practical tips on food preparation and various recipes useful in helping their children enjoy nutritious meals and snacks.

I congratulate the authors for a well-written book which should prove to be the "must read" book for young parents and parents-to-be. Healthy children with good eating habits will grow up to be healthy adults.

Quak Seng Hock
MBBS, MMED (Paediatrics), MD, FRCP (Glasg),
FRCPCH, FCPCHS, FCPCHM
Assoc Professor and Head, Department of Paediatrics
Yong Look Lin School of Medicine
National University of Singapore
Chief and Senior Consultant
Department of Paediatrics, Children's Medical Institute
National University Hospital, Singapore

Introduction

The revised edition of this book comes at a most opportune time when good nutrition and dietary practice has gained widespread recognition as a key component of a healthy lifestyle, and as a determinant factor in the prevention of certain diseases, starting from infancy.

Many books on infant feeding are available but these cater mainly to Western parents. We therefore felt there was a need to provide Asian parents with relevant advice on how to ensure a healthy nutritional start in life for their children based on local food habits and customs. With the advances in nutritional science over the past decade, we have updated certain information in the book to reflect new knowledge and revised recommendations established by the international health authorities.

Our mothers, and their mothers before them, no doubt fed their children on exactly the same nutritious foods that we are recommending in this book. Unfortunately, modern lifestyle often necessitates living at a distance from our extended family, so not all of us are able to have our mothers close at hand when we are bringing up our children. It can be daunting to be faced with the responsibility of feeding your child with no one to reassure you that you are doing it right. That is why we hope this book will be useful to young mums coping on their own.

In this book, we have introduced the basic principles of nutrition, and since nutrition for your child starts in the womb, we have devoted the second chapter to your nutrition during pregnancy. Breastfeeding has been covered extensively in order to provide you with all the information you need to make this a successful and rewarding experience.

We have then followed your child's introduction to complementary foods, providing step-by-step charts to guide you through the weaning process. Toddlers often become finicky eaters and parents understandably worry if their child eats poorly. We have addressed this issue in Chapter 5.

Feeding older primary school children has its own challenges too, as your child will now be eating some meals outside the home. School lunch-boxes, fast-food and hawker food have all been discussed in the book. We have also covered situations when you need to modify your child's diet, for example, due to illness or other special circumstances.

Since this book is intended primarily for Asians, it would have been incomplete without including a section on traditional food beliefs. It will be reassuring for parents to know that many of the practices are safe and we have given advice on some of the possible drawbacks. As many Asians are vegetarians, we have included information on planning nutritionally balanced vegetarian meals.

Because we aim to provide practical advice, we have devoted the entire second part of the book to an extensive recipe collection. Simple recipes for the early complementary feeding in baby's first year are followed by popular family recipes which have been adapted to suit young children. The fun element of food is very evident in the recipes. We hope your task of providing meals for your family will be made more enjoyable as a result!

Feed Your Child Right is first and foremost for parents but we hope health care personnel including doctors and nurses, and other caregivers in the family will also find it a useful reference.

Lynn Alexander and Yeong Boon Yee

Part I
Guide to Good Nutrition

01 Nutrition Basics

- Why we need food
- All about the food groups
- Safeguarding your child's future health
- Eating should be enjoyable as well as healthy

Everyone knows food is essential for life, but what types of food are best for us and for our children? A visit to the market or supermarket reveals an amazing array of foodstuffs. Our young children depend on us to make their food choices for them and so it is very important for us to choose foods wisely and prepare meals that will be nutritious and healthy. This becomes possible with some basic knowledge of nutrition. As it can be very difficult to change bad habits developed in childhood, a firm foundation in good dietary habits will help to ensure that the food choices one makes later on in life will automatically be healthy ones. ● ● ● ●

Why we need food

Food supplies energy

Energy is needed for all living processes such as the beating of our hearts, the digestion of food and the making of new cells. Over and above these basic energy needs, energy is also needed for physical activity. Energy is measured in units called kilocalories (kcals). The energy as well as the protein needs of some population groups by age are shown in Table 1.

Table 1: Recommended Daily Energy and Protein Allowances[a] for Various Age Groups

Age Group		Energy (kcals)	Protein (g)
Infants	3–12 months	700–950	16–18
Younger children	1–2 years	1150	19
	2–3 years	1350	22
	3–5 years	1550	25
Older children	Boys 5–7 years	1850	30
	7–10 years	2100	39
	Girls 5–7 years	1750	30
	7–10 years	1800	39
Men	18–30 years	2550–3450	68
Women	18–30 years	2000–2350	58
Pregnant women		+ 200–285	+9
Lactating women	First 6 months	+ 500	+25
	After 6 months	+ 500	+19

[a] Based on Recommended Daily Dietary Allowances for Normal Healthy Persons in Singapore (Health Promotion Board, Singapore, 2007).

Food supplies nutrients

At least 40 nutrients are required by our bodies. If not supplied in adequate amounts, our health and, in the case of children, their physical and mental growth will be affected.

Food supplies the "bricks" for building the body. These include materials for the developing brain. In fact, the most important period of brain growth occurs during a child's first three to four years. Good nutrition also helps us avoid deficiency diseases such as scurvy, resist infections, and recover from illness faster.

The major nutrients and energy, together with a summary of their functions in the body, are set out in Table 2. The chart also indicates which foods are especially rich in each nutrient and explains the importance of two other substances we obtain from our diet, namely *fibre* and water.

Table 2: Functions and Sources of Energy, Major Nutrients, Fibre and Water

Key Nutrients	Some Reasons Why We Need Them	Good Food Sources
Energy (Calories)	• For internal bodily functions • For activity and movement	All food containing protein, fat or carbohydrate.
Protein	• Builds and repairs body tissues • Helps form hormones and enzymes, and antibodies to fight infection • Excess protein used as energy	Best quality protein found in lean meat, poultry, fish, eggs, milk, cheese. Next best are soyabeans and soyabean products (e.g. bean curd), dried peas or beans (pulses), nuts, gluten and *dhal* (lentils).
Carbohydrate	• Supplies immediate energy • Spares protein for body building and repair • Gives bulk to diet	Rice, bread, noodles, cereals, potatoes, vegetables, fruit. (Sugar is a simple carbohydrate.)
Fat	• Concentrated energy source • Supplies essential fatty acids and enables fat-soluble vitamins to enter the body • Pads body organs against shocks	Butter, margarine, cooking oils, milk, ice cream, meat, eggs, nuts and seeds.
vitamin A	• Helps keep skin clear • Helps keep linings of mouth, throat and intestines healthy and free from infection • Helps eyes adjust in dim light • Promotes growth	Liver, margarine, butter, milk, eggs, yellow and red fruit and vegetables, (e.g. papaya, mango, carrot, pumpkin), green leafy vegetables.
vitamin B_1 (Thiamin)	• Promotes good appetite and digestion • Helps keep nerves healthy • Helps body cells obtain energy from food	Meat, poultry, fish, eggs, wholemeal bread, brown rice, milk, potatoes, dried beans or peas, nuts.
vitamin B_2 (Riboflavin)	• Helps cells use oxygen • Keeps eyes healthy	Milk, poultry, meat, liver, fish, eggs, green leafy vegetables.
Other B vitamins (niacin, B_6, B_{12}, folic acid, pantothenic acid, biotin)	• Necessary for normal metabolism and healthy blood	Liver, meat, eggs, nuts, green leafy vegetables.
vitamin C	• Helps hold body cell walls together • Helps resist infection and heal wounds • Helps bones and teeth to form	All fruit, especially kiwi, oranges, limes, papaya. Most vegetables, e.g. tomatoes, potatoes and green vegetables

vitamin D	• Helps body use calcium and phosphorus to build strong bones and teeth	Fish and fish-liver oils, foods fortified with vitamin D (e.g. powdered milk, margarine), sunshine on the skin.
vitamin E	• Necessary for normal metabolism • Keeps cells healthy	Widespread in foods, especially vegetables, cereals, oils and eggs.
vitamin K	• Needed for clotting of blood	Dark green leafy vegetables. Produced in the intestines by bacteria.
Calcium	• Builds bones and teeth • Helps blood to clot • Helps nerves, muscles and heart to function	Milk, dairy products, bean curd, green leafy vegetables, *ikan bilis* (dried anchovies).
Iron	• Combines with a protein to make haemoglobin in blood which brings oxygen from lungs to body tissues	Meat, poultry, fish, liver, green leafy vegetables, dried fruit, *dhal*, fortified cereals or beverages.
Fibre	• Regulates bowel movements • Certain types effective in helping lower blood cholesterol	Wholemeal bread, unmilled rice, bran cereals, oats, vegetables, fruit, nuts and pulses.
Water	• Important part of body cells and fluids • Carries nutrients to and wastes from cells • Aids in digestion and absorption of food • Helps to regulate body temperature	Water, beverages, jelly, soup, fruit, vegetables. Most foods contain water.

In addition, our bodies also require other minerals. All the major minerals required are so easily found in foods that deficiency is seldom a problem. The major minerals are:

• Sodium
• Potassium
• Chlorine
• Phosphorus
• Magnesium

Trace minerals are required in such tiny quantities that we can safely assume they will be obtained in adequate amounts provided a balanced, varied diet is taken. The major trace minerals are:

• Iodine
• Zinc
• Copper
• Chromium
• Manganese
• Molybdenum
• Cobalt
• Selenium

It is important to stress that although a certain amount of these nutrients is essential, taking more than the body requires will have no added benefits and may even be harmful. This is because many vitamins and minerals become toxic if taken in large doses over a long period of time.

Note too that all foods contain varying amounts of different nutrients and no one food contains all the nutrients. (The only exception is breast milk, which is a complete food for babies under six months.) Some foods are also more complete than others. Eggs, for example, containing protein, fat, minerals and vitamins, are much closer to being a complete food than sugar which contains only carbohydrate.

All about the food groups

The variety of food available in our wet markets and supermarkets is enormous, so it is useful to classify food into groups. The three main groups that nutritionists talk about are cereals and starchy foods; protein-rich foods; and fruit and vegetables. Since our book is about nutrition for children, we have added dairy foods as an important fourth group. These groups are described in detail in the following sections. They are all important and so the first step towards giving your family a healthy diet is to include foods from each of these groups every day. A balanced meal is generally one which contains foods from the cereals/starchy food group, the protein-rich or dairy food group and the fruit and vegetable group. Within the food groups, we should try to vary, as much as possible, the foods taken.

In addition to the four main food groups, there are other minor food groups which contribute to our diet. One of these is fats and oils. Some fat in the diet is necessary for the reasons given in Table 2 on page 13. Fats and other foods like sugar, seasonings, sauces, spices and herbs, if taken in moderate amounts, also make food more palatable and help increase the variety of dishes in the diet. As will be discussed later, however, fats, sugar and salty seasonings have to be limited, otherwise they can lead to ill-health.

1. Cereals and starchy foods

Cereals and starchy foods such as rice, noodles, oats, bread and potato, give bulk to our diet. It is recommended that the largest proportion of our energy intake comes from these foods. Cereals and starchy foods contain mainly carbohydrate and small amounts of protein, with hardly any fat. They are often thought to be fattening but, gram for gram, they supply much fewer calories than meat or fat.

Eating the whole grain is preferable to eating the refined or milled product because the outer layers of the grain are more concentrated in vitamins and minerals. Take rice for example. Milled white rice has only two-thirds the vitamin B_1, half the iron and niacin, and less than a third of the vitamin B_2 in the original unmilled brown rice. Milling also removes more than half the fibre.

One type of food in this category which appeals particularly to children is ready-to-eat breakfast cereals. These are a good, low fat source of energy and protein, fortified with iron and B vitamins, and sometimes with vitamins A, C and D. They are convenient for serving at breakfast since they require no cooking. They also encourage milk consumption and their crunchy texture is most appealing to children. It is preferable to buy plain unsweetened varieties as the sugar-coated or flavoured ones are rather high in sugar. The whole grain varieties are a good source of dietary fibre. It is not necessary, however, to give children high-bran or bran-added types.

2. Protein-rich foods

This group includes the foods which are major sources of protein. Other foods like cereals and some vegetables do contain small amounts of protein and their contribution can be quite substantial if eaten in large quantities, as in the case of rice, for example.

a) Animal protein

Animal protein is termed "first class protein", as the range of amino acids it contains is more complete than that of plant protein. Amino acids are the smaller units of which proteins are composed. We need 22 amino acids. Our bodies can only make 14 of these and so it is essential that the other eight are supplied in our diet.

Meat, offal and poultry

All meats contain fat as well as protein, and even a lean cut with no visible fat has invisible fat running through it. This means that meat is quite high in calories. Animal protein foods contain cholesterol, a fat-like substance required for a number of important body functions. Cholesterol is obtained from animal foods in the diet but is also made by our bodies. However, a high level of cholesterol in the blood is associated with heart disease (see page 22). Offal, such as liver, is much higher in cholesterol than meat and poultry. An important nutrient in meat is iron, which is highest in offal. Meat is also a major source of vitamin B_{12}.

Fish and other seafood

While fish is lower in fat than meat, some fish and other seafood do contain a considerable amount of cholesterol. However, fish and, to a lesser extent, seafood contain some beneficial fats (see page 23). Small fish which are eaten with the bones, like *ikan bilis* and sardines, are a good source of calcium.

Eggs

Eggs have suffered a bad reputation over recent years due to their cholesterol content. But as will be explained later, there is no necessity to give up eggs altogether. In fact, it would be a shame not to eat eggs, as they are one of the most complete foods available. Egg protein is of very high quality as it contains all the essential amino acids and is easily digested and utilised. Both the egg white and yolk contain protein, minerals and water-soluble vitamins. Fat is only found in the yolk, which also contains fat-soluble vitamins, iron and cholesterol. An added bonus of egg is that it is a more economical source of protein when compared to meat, fish or milk.

b) Plant proteins

Pulses

Pulses are dried/matured peas, beans and lentils (*dhal*). They used to feature more in the Asian diet as they are a less expensive source of protein than meat. Now, however, their consumption has gone down. An advantage of pulses is that they are much lower in fat when compared to meat. Moreover, pulses contain a particular type of dietary fibre which has been found to be beneficial in lowering blood cholesterol (see page 22).

A wide range of products is made from one familiar bean in this part of the world—the soyabean. To some extent, the soyabean can be thought of as a replacement for dairy products; there is of course soyabean milk, and bean curd has some similarities with cheese. Bean curd is high in calcium, as it is coagulated with a calcium salt. Soyabean milk, unless fortified, does not contain substantial calcium.

While there is no need to go completely vegetarian, it would be beneficial to have one or two vegetarian meals based on pulses each week, or to use pulses together with small amounts of meat in dishes.

Nuts and seeds

These contain fat as well as protein. They are a good alternative to sweets for an in-between snack, but too high in calories to be nibbled often! The salted nuts are not very suitable, particularly for children. Peanut sauces and nuts such as cashews added to dishes boost the protein and fibre content and allow less meat to be used.

3. Fruit and vegetables
a) Fruit

No other class of food has a greater variety of pleasant flavours and attractive colours than fruit. The cultivation of many local fruit has decreased in recent years in Singapore. One fruit which had practically disappeared from the market-place but is now enjoying a limited comeback is the guava. This fruit is very rich in vitamin C and fibre. Starfruits and chikus, although not so widely available as they once were, are highly nutritious—starfruit for its vitamins C and A content, and chiku for its rich content of dietary fibre.

Vitamin C in fruit

Almost all fruit contain significant amounts of vitamin C and some local fruit are among the richest, as Table 3 illustrates.

Children up to the age of 12 require 20 mg of vitamin C per day and older children and adults, 30 mg. As can be seen from Table 3, a portion or two of most fresh fruit will easily meet the daily vitamin C requirements.

Since vitamin C is a water-soluble vitamin, it is not stored in the liver in the way fat-soluble vitamins are, and excess is excreted in the urine. It is therefore necessary to take some vitamin C every day. In situations of stress, such as an injury or illness, vitamin C is metabolised more quickly by the body and requirements increase.

Vitamin C is also found in vegetables but a large proportion of it is lost during cooking. Since fruit are usually eaten raw, they provide large amounts of vitamin C and are therefore a more reliable and convenient way of obtaining our requirements of this important vitamin.

Unsupported claims about vitamin C

Vitamin C is popularly reputed to prevent and fight off the common cold and influenza. There has been much publicity about the so-called benefits which may be derived from taking large doses of vitamin C. Many people take vitamin C tablets in doses up to 100 times the recommended levels.

These claims, however, are not warranted. There is no conclusive evidence that extra vitamin C prevents the onset of colds or shortens the duration of symptoms. In fact, taking high doses of vitamin C over the long term has some deleterious effects on health. The higher the dose taken, the less vitamin C is absorbed and the unabsorbed vitamin C passing through the digestive tract causes diarrhoea. Kidney and urinary tract stones are further risks related to high doses of vitamin C. Large doses of the vitamin may also inactivate and destroy vitamin B_{12} and interfere with the absorption of copper. On a more serious note, some studies have shown that large doses of vitamin C taken in pregnancy may have adverse effects on the newborn infant (see page 36).

The conclusion from all of this is that vitamin C should ideally be taken from dietary sources, and any self-medication with the vitamin is not advisable unless deemed necessary by a doctor.

Table 3: Vitamin C Content of Fruit

Fruit	Servings	Vitamin C (mg)
Guava	½ large	200
Papaya	1 slice[a]	102
Orange	1 medium	80
Pomelo	2 large segments	74
Kiwi	1 medium	74
Rambutan	5 fruits	38
Starfruit	½ medium	38
Mango	½ medium	36
Pineapple	1 slice[a]	30
Soursop	1 slice[a]	30
Banana	2 small	10
Jackfruit	3 seeds	10
Watermelon	1 slice[a]	8
Apple	1 medium	8
Grapes	½ cup	8

[a] As sold in cut-fruit stalls

Other nutrients in fruit

Fruit are rich in dietary fibre, and some local fruit are among the top in terms of fibre content. Yellow and red-fleshed fruit, such as mango and papaya, also contain large amounts of carotene, which is converted to vitamin A in the body. Figure 1 shows the carotene content of local fruit and how one serving contributes to the recommended daily allowance of vitamin A for a child.

While canned and frozen fruit usually contain most of the vitamin C content of the original fruit, dried fruit contain little or no vitamin C. Iron, however, becomes more concentrated in dried fruit and vitamin A and fibre remain intact.

b) Vegetables

Some children do not like vegetables of any description and parents are often concerned that their child's health will be affected if he does not eat vegetables.

For most of the nutrients that can be found in vegetables, however, more than enough can easily be obtained from other foods. Milk, for example, provides more calcium than vegetables; fruit are generally better sources of vitamin C; and meat is a better source of iron.

Nevertheless, vegetables still play an important complementary role and there is a concern that the "no-veg" child will continue to avoid vegetables into adulthood, which could result in a low fibre intake. There is also increasing evidence to show that vegetables contain factors which protect against certain forms of cancer.

The nutritional value of vegetables

Most vegetables are very low in protein and fat but are good sources of several important vitamins, minerals and dietary fibre. Vegetables are generally low in calories. However, the common method of cooking

Figure 1: Contribution of Red/Yellow Fruit to a Child's Daily Vitamin A Requirements[a]

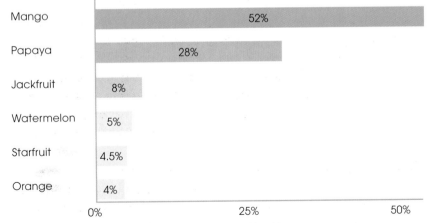

Percentage of RDDA[a] met by one serving[b]

Fruit	Percentage
Mango	52%
Papaya	28%
Jackfruit	8%
Watermelon	5%
Starfruit	4.5%
Orange	4%

[a] Based on the Singapore Recommended Daily Dietary Allowance of 300 micrograms for a child aged 3–7 years.
[b] Serving sizes are half of those in Table 3 on page 17.

vegetables in Asian diets—frying—can add a lot of calories to the diet. For example, an average bowl of vegetables fried with two Chinese spoons (a flat-bottomed spoon usually used for eating soup) of oil contains roughly 280 kilocalories, compared with 155 kilocalories when one Chinese spoonful of oil is used, and 50 kilocalories when steamed!

Iron
Iron is highest in green leafy vegetables, especially broccoli, spinach, *tang oh* (chrysanthemum leaves), *kai lan,* sweet potato leaves, *kangkong* (water convolvulus) and watercress. The iron in vegetables, while not absorbed as well as the iron in meat, can still contribute significantly to iron intake. Besides, it is known that vitamin C, which is also present in vegetables, increases iron absorption.

Calcium
Dark green leafy vegetables, particularly spinach, *kai lan,* broccoli and watercress, are good sources of calcium.

Vitamin A
Many local vegetables are good sources of vitamin A, which is present in the form of carotene. The carotene content of vegetables varies widely and is roughly related to the colour of the vegetable. Green vegetables such as broccoli and lettuce contain large amounts, but pale vegetables like cauliflower, gourds and cucumber contain very little. Red and yellow vegetables are also very high in carotene; these include carrots, yellow sweet potato, pumpkin and tomato.

Vitamin C
Most vegetables contain a substantial amount of vitamin C, although it is not as high as that in some fruit. The highest amounts are found in broccoli, green pepper and green leafy vegetables. The vitamin C in vegetables, however, is easily destroyed by careless preparation and prolonged cooking.

Folic acid
This B vitamin is present in most vegetables in small quantities but is highest in green leafy vegetables like watercress, spinach, and also in broccoli, cauliflower and lady's finger. As there are few good sources of folic acid in other foods, vegetables are an important source, particularly when requirements are increased, such as in pregnancy.

Are green leafy vegetables better than other vegetables?
We have all been brought up to believe that greens are essential. While it is true that green leafy vegetables are generally richer in nutritional value than other vegetables, there are many exceptions. Carrots and sweet potato, for example, are by far the highest providers of vitamin A. Even frozen green peas are surprisingly rich in vitamin C. Therefore variety, rather than limiting to a few types, is the order of the day.

What about the nutritional value of vegetable soups?
Boiling vegetables in water causes leaching of the water-soluble vitamins B and C into the water. However, if this water is then used in a soup or gravy, the nutritional value of the vegetable is not entirely lost. Some vitamins, especially vitamin C, are also sensitive to heat and more will be lost with longer cooking times.

Table 4 on page 20 shows the percentage losses of different vitamins in vegetables when boiled. Of the B vitamins, folic acid is the most heat-sensitive and up to 90 per cent of it can be destroyed in cooking. Carotene is not affected by boiling but is destroyed during shallow frying when exposed to air.

Vitamin C is also destroyed by heat and exposure to air. Chopping vegetables into small pieces will increase vitamin C loss as more surface area is exposed to the air. The destruction of vitamin C in a

Table 4: Losses of Vitamins in Vegetables During Cooking by Boiling[a]

Fruit	Percentage Lost		
	Root Vegetables	Leafy Vegetables	Seeds e.g. peas
Vitamin A	0	0	0
Vitamin B_1	25	40	30
Vitamin B_2	30	40	30
Vitamin B_6	30	40	30
Folic acid	90	90	90
Pantothenic acid	30	30	30
Biotin	30	30	30
Vitamin C	40	70	50
Vitamin E	0	0	0

[a] Note: These are representative values and actual loss depends on:
   a. volume of cooking water
   b. length of cooking time
   c. whether food is chopped or whole

vegetable, therefore, will be less if the vegetable is not chopped up too much and is placed immediately in boiling water rather than in cold water which is then brought to the boil slowly.

4. Dairy foods

Milk pours a lot of nutrients our way! It contains protein, carbohydrate, fat, several important vitamins and over 14 minerals. The protein in milk is of a very high quality and is easily digested by most people.

Milk is also by far the best source of calcium. Calcium is needed not only for growing bones and teeth but right throughout life as bone tissue is constantly being broken down and remodelled.

Of the vitamins in milk, vitamin B_2 is particularly important as there are few other good sources which are commonly eaten in this part of the world. By drinking milk, it would be easier to ensure that we have sufficient vitamin B_2 in our diet.

Is it wise to cut down on dairy foods because of their saturated fat and cholesterol content?
Milk normally contains 3.4 per cent fat. Fat-reduced milk (sometimes called low fat or "semi-skimmed") contains 2 per cent fat, while skimmed milk is practically free of fat, at below 0.2 per cent. The answer therefore for those needing to watch their fat intake is to switch to skimmed milk, which contains all the goodness of the original milk minus the fat. Note that children under seven years should not be given skimmed milk because the milk fat is an important source of energy for them.

An aspect of milk which often gives rise to concern in this part of the world is its lactose content.

Some Asians have difficulty digesting this sugar but, as explained later in Chapter 7, there are ways to get around this. Hydrolysed (lactose-reduced) milk is now available. Moreover, yoghurt and cheese do not usually present a problem for lactose intolerance sufferers as the lactose in these products is already in a digested form.

Types of milk and milk products
There are many types of milk on the supermarket shelves—pasteurised, sterilised, ultra heat treated, reconstituted, evaporated, condensed and powdered. All of them basically contain the same amounts of the major nutrients like protein and calcium. An exception is sweetened condensed milk which contains considerably less nutrients, weight for weight, than other milks as it is roughly 50 per cent sugar.

Vitamin losses in the various types of milk will vary according to the degree of heat treatment the milk has undergone. In powdered milk and some liquid milks, however, these vitamins are often added back by the manufacturer, and some are even enriched with iron.

Cheese is produced by clotting milk, pouring off the whey and pressing the curds, allowing them a period to "ripen" and develop flavour through fermentation. Cheese contains the fat and protein of milk but not the carbohydrates. Its fat content is usually high, unless it is made from skimmed milk, e.g. low fat cottage cheese, or from low fat yoghurt (see recipe for fresh yoghurt cheese on page 228).

Yoghurt is made by allowing milk to ferment after the addition of a bacteria called *Lactobacilli acidophilus*. When consumed, this bacteria suppresses the harmful bacteria which sometimes find their way into our intestines. Most yoghurts are made from skimmed milk. However, note that the fruit flavoured varieties, together with the cultured milk drinks that are so popular with our children, have a lot of sugar added. You can learn how to make your own yoghurt by turning to the recipe section on page 228.

Safeguarding your child's future health

As we have stressed all along, a good diet plays a vital role in promoting health. Similarly, a poor diet can cause ill-health, which is not only related to deficiencies of particular nutrients but excesses too. Although you cannot guarantee your child a 100 per cent healthy life, you can at least take preventive dietary measures. There are a number of measures currently recommended by leading nutrition authorities which may help avoid some of the more common diet-linked diseases. Four dietary factors have come to the fore recently because of the role they are believed to play in protecting against or causing disease. They are fibre, fat, sugar and salt, and we discuss each one in detail in the following pages. We also touch briefly on another area of concern in our diet—the processing of foods and the safety of food additives.

1. Fibre in your child's diet
Fibre is the indigestible part of plant foods—vegetables, fruit, nuts and grains—which provides bulk to the diet and promotes healthy bowel function. Increasing the amount of fibre in one's diet can help prevent constipation and possibly reduce the incidence of colonic disease including haemorrhoids and colon cancer.

With more fibre in their diet, there is less risk that children will overeat and become obese. This is because high-fibre foods are bulky, require more chewing and therefore give a more long-lasting feeling of fullness than low-fibre foods.

Certain types of fibre can lower blood cholesterol and so play a part in preventing heart disease. These are the soluble fibres found in pulses, oats and, to a lesser extent, fruit.

There is no recommended level of fibre intake for children, but you will know that your child's fibre intake is adequate if your child's bowel movements are regular, and the stool is bulky and well-formed yet soft. If your child suffers from constipation, encourage him to eat more of the following foods:

• Whole grains and wholemeal products—These include breakfast cereals, wholemeal bread, oats, wholemeal crackers and biscuits, and even unmilled (brown) rice.

• Vegetables and fruit—All fruit and vegetables contain some fibre. Lady's fingers, snow peas and long beans are particularly high in fibre. Among fruit, chiku, guava and jackfruit are the highest in fibre, while the good old banana also gives substantial amounts. Prunes,

in particular, usually help relieve constipation quite quickly as they contain a natural laxative substance, besides their high fibre content.

• Pulses—These include lentils, baked beans, split peas, green peas, green or red beans.

If the idea of switching completely to brown rice is not appealing, try cooking it occasionally for a change or mixing brown and white rice together. And if you do use only white rice, it is important to use other whole grains, such as oats, which can be taken as porridge or in cookies, wholewheat or rye bread, and bran-containing breakfast cereals.

A word of warning, though. Do not go overboard with fibre in your child's diet, as too much can cause wind, stomach cramps and even diarrhoea. Fibre must always be accompanied by adequate fluid intake, to ensure that the fibre can absorb water and become soft. Too much fibre may also hinder the absorption of minerals, including iron. Finally, since children's capacity for food is smaller than ours, too much fibre will make their food too bulky and reduce the overall amount of calories they consume. Therefore, we do not recommend the use of fibre supplements or bran for children, unless your doctor prescribes them for an acute case of constipation.

2. Fat and the heart

You would have no doubt heard that too much fat may lead to heart disease. The reason is that excess fat, especially saturated fat and cholesterol, is associated with a high level of cholesterol in the blood. This in turn leads to cholesterol deposits on the lining of blood vessels (atherosclerosis). The deposits can eventually cause blockage of an artery, which is when a heart attack happens.

While heart attacks do not usually occur until middle age, many nutritionists feel that it is best to take preventative measures from young. Autopsies performed on teenagers and young adults who died in accidents have revealed the beginnings of atherosclerosis, leading to the conclusion that watching the diet even in childhood can stand one in good stead for the later years.

There are three main considerations in the early dietary prevention of heart diseases.

a) Watch total fat intake

High intakes of fat should be avoided. Some fat, however, is essential and so children should not be placed on very strict low fat diets. Our advice is therefore simple—avoid excessive fat intake. Do not fry all your food or allow your child to consume fried

Table 5: Main Dietary Sources of Fat

Visible Fat	Invisible Fat
Meat fat	Meat
Butter	Oily fish
Margarine	Egg yolk
Vegetable oils	Milk, cream, cheese
Lard	Chocolate
Ghee	Cakes, pastries, biscuits
	Gravies, sauces, dressings

hawker or fast foods every day. Keep fatty foods like ice cream, chocolate and cream cake to a weekly rather than a daily affair. The main sources of fat in foods are listed in Table 5 above.

You may be wondering if it would be beneficial to use low fat milk for your child. As mentioned earlier, low fat or skimmed milk should not be given to children under seven. Even after this age, two glasses a day of full-cream milk is generally acceptable. Only if your child is overweight or there is a family history of heart disease, is it recommended that you switch to a reduced fat milk.

b) Replace some saturated fat in the diet with unsaturated fat
High intakes of saturated fats contribute to high blood cholesterol. On the other hand, unsaturated fats can actually help to lower blood cholesterol. A good way to achieve a higher intake of unsaturated fat

is to use unsaturated margarine instead of other margarines and butter, and to cook with an oil high in unsaturates, such as olive, canola, corn or soya oil. To ensure that you minimise saturated fat, trim all fat from meat and remove chicken skin before cooking.

Saturated fat will still be present in the diet in the fat of meats and also dairy products. But this is fine since it is acceptable for roughly one-third of our fat intake to be saturated and the rest unsaturated.

Unsaturated fats consist of polyunsaturated and monounsaturated fats, and it is recommended that at least one third of our total fat intake is the monounsaturated type as this is felt to be even more beneficial than the polyunsaturated type. Table 6 on page 24 shows the dietary sources of the various types of fat as well as cholesterol.

Cook fish more often, as fish has less fat than meat and also contains some very beneficial omega-3 unsaturated oils, including eicosapentanoic acid (EPA), which have been found particularly effective in helping reduce the risk of heart disease.

You should minimise your usage of products containing *hydrogenated and trans fats*. These are fats which have been saturated to some extent during processing to make them more solid at room temperature. Examples are hard, block margarines and fats or shortenings used in commercial baking.

c) Avoid excessive cholesterol
From Table 6, it will immediately strike you that foods high in cholesterol are also foods recommended for children because of their valuable protein and vitamin contents. Therefore, the main word of caution is that you should not give more than one egg

Table 6: Major Sources of Saturated and Unsaturated Fat and Cholesterol

Saturated Fat	Unsaturated Fat	Cholesterol
Dairy fat Meat fats Hard margarines Coconut oil Palm oil Blended "vegetable oil" Commercially prepared cakes, pastries, biscuits and chocolates	**Polyunsaturated:** Corn oil Soyabean oil Sunflower seed oil Safflower seed oil Fish oils Polyunsaturated margarines **Monounsaturated:** Peanuts and peanut oil Olive oil Canola oil Monounsaturated margarines Almonds Salmon Egg yolk Avocado **NB:** *There are small amounts of monounsaturated fats in most other foods.*	Brain Egg yolk Offal (e.g. liver, kidney) Red meats Fish roe Some seafood (e.g. prawn, crab) Butter Cream Cheese

a day on average, or cook liver and shellfish more than twice a week. Since children do not usually eat big portions of meat and shellfish anyway, there is little need to restrict their intake of these foods.

3. Salt and blood pressure

Salt is a combination of the two elements, sodium and chlorine. Sodium, although an essential mineral for the body, is believed to be related to the development of high blood pressure in susceptible persons when taken in excess. High blood pressure is a common problem in adulthood and while usually symptom-free, it is a dangerous condition as it increases the risk of coronary heart disease, stroke and kidney disease.

Besides being present in salt, sodium is also found in most foods, some of which contain more than others. For example, some foods like ham or bacon are preserved by being heavily salted or being soaked in brine (salt solution). Many modern processed foods, sauces and seasonings contain a lot of salt and sodium additives.

It will be beneficial for your child's future health if he does not develop a liking for salty food. Therefore, make sure your child's diet is only lightly salted; this way you will help ensure that he actually prefers a diet low in salt throughout his life.

To curb salt intake:

- Add just a little salt in cooking.
- Avoid using monosodium glutamate (MSG)
- If you use soya sauce, oyster sauce, fermented bean curd paste or a commercial stock or seasoning cube, taste before adding additional salt; often it is not necessary.
- Discourage your children from drowning their food in ketchup and soya and chilli sauces. Bring these to the table only for a few particular dishes and use them sparingly.

- Do not keep a store of salty snacks in the house such as potato chips or salted nuts.
- Cut down your use of processed and tinned meats, including luncheon meat. Instead, use fresh or frozen meat.
- Use shallots, garlic, ginger, lime juice, pepper, tomato and mushroom to enhance the flavour of your dishes and reduce the need for salt.
- Do not make it a habit to add salt to cut fruits such as pineapple and do not soak apples and pears in salt water to prevent browning. Lemon or lime juice does the job just as well.

4. Myths and truths about sugar
a) Myths

- Myth 1—*Sugar is essential for energy*
  Sugar is broken down in our bodies to glucose which then provides energy. However, all carbohydrates, not only sugar, provide glucose upon digestion. So rice, bread, potatoes and noodles are energy foods too. Protein and fat also provide the body with energy, so avoiding sugar is not going to result in a lack of energy.

- Myth 2—*Glucose is superior to sugar and is good for children*
  Being the simplest form of sugar, glucose is a rapidly absorbable

source of energy. However, it is still simply sugar in another form.

- Myth 3—*Honey is more healthy than sugar*
  Because honey is a natural food, it is often equated with being a health food. In fact, it too is just sugar in another form and contains very little else in the way of nutrients.

b) Truths

Excess sugar intake has been implicated in a number of major diseases. It is easy to take a lot of sugar and sugary foods like soft drinks and ice cream, as they do not require chewing and usually taste good. However, the concentrated calories they provide can lead to obesity.

Tooth decay is the second reason why sugar should be curbed in a child's diet. The teeth your child has from around eight years onward are going to be with him the rest of his life—it is thus in his best interest to take good care of them from the start. Even baby teeth (milk teeth) should be well taken care of as they create the spaces into which the adult teeth eventually grow. Early loss of baby teeth to tooth decay could be detrimental to the growth of adult teeth, not to mention the nightmare of having to undergo dental treatment for cavities at that young age!

Sugar and sugary foods are by nature sticky and they adhere to the teeth. Bacteria present on the surface of the gums and teeth ferment the sugar, producing a corrosive acid which eats away at the teeth and causes cavities. Generally, the stickier the food, the more likely it is to contribute to cavities. For example, toffees are worse than a sweet drink. If sweets are eaten, it is important to confine this to a short period and make sure your child brushes his teeth afterwards, rather than allowing him to continually suck on sweets, say for a whole afternoon.

Sugar is often associated in our minds with diabetes. High sugar intake does not in itself cause diabetes. In individuals who have a family history of the disease, however, a high sugar consumption may trigger earlier development of diabetes. It may also be an indirect cause of diabetes if it leads to obesity, since obesity increases the risk of getting diabetes.

As with salt, discouraging your child from developing a sweet tooth will help safeguard his future health.

Ways to cut sugar
- Instead of desserts and sweets, serve fresh fruit after meals and as snacks. Fruit is naturally sweet and nutritious too!

- When children are hungry between meals, offer a substantial savoury snack such as a sandwich rather than cake or sweets.
- Avoid sugar-coated cereals. If the plain variety is not liked, try adding raisins or a little chopped apple or banana for sweetness.
- Avoid heavily sweetened drinks like flavoured milks, soft drinks, syrups and cultured milk drinks. Encourage your child to drink plain water, milk and unsweetened fruit juice instead. Often, when the family goes out, sweet drinks are the only choice so it is worth providing your child with his own supply of drinking water or fruit juice when he goes out.
- Do not add sugar to your child's malted milk or chocolate-flavoured beverages. These drinks are already sweetened. And no condensed milk!
- Reduce the use of sweet spreads such as jam and *kaya*. Alternate with cheese spreads or peanut butter.

5. Processed foods and additives

People generally believe that "fresh is best". This is true to a large extent, as the nutrient contents of foods may be affected by processing which involves drying or cooking.

Freezing, however, preserves nearly all the nutrients in foods. Vegetables frozen immediately after picking, such as peas, may even have more Vitamin C than their fresh counterparts since cold temperatures stop the action of the enzyme that destroys the vitamin. On the other hand, fresh produce gradually loses vitamin C as it is transported in trucks, then moved from warehouses to markets and finally sits in your refrigerator for a few days. A slight drawback with frozen foods, however, is that some of the nutrients may be lost during thawing.

a) Fortification of foods

For some processed foods, manufacturers replace the nutrients lost during processing. Sometimes products are even fortified beyond the level of nutrients that would be found in the natural food. Breads, margarine, milk powder and ready-to-eat breakfast cereals are all examples of fortified processed foods. Manufactured baby foods, too, are often fortified.

b) Additives

People are naturally concerned about additives in preserved foods. Although we may rest assured that the additives used in foods are only those that the authorities believe to be safe for human consumption, we can try, wherever possible, to choose foods labelled "no preservatives", "additive-free" or "no artificial flavouring or colouring". Bear in mind, however, that preservatives are sometimes essential, and in fact can make our food safer as they prevent spoilage and growth of harmful bacteria.

Fresh produce may also be a source of some additives, such as pesticide residues on leafy vegetables and the skins of certain fruit like apples. Again, these are strictly regulated but, to be on the safe side, always wash fresh fruit and vegetables thoroughly in running water before eating.

Help children develop good dietary habits so they will make healthy food choices later in life.

Eating should be enjoyable as well as healthy

Having briefly covered the basics of nutrition, it must be stressed that food is not just nutrition. Food provides a learning medium for children, serves as an avenue for social interaction at mealtimes and, above all, should be a source of pleasure and enjoyment. And no one has yet defined the nutritional value of that very important ingredient every parent puts into his or her cooking—love!

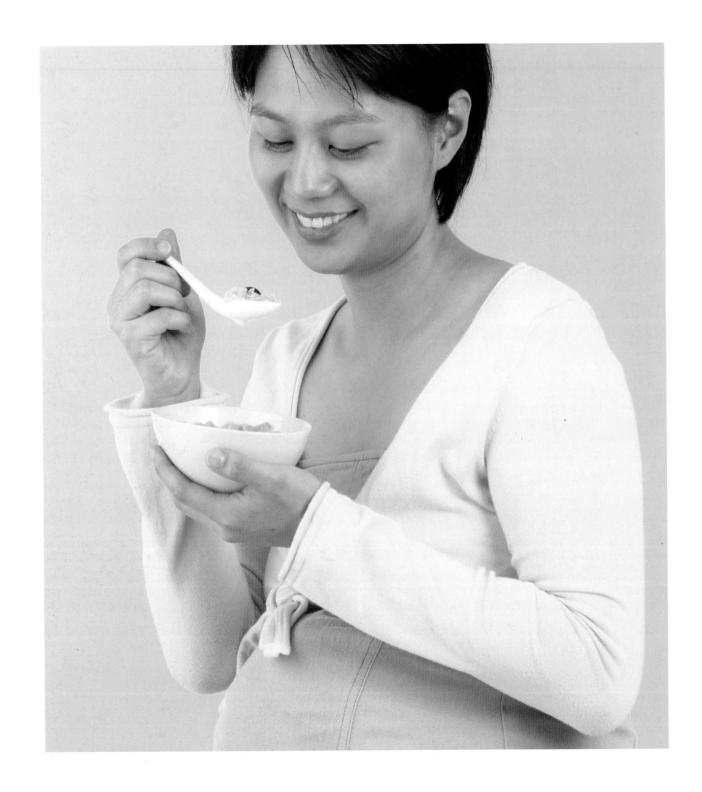

02 Nutrition in Pregnancy

- Meeting the extra needs of pregnancy
- Dietary supplements in pregnancy
- Weight gain in pregnancy
- Foods to avoid in pregnancy
- Alcohol, tobacco and caffeine
- Diet-related problems in pregnancy

Being pregnant would probably top any woman's list of reasons for re-examining her eating habits and embarking on a sensible and well-balanced diet. After all, another life will benefit from it. Every woman hopes for a healthy, comfortable and stress-free pregnancy, with a beautiful bouncing baby at the end of it. Being optimally nourished is a very important factor in achieving this goal. ● ● ● ●

During pregnancy, all your baby's nutrients are supplied solely from your body via the placenta. However, the effect of nutrition on the outcome of pregnancy actually starts long before you are pregnant. If a healthy diet is followed throughout childhood and early womanhood, nutritional status will be good right from the moment you conceive and the body will have plenty of nutrient reserves to meet the early demands of pregnancy. In this regard, adequate spacing of pregnancies is also beneficial as it allows time for replenishment of body stores between pregnancies.

Severe malnourishment will definitely have an adverse effect on the development of the foetus. However, even being mildly undernourished during pregnancy can jeopardise your health as well as your baby's. While your own body stores will be drawn upon to meet most of the baby's needs, remember that this is at the expense of your own health. Ultimately, this may affect the baby too as mothers in poor health are more likely to have birth complications.

On the other hand, too much of a good thing can also lead to a less than ideal pregnancy. In other words, avoid putting on too much weight! So, how should you best meet the nutritional needs of your baby during his nine months in the womb?

Meeting the extra needs of pregnancy

Figure 1 on page 31 shows the additional needs of the pregnant woman for various nutrients. At a glance, it can be seen that eating for two does not mean eating double of everything! Requirements for energy (calories) are not increased so much as are requirements for some nutrients. This means that the food a pregnant woman eats should be of high quality, rich in vitamins and minerals rather than being purely high in calories. A mother-to-be should therefore minimise her intake of foods containing high levels of sugar and fat, which contain mainly calories.

Energy
All the metabolic processes encompassing growth and development of the foetus and the changes in the mother's own body require energy. These essential processes include the making of new cells, the passing of nutrients across the placenta from mother's bloodstream to baby's, and the manufacture of enzymes and hormones which regulate baby's growth.

It is normal for the appetite to increase during pregnancy so as to ensure that the calorie intake will be adequate. The body also seems to make more efficient use of the food eaten. Therefore, women who do not increase their calorie intake to the recommended level often continue to maintain satisfactory weight gain through their pregnancy. If energy intake is too low, however, dietary protein will be wasted on energy production, and this should be avoided.

Protein
Proteins are the "building blocks of life" and therefore basic to the growth process. Protein is needed for building baby's muscles and tissues as well as for the expanding maternal tissues. It is also necessary for the manufacture of all the essential regulating substances, such as hormones, in both mother and baby.

Because we normally eat considerably more protein than we need, it is not necessary to suddenly start eating huge steaks to meet the increased requirements of pregnancy. It is generally sufficient to

Figure 1: Additional Dietary Requirements in Pregnancy[a]

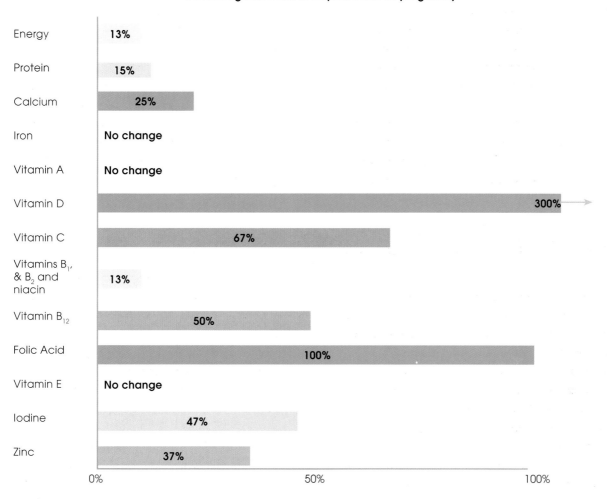

Percentage increase in requirements for pregnancy

Nutrient	Increase
Energy	13%
Protein	15%
Calcium	25%
Iron	No change
Vitamin A	No change
Vitamin D	300%
Vitamin C	67%
Vitamins B_1, & B_2 and niacin	13%
Vitamin B_{12}	50%
Folic Acid	100%
Vitamin E	No change
Iodine	47%
Zinc	37%

[a] Based on Recommended Daily Dietary Allowances for Normal Healthy Persons in Singapore (Health Promotion Board, Singapore, 2007), for all nutrients except vitamin E, iodine and zinc, which are based on US Dietary Reference Intakes (DRIs): Recommended Intakes for Individuals; Vitamins and Elements. Food and Nutrition Board, Institute of Medicine, National Academies, 2005.

ensure that each of the three daily main meals contains a protein rich food (see Food Plan (Table 1) below and Sample Daily Menu (Table 2) on page 33). Drinking the recommended amount of milk will automatically cover the increased protein needs of pregnancy.

Calcium

Demands for calcium rise because calcium is necessary for the formation of baby's skeleton and teeth. If dietary calcium is insufficient, calcium is drawn from the mother's bones to meet the baby's needs. This leaves the mother with a calcium-depleted skeleton which, particularly if further deprived in subsequent pregnancies, can make her susceptible to osteoporosis (brittle bones) in later life.

Half of the daily calcium requirement in pregnancy can be met by drinking two glasses (240 ml per glass) of milk. The rest can usually be obtained by including some of the other calcium-containing foods daily, as illustrated in the Sample Menu. Many Asians, however, particularly the Chinese, cannot drink this amount of milk, as they have problems digesting it due to lactose intolerance. If this is the case, it would be worth experimenting with other dairy products in which the lactose is already partly digested, such as cheeses, plain or fruit yoghurt

Table 1: A Food Plan to Supply Daily Nutrient Needs During Pregnancy

Food Group	Number of Servings Required Daily	Example of Serving Size	Notes
Milk	2	1 cup (240 ml)	For calcium. If less is taken, substitute with alternative sources or take a calcium supplement.
Meat, fish, egg, pulses, nuts, bean curd	3	90 g meat/fish ¾ rice bowl of cooked pulses 60 g nuts 1 bean curd cake 1 egg = ½ serving	Include seafood weekly for iodine.
Cereals and starchy foods	3–4	1 bowl rice 2 slices bread 2 small potatoes 1 bowl oats or cereal	Wholegrain preferred for more B vitamins and fibre.
Vegetables	1 green leafy + 1–2 others	3 Ch sp (cooked)*	For folic acid, iron, calcium, vitamins A and C and fibre.
Fruit	1 red or yellow + 1–2 others	1 orange, apple or starfruit 1 slice papaya or melon	For vitamin A and fibre. For vitamin C, fibre and to aid in iron absorption.
Butter, margarine, oil	2–3	1½ tsp butter or margarine 1 Ch sp oil	For use in cooking and as source of vitamins A, D, E, and essential fatty acids.

*Ch sp = Chinese spoon (see page 129)

Table 2: Sample Daily Menu During Pregnancy

Menu	Portion Size
Breakfast	
Wholewheat or bran cereal (fortified) with milk	1 bowl ½ cup
Half-boiled egg	1
Fresh orange juice	1 small glass
Morning Snack	
Digestive biscuits	2
Milk*	1 cup
Lunch	
Boiled rice or noodles	1 bowl
Lean beef or pork	4 Ch sp
with green pepper	1 Ch sp
and tomato	1 medium
White cabbage	3 Ch sp
Honeydew melon	1 slice
Afternoon Snack	
Fruit yoghurt (or milk)	1 carton/l cup
Groundnuts	1 small packet
Dinner	
Boiled rice	1 bowl
Steamed or curried fish	1 medium fish or fish slice
Kai-lan (Chinese broccoli)	3 Ch sp
in oyster sauce	
Bean curd cake	1 small cake
fried with shredded chicken	1 Ch sp
Papaya	1 slice
Oil in cooking	2 Ch sp

* This could be taken as a milky beverage at bedtime instead. Make use of recipe section for more ideas and variety.

and frozen yoghurt. Lactose-reduced (hydrolysed) milk is also available for the lactose-intolerant (see Chapter 7).

Besides dairy foods, the other sources of dietary calcium include dark-green leafy vegetables and bean curd. Table 3 on page 34 shows how much of these foods is needed to replace milk. Note that soyabean milk is not a good substitute for cow's milk. Since these alternative sources, while useful, are not nearly as rich in calcium as milk and dairy products, your doctor may prescribe calcium supplements if you do not drink milk. Taking care to get adequate vitamin D will help maximise the absorption of calcium from food and supplements.

Iron

Overall iron needs of a pregnant woman are roughly twice that of a non-pregnant female of child-bearing age. The growing foetus needs iron for its developing blood supply, and the mother's own blood volume increases massively during pregnancy by up to 30 per cent. The placenta, full of tiny blood vessels from which the foetus obtains its oxygen and other nutrients, accounts for further iron requirement. Finally, at delivery, quite a lot of blood may be lost. However, the recommended intake does not actually rise because there are no blood losses through menstruation. Furthermore in pregnancy, the body absorbs proportionately more iron from foods than usual. Instead of 5 to 10 per cent, up to 20 per cent iron is absorbed from the diet in pregnancy.

In practice, even when not pregnant, many women fail to meet their iron requirements, and it has been estimated that up to half of all women of child-bearing age are iron-deficient. The resulting anaemia causes fatigue and breathlessness on exertion. Headaches may also occur. If you are "run-down" like this in pregnancy, apart from feeling tired and irritable, you will be much

Table 3: Calcium in Foods: Food Portions with Calcium Content Equivalent to Milk

Menu	Portion Size
Equivalent to 1 cup (240 ml) full cream milk: (280 mg calcium)	
Skimmed milk	1 cup
Hard cheese, fresh or processed	2 slices
Yoghurt	1 carton
Ikan bilis	3 Ch sp
Sardine	1½ fish
Bean curd (*tau foo*)	½ large square
Bean curd cake (*tau kwa*)	2 small cakes
Unpressed bean curd (*tau huay*)	1 bowl
*Kai-lan**	5 Ch sp
Equivalent to ½ cup milk: Soyabean milk (home-made style)	3 cups
Tempeh (fermented soyabean cake)	1 cake
Spinach, mustard green*	4 Ch sp
Chocolate or malt flavoured beverages	6 tsp powder

* Calcium from vegetables is not as well absorbed as that from dairy foods

more susceptible to infections, which could harm the unborn baby and even trigger miscarriages. It is thus extremely important that you meet your iron requirements. For this reason, doctors will often prescribe an iron supplement from the beginning of the second trimester or earlier. If you are in good health at the start of your pregnancy, however, following the food plan suggested will help to ensure your iron needs are met.

Study the sample menu in Table 2 on page 33 and Table 4 on page 35 showing the iron contents of foods, to become more familiar with the sources of iron. It is important to note that absorption of iron is hindered by tea, and increased by vitamin C. Therefore, avoid taking tea at meal times and try to have a vitamin C-rich food, such as fresh fruit, with each meal.

Vitamin A
This vitamin is essential for normal growth. Its requirements can be easily met by following the daily food plan suggested, with eggs and milk supplying substantial amounts.

Vitamin D
This is very important during pregnancy as it is necessary for calcium absorption. We do not need to depend entirely on our diet for this vitamin, provided we spend some time outdoors regularly to allow the sun's rays to help our bodies manufacture the vitamin. If getting out in daylight hours is difficult, it is important to get plenty of vitamin D in the diet—powdered milk is a good source, as it is usually fortified. Fresh milk, however is naturally low in vitamin D. Other good sources include eggs, butter, fortified margarine and fortified breakfast cereals. Fish, particularly dark-fleshed fish like *ikan tenggiri* and sardine, also contain vitamin D. It is recognised that pregnant women may be at risk of not getting enough vitamin D, and some countries have in recent years recommended that all pregnant

Table 4: Your Guide to Iron-Rich Foods

Food	Serving	Iron Content[a] (mg)
Animal foods		
Pork, beef, mutton	3 Ch sp	2
Sardine	1 fish	2
Ikan bilis, dried	3 Ch sp	3
Egg	1	1
Cereals		
Unpolished rice, cooked	1 bowl	2
White rice, cooked	1 bowl	1
Fortified breakfast cereals	1 bowl	1–3
Wholemeal bread	1 slice	1
Vegetables/pulses (cooked)		
Dark green leafy vegetables	3 Ch sp	1–2
Dried beans, *dhal*	4 Ch sp	2
Baked beans, canned	3 Ch sp	1
Bean curd	½ large cake	3
Tempeh	½ cake	3
Miscellaneous		
Groundnuts	3 Ch sp	1
Prunes, raisins	7 pc or 2 Ch sp	1
Chocolate flavoured beverages	3 tsp powder	2
Meat extracts	1 tsp	1

[a] The Singapore daily dietary allowance for iron in pregnancy is 19 mg.

women take a daily vitamin D supplement.

Vitamin C

As well as protecting against anaemia by helping in the absorption of iron, vitamin C is important in pregnancy as it promotes bone and ligament formation. Two portions each of fresh fruit and vegetables daily will take care of the increased requirements.

Vitamin B-complex

Vitamins B_1 and B_2, and niacin are needed for the production of energy, so when energy requirements go up, the requirements for these vitamins automatically increase too. While it is the general rule that baby's needs are met at the expense of the mother's, this is not the case with vitamins B_1 and B_2. For these two B vitamins, mother's needs are taken care of first, so a deficiency could have serious consequences for the growing foetus.

Vitamin B_6 is concerned with the manufacture of body proteins and requirements for this vitamin during pregnancy increase accordingly.

Vitamin B_{12} and folic acid are necessary for the formation of new blood cells and so play a crucial role in cell multiplication. Vitamin B_{12} is found only in animal foods, so vegetarians should take a supplement. Folic acid is plentiful in only a few foods and it is difficult to meet the recommended intake.

Dark-green leafy vegetables have reasonable amounts of folic acid but, unfortunately, up to 80 per cent is destroyed by cooking. Among fruit only oranges, honeydew melon and avocado have substantial amounts of folic acid. Folic acid is important in reducing the risk of birth defects of the central nervous system, such as spina bifida. Because the crucial time for these defects to occur in the developing baby is in the first trimester, a daily folic acid supplement should be taken before and during the first 12 weeks of pregnancy. This effectively means commencing folic acid supplements from the time when you begin trying for a baby.

Trace minerals

There is still not much known about the requirements for many of the trace elements for maintaining normal health, let alone during pregnancy. Therefore, a well-balanced diet with plenty of variety becomes especially important during pregnancy to ensure that the trace minerals are supplied in sufficient quantities. Zinc and iodine are the two most likely to be deficient. Zinc is plentiful in milk, meat and liver, and iodine is found in seafood and seaweeds. There is some concern that zinc absorption may be reduced by high iron levels, so if your doctor prescribes iron tablets, he will usually also prescribe a preparation which contains zinc.

Dietary supplements in pregnancy

Do not buy your own nutritional supplements without consulting a doctor. There are a bewildering number of preparations around, all with varying doses, and some are less suitable than others. You could end up taking dangerously high levels of vitamins A and D which have been shown to cause foetal abnormalities. Even vitamin C, in doses greater than 1000 mg per day, can have a harmful effect on the infant who may get used to the high levels available to him in the womb and suffer vitamin C deficiency (scurvy) temporarily after birth.

Similarly, an overdose of vitamin B_6 can cause over-dependence in the baby, resulting in fits after birth.

Your doctor will generally prescribe one of the specially formulated antenatal vitamin/mineral preparations. Additional calcium may need to be taken, as the calcium in the antenatal supplement may not be high enough. If your supplements seem to be causing an adverse reaction, such as constipation, report this to your doctor who can then let you try a different preparation.

It is important not to regard multivitamin/mineral supplements as a substitute for a balanced diet. Supplements *supplement* what you are already obtaining from your food, and often only a percentage of your total daily requirement is supplied by them. Even the most "complete" multivitamin/mineral supplements generally do not contain more than 20 of the nutrients known to be essential for health. Thus, even though we may feel secure taking a vitamin pill, we still need to pay utmost attention to the quality of our diet.

Weight gain in pregnancy

Ideally, you should gain 11 kg to 12.5 kg during pregnancy. Weight gain starts off slowly, with hardly any gain in the first three months. There is then usually a spurt over the next three months and, by six months, between 7 and 9 kg have usually been gained. The rate slows down after that, to about 1 kg per month. It is helpful to monitor your weight gain by checking your weight fortnightly —refer to Figure 2 to check whether you are putting on weight at the correct rate.

If too much weight is gained, hypertension (high blood pressure) becomes a greater risk, not to mention the fact that you will feel most uncomfortable carrying all that extra weight around, especially in this climate. It will also take longer for you to regain your pre-pregnancy figure after delivery.

If you are already overweight when you find you are pregnant, you must not diet. Instead, make sure the foods you eat are rich in nutrients rather than just being high in calories. During pregnancy, there is a tendency to think that at last here is an excuse for eating all you want and indulging in all those naughty-but-nice foods. Weight-wise, however, foods high in calories but low in protein, vitamins and minerals are luxuries you just cannot afford.

If you drink a lot of milk, it may be advisable to take skimmed milk, which will still give you the same amount of calcium and protein as full-cream milk, without the fat. Two glasses of full-cream milk a day supplies your entire extra calorie allowance during pregnancy, whereas skimmed milk provides only half this amount of calories.

Figure 2: Recommended Weight Gain in Pregnancy

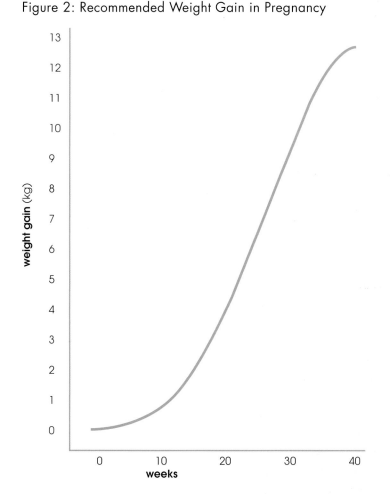

Foods to avoid in pregnancy

In pregnancy, certain foods should be avoided, either to prevent being exposed to the risk of food poisoning, or because they can be potentially dangerous to your unborn baby.

Pâté and soft cheese

Pâté (any type) and soft and blue-veined cheeses, such as Camembert, Brie and Stilton, should be avoided as they could be sources of a bacteria known as listeria. Listeria infection known as listeriosis, although rare, can cause stillbirth, miscarriage, or severe illness in newborn babies.

Other foods that should be avoided due to possible listeria contamination are:

- pre-prepared salads such as potato salad and coleslaw
- ready-prepared meals or re-heated food, unless they are heated thoroughly

Unpasteurised milk and raw eggs

Salmonella, a food poisoning bacteria, can be found in unpasteurised milk, raw eggs and raw egg products, raw poultry and raw meat. This type of food poisoning is unlikely to harm your baby, but you may suffer unpleasant symptoms. To reduce the risk of salmonella, avoid:

- food containing raw or partially cooked eggs, such as homemade mayonnaise, and some mousses and sauces. Eggs should be cooked until both white and yolk are solid, e.g. hard boiled eggs
- unpasteurised dairy products
- undercooked meat and poultry, including any meat which is still pink after cooking.

Raw shellfish

Raw shellfish can sometimes contain harmful bacteria and viruses that could cause food poisoning.

Unwashed raw fruit and vegetables

Traces of soil left on unwashed fruit and vegetables could be a source of toxoplasmosis infection. This is transmitted from a parasite found in cat faeces. Although rare, it could cause serious harm to the unborn baby.

Foods containing too much vitamin A

Although vitamin A is essential in the diet, having too much in pregnancy can harm your unborn baby. It is recommended therefore, that you avoid liver and liver products such as pâté because liver is very high in vitamin A. Cod liver oil supplements also contain high levels of vitamin A, and so check with your doctor before taking these or any other supplements.

Certain oily fish

Fish has many health benefits and in pregnancy, it is good to eat at least two portions of fish a week, including one portion of oily fish. But because harmful levels of mercury have been found in certain oily fish, it is recommended to have no more than two portions of oily fish per week. In particular, avoid shark, swordfish and marlin, and limit tuna to one tuna steak or four medium-sized cans (140 g per can) a week. High levels of mercury could have a damaging effect on your baby's developing nervous system.

Alcohol, tobacco and caffeine

Alcohol is best avoided in pregnancy, as even in moderate amounts it may cause foetal abnormalities. It is particularly dangerous in the early stages of pregnancy, which means, in effect, you should abstain from alcohol from the time you start trying to conceive.

Tobacco has an adverse effect on the nutrition of the unborn baby. The nicotine inhaled into the bloodstream when one smokes tobacco has a constricting effect on the blood vessels. It may therefore interfere with the blood supply to the placenta, which of course is the source of the foetus' nutrients. It has been observed that infants born to mothers who smoked during pregnancy are lighter in weight than normal. If the babies are full-term, this does not usually affect their survival or permanently stunt their growth. If they are born prematurely, however, such infants may not have such a good chance of survival as those born to non-smoking mums.

The ingestion of high amounts of caffeine during pregnancy (more than three cups of coffee or 300 mg caffeine a day) has recently been cautioned against by the Food and Drug Administration (FDA) in the USA. This warning stemmed from the results of studies which showed the harmful effects of caffeine on the developing unborn of some animals. Besides this, caffeine may raise blood pressure—an undesirable effect in pregnancy. It is also one of the substances which may contribute to heartburn.

Diet-related problems in pregnancy

Morning sickness

In the first few months of pregnancy, nausea and vomiting are sometimes experienced. While the causes are not clear, symptoms are usually worse when the stomach is empty, for example upon waking in the morning. They can usually be alleviated or prevented altogether by eating smaller meals more frequently and, in particular, taking a good breakfast first thing in the morning and a small snack last thing at night.

During the early months of pregnancy, it is common to experience hunger pangs more frequently, and these can turn to nausea if not satisfied. So listen to your body and eat something at these times even if it is just a plain biscuit or a piece of fruit.

Remember, it is not inevitable that you will experience sickness. In fact, only about half of pregnant women do. Unfortunately for a few, the symptoms do not subside after the first few months but continue right up to delivery. The vomiting is not harmful provided it does not lead to excessive losses of food. If the latter is the case, or if appetite is severely reduced, weight loss may occur. This is acceptable during the first trimester of pregnancy but definitely not after that. Your doctor should be informed if vomiting becomes severe, and he can then prescribe some medication to relieve it. He would then also prescribe a nutritional supplement.

Food cravings and aversions

The hormonal changes that occur during early pregnancy can play havoc with our sensory perceptions, and foods we normally enjoy can become offensive overnight. This can be a real nuisance, as you may get to the stage when you have gone off nearly everything and just do not know what to eat! Fortunately, in this part of the world there is such an endless variety of food available that you will usually be able to find something acceptable to sustain you through this temporary state of affairs.

Food cravings, like morning sickness, are normally confined to early pregnancy. For some unknown reason, pregnant women typically crave sour foods with pickles, *achar* (pickled vegetables) preserved plum and unripe mangoes usually topping the list. It is not unknown, however, for women to conveniently "crave" durians, ice cream, chocolate or other such foods! Poor husbands feel obliged to entertain these cravings when they occur, as it is traditionally held in Asian society that a pregnant woman should be given whatever she wants to eat!

Cravings are not harmful so long as they do not get out of hand, with one food being consumed in huge quantities at the expense of a variety of other foods in the diet.

Constipation

During pregnancy, the intestines become relaxed, causing the contents to move through sluggishly. Therefore, constipation can be a problem, particularly in the last three months when the enlarged uterus presses on the lower intestine. Another cause of constipation may be the vitamin and mineral supplements, iron being the commonest offender. However, only a few women are affected by supplements in this way, however, and a change of brand will usually bring relief.

To prevent constipation, taking adequate fluids and fibre-containing foods (see Chapter 1) will help. Do not take over-the-counter commercial laxatives without consulting your doctor.

Haemorrhoids

Haemorrhoids or "piles" are enlarged veins in the anus. They occur in pregnancy due to the pressure exerted by the uterus and its contents on the rectum. They are made worse by constipation as straining to pass a stool may cause the veins to rupture. It is therefore extremely important to follow a fibre-rich diet for the prevention of constipation.

Heartburn

The opening at the top of the stomach becomes slack during pregnancy and this makes it easier for stomach contents to come into contact with the oesophagus. This causes an uncomfortable burning feeling due to the acid which has mixed with the food in the stomach. In later pregnancy, the problem may worsen as the enlarging uterus begins to put pressure on the stomach.

Heartburn can be relieved to some extent by eating smaller meals than usual. So, instead of three main meals a day, have five or six small ones. Relax during mealtimes and eat slowly. Lying down, sitting or stooping just after a meal may increase heartburn so it may be helpful to take a stroll instead. Fatty foods, chocolate, coffee and alcohol usually aggravate heartburn so steer clear of these foods.

Diabetes

Diabetes can sometimes develop in pregnancy, triggered by the sudden

The practice of good nutrition from childhood into early womanhood would ensure good nutritional status from the moment you conceive.

extra demands of pregnancy. It often disappears after the pregnancy and is then termed "gestational diabetes".

It is very important that a pregnant woman with diabetes has regular check-ups with her doctor and access to a dietitian. Diet is the cornerstone of treatment in diabetes and this is true for diabetes in pregnancy too. The diabetic mother-to-be must follow a diet that will meet her nutrient needs yet not cause too high or too low a blood sugar level, which could affect the growth rate of the baby. Incidentally, diabetes presents no problem for breastfeeding but again, close medical and dietary supervision is needed.

Toxaemia

Toxaemia is a disorder of late pregnancy characterised by high blood pressure, loss of protein in the urine and fluid retention. Excessive weight gain and high salt intake were at one time thought to contribute to toxaemia. It is now believed, however, that these factors have no direct effect on the incidence of the condition.

Leg cramps

It is widely held that low levels of calcium in the blood are responsible for the leg cramps commonly experienced by pregnant women.

While there is lack of evidence that extra dietary calcium prevents cramps, it is wise to ensure that intake of this nutrient is at least adequate.

03 Milk—Baby's First Food

- Benefits of breastfeeding
- Diet during lactation
- Getting started with breastfeeding
- Breastfeeding under special circumstances
- Breastfeeding and the working mother
- Bottle feeding

Meeting babies' dietary needs for the first six months of life is simple. All they need is milk, preferably breast milk. There is no doubt whatsoever that breast milk is the best you can give your baby. Infant milk formulae have come a long way since the diluted evaporated cow's milk-plus-sugar formula common in the 50s and 60s, but even the modern "humanised" infant milks are still substitutes. Why settle for a substitute when you can give your baby the real thing? ● ● ● ●

Benefits of breastfeeding

A recent study indicated that the number of children who are breastfed in Singapore is just over 50 per cent. The number of children breastfed for more than three months is considerably less than this, at around only 15 per cent.

Many mothers are aware of the importance of breastfeeding and express their willingness to breastfeed but feel they are unable to produce sufficient milk. However, when attempted correctly, and with support and encouragement, almost every mum can breastfeed her baby. The only exceptions are the very few women who have a genuine medical problem which might prevent them from doing so.

Have a look at the following benefits that breastfeeding will give you and your baby and decide whether or not it is worth giving it a try.

Benefits for the baby
a) Breast milk is the best form of nutrition for babies
The nutritional composition of breast milk is just right for your baby. Infant formulae come pretty close to having the same nutrient composition, but they can never get it completely right. There are two main reasons for this. Firstly, the composition of breast milk varies a lot depending on the age of your baby. For example, the milk that you produce initially after birth is in the form of colostrum, a thick yellowish milk containing all that baby needs in the first few days. As baby's fluid and nutrient needs increase, the milk composition changes accordingly.

Secondly, the composition changes during a feed. Milk becomes higher in fat towards the end, thus making baby feel full and stop sucking. It has been suggested that this may help babies develop control of their appetite, and so may have an important bearing on future eating habits.

Breast milk is much higher in cholesterol than infant formula. While we always think of cholesterol as something harmful for the body due to its association with heart disease, it is an essential compound needed for the proper development of the baby's nervous system. Cholesterol in the diet enables the infant's body to "learn" how to process or metabolise it. If cholesterol intake is low in infancy, the necessary enzyme systems for metabolism of cholesterol may not develop and this may lead to a tendency to high blood cholesterol in later life.

b) Breastfeeding promotes better digestion and absorption of nutrients
The nutrients in breast milk is better absorbed and digested than that of formula milk. This is because breast milk contains certain biological compounds for which there are no synthetic substitutes. The fat in breast milk, for example, is easier to digest and absorb than fat in formula milk due to the presence of a fat-digesting enzyme called lipase in breast milk. The body is also able to absorb 50 per cent of the special iron-binding protein that comes from the iron present in breast milk as compared to the 10 per cent that comes from iron in formula milk. Breast milk also contains higher lactose content than formula milk, which enables greater absorption of calcium, magnesium, phosphorus and other minerals.

c) Breastfeeding protects the baby against illnesses
When you breastfeed your baby, you are not just giving him more than the nutrients required for normal growth. You are also passing on a number of biological substances which

can increase his resistance against infectious diseases, particularly the common tummy upset with diarrhoea and vomiting known as gastroenteritis.

Breast milk, therefore, may be thought of as a living fluid or, in the words of the Koran, "white blood". Some of these substances and what they do are listed in Table 1. Note that colostrum is particularly rich in these vital factors, and so if you delay breastfeeding until your milk comes in, your baby will be missing out on early immune protection.

Whilst there is no absolute guarantee that the breastfed baby will be free from illness, studies have shown that fewer illnesses, such as diarrhoea, occur in the first year of life in infants breastfed for at least four to five months.

d) Breastfeeding develops a sense of security
Breastfeeding may be thought of as a logical continuation of pregnancy. In other words, you are still nourishing

Table 1: Substances in Breast Milk which Protect Against Disease

Substance	Role
Bifidus factor	Promotes the growth of "good" bacteria in the infant's intestines, thus preventing growth of harmful bacteria.
Lactoferrin	Binds the iron in breast milk so that it is not available to harmful bacteria which need it for growth.
B_{12}-binding protein	Renders vitamin B_{12} unavailable to bacteria.
Lactoperoxidase	Kills harmful bacteria.
Anti-staphylococcus factor	Inhibits growth of harmful staphylococcus bacteria.
Phagocyte cells	Swallow up bacteria.
Complement	Enhances the activity of phagocytes.
Lymphocytes and macrophage cells	Secrete antibodies which give immunity to certain diseases.
Lysozyme	Helps prevent infection.
Interferon	Inhibits growth of viruses.
Epidermal growth factor	Helps keep lining of infant's intestines intact as a barrier to stop harmful substances entering the bloodstream.

your baby from your own body. For many women who are busy with other things and leave their baby's care largely to someone else such as a maid or mother-in-law, breastfeeding is a good opportunity for them and their babies to spend some time exclusively together. The baby will also enjoy a sense of security as a result of this regular close contact with his mother.

Benefits for the mother

You are likely to regain your pre-pregnancy figure faster as breastfeeding uses up fat stores laid down in pregnancy. Furthermore, the hormones secreted when you breastfeed act on the uterus, causing it to contract. This helps it return to its normal size faster. While there is no conclusive evidence, some studies have suggested that there may be less risk of getting breast cancer if you have nursed your baby.

Breastfeeding also cultivates a strong emotional bond between you and baby and is found by most mothers to be a very satisfying and enjoyable experience. Finally, breastfeeding is convenient, available anywhere and anytime at the right temperature, and is free of charge.

Diet during lactation

Milk is an excellent source of the extra energy, protein and calcium needed by lactating mothers. However, lactating mothers need not drink milk in large quantities to meet these extra requirements.

The energy needs as well as additional nutritional requirements of the lactating mother are shown in Figure 1 on page 47. The recommended energy figures take into consideration the fact that the woman's stores built up during pregnancy will be used at this time. Thus, mothers who put on very little extra weight during pregnancy may have energy requirements higher than the recommended value.

Fluid requirements are much higher than normal too, so take plenty of drinks such as milk, fruit juices or plain water throughout the day. Thirst will usually let you know when you need to drink but, as a guide, at least eight cups a day should be taken. A Food Plan for lactation is given in Table 2 on page 48.

You may still need to continue taking the vitamin and mineral supplements recommended during pregnancy, especially iron and calcium, since requirements will continue to be as high as, and in several cases, higher than in pregnancy. Guidelines in countries recommending a vitamin D supplement in pregnancy also state that this should continue to be taken while breastfeeding.

Does diet affect the composition of breast milk?

Generally, the nutrient composition of breast milk is not dependent on the mother's diet, as her body stores will be drawn from to keep the composition of the milk constant. In the case of fat, however, if your intake of saturated fat—from foods like meats, ice cream, butter and chocolate—is very high, this will be reflected in the saturated fat content of your breast milk. Since too much saturated fat is generally believed to be harmful to health, It is wise to avoid foods with excessive saturated fats. Replace saturated fats with unsaturated fats such as olive, canola or soya oils and fat from fish.

Figure 1: Additional Dietary Requirements for the Lactating Mother[a]

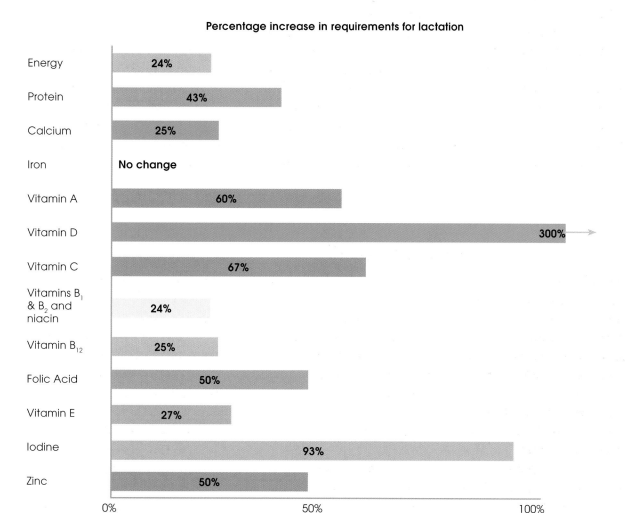

Percentage increase in requirements for lactation

Energy	24%
Protein	43%
Calcium	25%
Iron	No change
Vitamin A	60%
Vitamin D	300%
Vitamin C	67%
Vitamins B₁ & B₂ and niacin	24%
Vitamin B₁₂	25%
Folic Acid	50%
Vitamin E	27%
Iodine	93%
Zinc	50%

[a] Based on Recommended Daily Dietary Allowances for Normal Healthy Persons in Singapore (Health Promotion Board, Singapore, 2007), for all nutrients except vitamin E, iodine and zinc, which are based on US Dietary Intakes (DRIs): Recommended Intakes for Individuals; Vitamins and Elements. Food and Nutrition Board, Institute of Medicine, National Academies, 2005.

Table 2: A Food Plan to Supply Daily Nutrient Needs During Lactation

Food Group	Number of Servings Required Daily[a]	Notes
Milk	2–3 cups	If less is taken, substitute with alternative calcium sources or take calcium supplements.
Protein-rich foods	3	May include liver once a week. One egg a day will be useful.
Cereals and starchy foods	3–5	Whole grain preferred.
Fruit and vegetable	2–4	Include one green leafy vegetables and one red or yellow fruit.
Fluids	8 cups	Includes milk if taken. Avoid excessive coffee.

[a] Serving sizes as in Food Plan for Pregnancy, Chapter 2.

The content of vitamin C, vitamins B_1 and B_2 and other B vitamins in breast milk also depends on your diet, so it is very important to take some good sources of these nutrients every day. Remember, these nutrients are water-soluble and cannot be stored in the body. An old wives' tale has it that brewer's yeast helps promote lactation and overcome fatigue. While this is totally unproven, brewer's yeast supplements are not a bad idea as they will certainly ensure a good supply of the B vitamins.

In all cultures of the world, many other beliefs about certain foods that increase milk production abound—local beliefs concerning these foods are discussed in Chapter 8.

Occasionally, a particular food or drink taken by the mother may have some adverse effects on the baby such as, making him restless or causing loose stools or giving him a patch of eczema. This may be a mild allergy to some protein present in the mother's diet—usually from cow's milk (especially if the mother drinks a lot of it), egg or seafood—which passes into the breast milk.

If a mother is not sure whether consuming a particular food is safe or not during lactation, she can simply avoid it for the time being and reintroduce it a little later, watching carefully for any reaction. Allergies are discussed more fully in Chapter 7.

Excessive caffeine intake (more than three cups of coffee or 300 mg a day) and smoking have been shown to adversely affect the "let-down reflex" (the reflex which causes the milk to flow when the baby sucks the breast). In addition, caffeine passes into the breast milk which may cause the baby to be restless.

The effects of traditional "confinement" practices on breastfed babies are discussed in Chapter 8.

Getting started with breastfeeding

Preparing for breastfeeding means simply taking care of yourself throughout pregnancy to maintain optimum health and to make sure your nipples are toughened up a little by regularly rolling each between the thumb and forefinger for a few minutes each day towards the end of pregnancy. The rest happens automatically. The amount of milk-producing tissue and the number of ducts in your breasts begin to increase right from the early weeks of pregnancy. In the last trimester, the milk-producing cells enlarge and then production of colostrum begins. You are all set to go!

The first feed

When baby is born, request that you be allowed to hold him straight away. Studies suggest that putting baby to the breast immediately after birth—within an hour if possible—increases the success of breastfeeding. The baby will initially give only a few sucks, but this is perfectly adequate. The sucking reflex is in fact stronger in infants put to the breast in the first four to six hours after birth than in those for whom the first breastfeeding is delayed.

You must let your doctor and the hospital staff know that you intend to breastfeed so that they will bring the baby to you for feeds or allow the baby to "room in" with you. Supplementary formula feeding, apart from exposing the baby unnecessarily to cow's milk, is undesirable as it fills baby up and reduces his demand for the breast. He may also become used to the different method of sucking required to get milk from the bottle and may subsequently refuse the breast.

Correct sucking position

If the baby does not take enough of the areola (dark area around the nipple) into his mouth when sucking (see Figure 1a on page 50), he will tend to pull on the nipple like a short teat, and this can cause friction and lead to a sore nipple. It also means he will not get the milk efficiently, which may reduce the milk supply and ultimately lead to refusal to feed.

To suck correctly, the baby must latch onto the breast when his mouth is wide open (see Figure I b on page 50), so that he can take in more of the areola. He then forms a long "teat" from the nipple and the surrounding areola. He does not pull on this but, instead, compresses it between his palate and tongue to gently squeeze out the milk. This causes no friction to the nipple, so sore nipples will not develop. It also stimulates a good milk flow and is therefore important for successful breastfeeding.

Colostrum

Colostrum is the yellowish fluid secreted by the breast before the milk comes in will satisfy all of baby's needs for the first few days. As we have mentioned earlier, colostrum is particularly valuable to the infant as it is abundant in antibodies and is rich in protein and minerals. The colostrum gradually changes to milk by the third day after delivery, although it may take up to a week, particularly if delivery had been very traumatic or a Caesarean delivery had been performed. It is seldom necessary to give baby supplementary formula feeds or even water in the first few days as he is born with nutrient stores to tide him over this period and thus his requirements are satisfied by the colostrum.

It is normal for babies to lose a little weight in the first few days after birth. It may take 10 to 14 days for them to regain their birth weight. After this, their rate of weight gain should be at least 0.5 kg per month for the first six months.

Figure 1: Correct and Incorrect Sucking Positions in Breastfeeding

a. Incorrect

Baby's mouth is almost closed, he is far from the breast and takes rapid, shallow sucks.

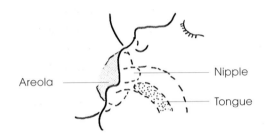

Areola — Nipple — Tongue

b. Correct

Baby's mouth is wide open, he is close to the breast and takes long deep sucks.

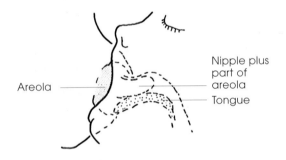

Areola — Nipple plus part of areola — Tongue

Establishing a routine

It is necessary to let the baby suck frequently at first—about eight to 10 times per day (roughly two-three hourly)—in order to stimulate the milk flow. On the first day, two minutes on each breast is adequate, slowly increasing to about eight to 10 minutes on each breast by the end of the first week. Start each feed on the breast which baby ended off during the previous feed.

The duration of the feed is not very important, as most babies get most of what they require in the first few minutes on each breast. Baby may like to suck longer for comfort and once your nipples have toughened a little, he can be allowed this privilege. For the first week, though, do not prolong the feeds unnecessarily as the nipples may be tender. Applying breast cream after feeds will help prevent any dryness or cracking of the nipples.

Engorgement

Engorgement, or swelling of the breasts, is common in the first week and can be relieved by applying hot towels to the breasts or bathing the breasts in warm water and allowing the baby to suck frequently. If you are still in hospital, an electric pump can give effective relief. Before using the pump, massage your breasts gently, rubbing the hard little milk sacs which you can feel within the breasts. Not all mothers will experience engorgement, however; the breasts can be full of milk and yet quite soft.

Inverted nipples

Having flat or short nipples does not necessarily mean that the nipples are inverted. As long as they can be pulled out when baby sucks, the nipples are fine for breastfeeding. A truly inverted nipple goes deeper into the breast when you try to pull it out. In the case of inverted nipples, nipple shields can be used when attempting to breastfeed. A nipple shield is like a teat with a wide base. The shield is placed over the nipple and the baby then sucks through the teat. This stretches the nipple and can in fact lessen the inversion. The shield can be used for a few days, after which the baby can try to suck directly from the breast.

Insufficient milk supply

Many mothers are doubtful from the start that their milk will be adequate because of small breasts or because the milk looks thin and watery. However, the size of the breasts is not important as even the smallest breasts have the same amount of glandular (milk-producing) tissues as large breasts have. Although human breast milk is thin and watery looking for the first part of a feed, it becomes whiter and creamier like cow's milk towards the end of a feed.

The "let-down reflex"

Baby fussing at the breast or refusing to suck does not mean that there is insufficient milk. Instead, this may be due to a slow let-down reflex. The let-down reflex causes the milk to flow when the baby sucks. It feels like a tingling, full sensation in the breast. Tiredness, anxiety or too little stimulation by the baby can delay the reflex.

Refusal of the breast

At any time, baby may go through a phase of refusing the breast. This is very upsetting to mothers and many are tempted to abandon breastfeeding when they find their baby is crying with hunger yet refusing to suck. If this happens, you should not feel rejected as there is usually a reason why baby is acting this way and there are many ways to overcome the problem. Start by asking yourself the following questions:

a) Have you or has your baby been sick lately?
Try short frequent feedings to build up your milk supply and your baby's appetite again.

b) Have you been worrying about something or are you overtired?
If so, your let-down reflex could be delayed. Relax! Lie down for a short while before a feed or put your feet up and have a hot drink.

c) Have you recently begun giving bottles for some of your baby's feeds?
Your baby could have grown used to the different sucking action and the fact that the milk flows immediately when bottle-feeding. Remember, with the breast, let-down of the milk is slightly delayed after the onset of sucking. To remedy this, you could try expressing your milk until it flows easily, so that your baby will get something as soon an he begins to suck.

d) Is baby refusing only in the daytime?
Particularly for babies who are three months and older, this is probably due to the fact that in the daytime they are more alert and easily distracted by any sight and sound in the room. If this is the case, try feeding in a quiet, darkened room, perhaps with some soft music in the background. Be sure that you are in a comfortable position—experiment

with different ways of holding baby till you find the one you both prefer.

Another possibility is that baby may be too hot, particularly around mid-day. Try feeding in a lying down position without your bodies touching, or give him a bath to cool him down before the feed.

e) Does baby suck a short while then cry as in pain?

This could be because he needs to be burped. Carrying baby around in an almost upright position to feed may be more comfortable for him.

f) Has baby been crying for a long time before his feed?

If so, he is probably too upset and impatient to suck long enough for your let-down reflex to occur. His crying may also have made you anxious, inhibiting the reflex. Give baby half an ounce of formula or a little expressed milk if you have it. Once quietened and sucking contentedly from the bottle, switch baby to the breast. Try waking baby for his feed so he is still sleepy at the start.

During a period of refusal, it is important to keep up your supply of milk by frequently expressing the milk. If you are still tense at feedtimes because baby is not sucking well, seek support and practical help

from an experienced mother. The Breastfeeding Mothers Support Group (Singapore) (www.breastfeeding.org. sg) or The Malaysian Breastfeeding Association (Persatuan Panggalak Penyusuan Susu Ibu Malaysia) (www. susuibu.com) can help.

If baby is not gaining weight

Only if baby is not gaining weight at the proper rate can you suspect he is not getting enough milk. There may be other reasons, however, for poor weight gain, and you should consult your doctor. Failure of baby to drink enough milk is not usually due to insufficient milk production by the mother but more often, it is because baby is not sucking properly. Make sure that he is sucking correctly. Check that baby's nose is not blocked. If baby has a cold it will be necessary to clean the nose with a soft cotton bud or nose drops from the doctor before feeding.

Mothers often fear that baby may not be getting adequate milk because they seem to be losing a lot of milk by leakage or because baby is regurgitating milk after each feed. The amounts lost in both these circumstances, however, are very small, and will not contribute to a failure of the baby to gain weight.

To know whether or not baby is getting enough milk, you can carry

out the wetness test. This involves checking to see that baby passes urine at least six times a day. The urine should be colourless or pale yellow. If the baby is fed solely on breast milk and is urinating at least six times a day, he is taking sufficient milk. However, this test will not be an accurate gauge if baby is being fed water or other drinks in addition to breast milk.

Increasing milk supply

If the milk supply is thought to be inadequate, it is always possible to increase it. The best way of doing this is to give the breast first, followed by a "filling up" feed of half-strength formula. Because it is only half strength, baby will be satisfied for a shorter time than usual and he will then take the breast again sooner, resulting in more frequent stimulation of the breast. So that baby does not come to prefer a teat to the breast, the diluted formula is best given with a spoon.

Breastfeeding under special circumstances

Baby delivered by Caesarean

Holding the baby and breastfeeding may be difficult the first few days after a Caesarean delivery due to the wound, but this should not present any major obstacle to breastfeeding. It should be initiated within 24 hours of the delivery.

Twins

There is no reason why a mother cannot breastfeed twins or even triplets successfully provided she has the time! As her milk production will be higher than normal, it is important that she eats plenty of nourishing food and drinks plenty of fluids.

Premature and small-for-dates babies

These babies do best on breast milk although they also require some nutritional supplements prescribed by a doctor to build up their nutrient stores. As they are often too small or weak to suck or swallow properly, the mother must express her milk which will then be fed to the baby by tube. Techniques for expression are discussed on page 56. The baby should be able to feed directly from the breast once he weighs 1.6 to 1.8 kg.

Due to the smaller stomach capacity of premature babies, they will need smaller but more frequent feeds.

Diarrhoea

Diarrhoea in a baby is no reason to stop breastfeeding. In fact, the baby with diarrhoea needs all the fluids he can get to prevent dehydration. Between feeds it may be necessary to give him glucose and electrolyte solution—which the doctor will prescribe—or just extra water. If the infant is vomiting, the doctor may advise stopping breastfeeding for 12–24 hours and giving only glucose and electrolyte solution.

Constipation

A breastfed baby may pass a stool after every feed or only once in a few days. Both patterns are perfectly normal and do not warrant any concern. Even if baby does not pass for up to five days, there is no cause for alarm so long as the stool is not hard. If stools are always very infrequent, however, and baby has difficulty in passing them, a little diluted fruit juice (for babies over two months), particularly prune juice, will help.

Green stools

The normal stools of a breastfed baby are bright yellowish-brown. Green stools may indicate an infection or may simply be because they have been exposed to the air and have undergone oxidation. After a cold, a baby may have green-tinged stools for a day or two.

Normally, stools of bottle-fed babies are greenish-brown, so when you shift from breast milk to formula milk or introduce some solid food to your baby, a change in stool colour is normal.

Fever

A baby with fever needs nourishment and may have higher than normal fluid requirements, but he may be unwilling to feed. After giving him paracetamol—as prescribed by the doctor—his temperature should come down and he may be more eager to suck. But if the feed is unsuccessful, express your milk. This will help maintain the supply. Keep it in the refrigerator, and try giving a little to the baby by cup and spoon or dropper.

If mother has a fever

Having a fever may sometimes reduce the milk supply but is not a reason to stop breastfeeding. As the need arises, however, temporary supplementation of formula milk should be resorted to. Furthermore, if the fever comes with a cold or mild infection there is no need to separate the baby from the mother as the baby will usually have been exposed to the virus or bacteria before the mother realised she had the infection.

If taking medication, one must check with the doctor if it is safe to breastfeed. If the doctor knows you are breastfeeding, he can usually ensure you are given a drug which is not harmful to the baby.

Mastitis

Mastitis, or inflammation of the breast, sometimes occurs in the first few weeks of lactation. If it occurs on the skin of the breast there is no reason to stop breastfeeding. But when the glandular tissue inside the breast becomes inflamed, it is usually because of a blocked duct and failure to empty off that part of the breast. Drainage of the milk is therefore the most important part of treatment and provided the mastitis has not been present for more than three days, the baby can still be breastfed. In fact, baby should suck more frequently on the affected breast. If an abscess develops and there is pus discharge, do not breastfeed from the affected breast. Normal nursing can be resumed once the abscess has been incised and drained.

Jaundice

It is common for babies to develop jaundice after birth. This is because their livers are slightly immature and unable to metabolise all the bilirubin which is released when old red blood cells are broken down. Bilirubin is yellow-coloured and so when excess builds up in the blood, the characteristic yellow tinge appears in the skin and the whites of the eyes. Jaundiced babies should continue to breastfeed normally. If they are very sleepy and unwilling to suck, the mother should express her milk and give it by spoon or dropper. Phototherapy is often used to treat jaundice, and this may mean that mother and baby cannot be together so much. The infant in this case is usually given supplementary water to replace water lost in sweat, but breast milk can provide all his other needs. A daily morning sunbath should help to clear up the jaundice in these babies.

There is another potentially more serious type of jaundice in babies which is due to a deficiency of the enzyme glucose-6-phosphate dehydrogenase (G6PD). This is discussed in Chapter 7.

Colic

Colic is sometimes described as "fussiness or crying for an unknown reason". Up to 30 per cent of infants in their first three months suffer from colic, which is usually limited to one fussy period at the same time each day. The infant cries and may draw up his legs as if in pain. Colic is not to be confused with "wind" or "gas" which occurs if the infant swallows air during a feed and which can be simply relieved by gentle patting on the back in an upright position after feeds.

Many mothers feel their baby's colic must be due to his feeds but this is not usually the case. It is no more common in bottlefed than breastfed infants, nor is it relieved by the introduction of solids. In a few severely affected babies, cow's milk may play a role and your doctor may advise changing to a soy-based formula. For most infants, however, only time can cure colic, and mothers should be reassured that it will pass. A colicky baby is comforted by more frequent small feeds and a lot of cuddling. Warm towels applied to the baby's tummy or placing baby on his tummy may help relieve abdominal pain. Gripe water, which contains a very small amount of alcohol, may help.

However, if you prefer something that does not contain any alcohol, you can easily buy one of the numerous preparations that are available in the pharmacies. Some mothers have also found it helpful to try rubbing a herbal ointment for wind—but just a little as baby's skin may be sensitive.

Breastfeeding and contraception

While menstruation does not usually occur when you are breastfeeding, it is not a 100 per cent guarantee against pregnancy. Ovulation can return at any time and the sign that it has done so will not be visible until menses follows two weeks later. If couples are considering taking some contraceptive measure at this time, bear in mind that the contraceptive pill tends to suppress lactation, and so an alternative form of contraception should be sought.

Breastfeeding and the working mother

If you intend to return to work within baby's first two to three months, do not let this put you off breastfeeding from the start. Even if you only breastfeed for these first months, you will have given your baby the best start in life. Once you establish breastfeeding, you will know what is involved and you will be in a better position to determine whether or not it will be possible to continue breastfeeding when you go back to work. It should be reassuring to know that many working mothers do successfully continue breastfeeding, with only minor inconvenience to their daily routine. Remember, you will only be away from your baby for two or three feeds each day. The other three to four feeds will be just as before, directly at the breast. These can be given once in the morning before you go to work, once as soon as you return in the evening, once before you go to bed, and then a night feed if required. Infants beyond two months do not usually need a night feed so interruption of your sleep will become less of a problem as you go on.

The daytime feeds

A logical way to solve the problem of the feeds you will miss is to express the milk at the usual feeding times and keep it for baby to have the next day. This is feasible if there is a refrigerator in your workplace to store the milk until you go home. You also need about 10 to 15 minutes to express enough for each bottle and a clean private place in which to do it. Access to a wash basin for washing your hands and rinsing the pump is a must. An extra precaution is to store your pump in a container of sterilising fluid between expressions, which will ensure that the pump is sterile before you use it again.

Refrigerated breast milk keeps for 24 hours. If your journey home is long and hot, then you should transport the bottles in an insulated container or "cooler".

If you have no way of storing your breast milk at work or find it difficult to express the milk, then baby can go on to mixed feeding—having formula milk during the day and breast milk when you are home. In this case, it may be necessary at first to express and discard some milk while you are at work in order to relieve the full breasts. The supply will soon adjust to the decreased demand, however. On weekends, it is probably best to keep baby on the routine he is used to, that is, formula milk in the daytime and breastfeeds at the same times as on the working days. While all this may seem very troublesome, keep in mind that it will only last until baby is about six months as by then, solids become increasingly important as a source of nourishment. By eight months you can usually dispense with daytime milk feeds altogether as baby will be having meals instead.

So that your babysitter will always have an extra bottle on hand for daytime feeds should the need arise, it is a good idea to express an extra bottle of milk occasionally and store in the freezer, clearly marked with the date. It will keep for up to three months and, if needed, it simply has to be left out at room temperature where it will quickly thaw. It can then be warmed up in the usual way—letting the bottle stand in a bowl of hot water. The milk should not be boiled as this will destroy some of its components. It is best not to use the microwave to reheat refrigerated milk as well because there is the danger of baby being scalded—the temperature of the milk inside the bottle may be much higher than the temperature of the bottle itself.

Expressing breast milk

Practice this before you go back to work. Expressing can be done easily by hand and this is preferred by many mums as it can be done anywhere at any time. Pumps are convenient, however, as the milk is usually collected directly into a bottle. But not all hand pumps work well. Some can cause discomfort. Thus, it is best to borrow a few different kinds of pumps from friends

so that you can see which is best. Practising beforehand will also give your baby opportunity to take breast milk from the bottle occasionally so he gets used to it.

Before returning to work, give yourself a week or so to get into a routine of expressing milk for the daytime feeds and keeping it until the following day.

Technique of hand expression
1. Wash hands.
2. Massage breast for a few minutes.
3. Cup one hand around breast, holding sterile collecting container in the other.
4. With thumb on edge of the areola above the nipple, and the fingers below, squeeze firmly. Repeat squeezing, moving around areola gradually to milk all the ducts.
5. Carry on for a few minutes then repeat process for the other breast. Alternate between breasts, working on each one for a few minutes at a time until enough milk is collected.

Weaning from the breast

If, for one reason or another, you have to stop breastfeeding before baby is ready, you can do so by dropping off one feed at a time with an interval of at least four to five days before dropping the next feed. When you are down to one or two feeds per

day, gradually reduce the duration of this feed to a minimum. If baby still frets for the breast occasionally, it may be possible to nurse once in two to three days, but note that milk production will gradually cease.

Babies are often said to wean themselves—they just begin to be less interested in the breast and more eager to try other foods and drinking from a cup. This can occur from about eight months onwards. Many babies, however, do not show any inclination to give up the breast and it is perfectly all right in such cases to allow them to continue as long as you feel comfortable doing so.

Bottle feeding

Despite the many disadvantages of infant formula compared to human breast milk, infants are hardy creatures and most seem to get by on formula without any problems. There are some precautions which bottle-feeding mothers should take, however, to ensure that they do not endanger their baby's health. These concern hygiene and concentration of the formula.

Hygiene

Milk is a highly nutritious substance and therefore an ideal medium for rapid bacterial growth. Care must be taken to keep all bottles and teats scrupulously clean and free of contamination and the milk powder tin should always be closed tightly immediately after preparing the feed. Make feeds with cooled boiled water and let your baby consume right away. Any milk that has been kept for longer than an hour without refrigeration should be discarded. You should also discard any milk left over after a feed.

If you want to make up feeds ahead of time, always make sure you refrigerate the feeds immediately after preparation. Milk that has been made up beforehand and refrigerated can be kept for 24 hours.

As it is often difficult to remove all traces of milk even by using the bottle and teat brushes, sterilising baby's bottles and teats is necessary. Sterilising can be done either by boiling in water or by soaking the bottles and teats in sterilising fluid. If you are boiling the bottles and teats, make sure that all of them are submerged in the water and boil for at least 10 minutes. When using a sterilising fluid, be sure to follow the manufacturer's instructions and soak the bottles and teats for the required time period.

Concentration of the formula

If the formula is not made up to the manufacturer's instructions, overfeeding or underfeeding will result. Over-concentration of formula milk is particularly dangerous for the baby. The extra protein and salts in the milk place too great a strain on his immature kidneys—in an effort to pass out the extra salt from the body, too much fluid may be lost. This could lead to dehydration. The scoops provided in each tin of formula milk are not to be packed tightly with powder nor are they to be heaped. As the instructions state, scoop up the powder and level it off with a clean knife.

The number of feeds and approximate amounts which a baby should be having from birth onwards are indicated in the weaning charts on pages 64 to 70 in Chapter 4. Just as in the case of breastfed babies, bottle-fed babies are usually capable of regulating their own intake, and should not be forced to take more than they really want just for the sake of finishing the bottle.

Bottle feeding and allergies

If your infant is not gaining weight and shows symptoms of allergies (see Chapter 7), the doctor may suggest a soya milk formula of which there are several on the market. Occasionally, this too may produce an allergic reaction, in which case a hydrolysed cow's milk formula can be tried. As allergy to cow's milk protein is often temporary, the doctor may recommend a test re-introduction of a standard cow's milk formula at a later date.

How long should a baby bottle-feed?

Your baby may gradually become more eager to drink from a cup in his second year. If not, you can try to wean him off the bottle gradually by offering his juice and mid-day milk drink from a cup and only allowing him his morning and evening milk feeds from a bottle. There is no reason why you should not allow him to have the bottle, but if your baby is still attached to his bottle after the age of two, offer him the choice between bottle or cup and explain that bottles are for babies and he is now a big boy!

Introduction of ordinary cow's milk

Infants who are not breastfed from six months of age should have infant or age-appropriate follow-on formula from this time. Ordinary unmodified cow's milk should not be used as the main milk drink until one year of age. While follow-on formulae may be continued beyond one year of age, there is no advantage in doing so.

If you have been breastfeeding and are introducing infant or follow-on formula or ordinary cow's milk for the first time, watch carefully for any allergic reaction.

Do breast- or bottle-fed babies need supplements?

In countries where there is little sunshine, vitamin D, found only in trace quantities in breastmilk, is given to breastfed babies. Some countries, including Canada, USA, UK and Ireland, have in recent years, recommended that all infants and young children up to age 5, take a daily vitamin D supplement. It is important to check with your doctor or health professional before commencing any supplement for your child, to ensure the correct dose is given, as too much Vitamin D could be harmful.

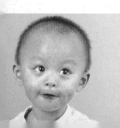

Breast milk is the best that you can give your baby.

04 Weaning

- When to start weaning
- Baby's first solids
- Weaning guides
- Food preparation for baby's first year
- Do's and don'ts of weaning
- Pros and cons of commercial baby foods
- When baby is in someone else's care
- A note on baby's growth
- Travelling with your baby

Weaning means the gradual switch from milk-only diet to a mixed diet. By the time baby is six months old, his weight will have doubled since birth. His calorie and nutrient requirements are therefore greatly increased and can no longer be supplied by milk alone. Your baby has an increasing natural urge to make use of his mouth as nature intended and this is satisfied with the introduction of complementary solid food.

When to start weaning

Opinions differ (and so do babies!) regarding the best time to introduce complementary foods, also known as weaning foods. (Although it is more appropriate to use the term "complementary foods", we have kept to the term "weaning foods" throughout much of the text as it is more familiar and widely used by the public.) Research on allergies suggests that weaning is best delayed until six months. Starting too late may reduce the infant's acceptance of weaning food. There is, however, no advantage in starting before six months. It is important to realise that milk still remains an important food; at least three cups (240 ml each) a day should be given until baby is into his second year, and at least two a day after that.

An infant is ready for semi-solid food when he is able to sit up with support and open his mouth when he sees food coming. The new technique of swallowing is not easy to master and takes a bit of practice. The infant must learn to close his mouth over the spoon, scrape the food from the spoon with his lips and move the food from the front to the back of his tongue. This can be very messy at first and very little solid food may actually be swallowed. However, since babies evidently enjoy the new experience, the messier it gets, the better! As they are now at the stage where everything they hold automatically goes into the mouth, it is fun to let them hold their own spoon and try to feed themselves; but time this before and not just after their bath!

If your infant shows signs of being ready for solid food before six months, you may start giving him weaning foods, but make sure this is not before the age of four months, and not at the expense of milk intake.

Baby's first solids

The first weaning foods should be:

1. Nutritionally right

Weaning foods should supply calories as well as protein, iron and vitamins, particularly vitamins C, B_1 and niacin. Cereals and fruits are suitable sources of calories, while protein can be given in the form of *ikan bilis*, beans or lentils, and egg yolk.

The infant's store of iron lasts only until about six months, so it is important to give more iron-rich foods after this time. Fortified infant cereals serve this purpose, as do egg yolk, liver and, later, meat and poultry. Since vitamin C is low in breast milk, fruit or fruit juice are also necessary additions to a child's diet from six months onward.

2. Not associated with allergies

It is best to begin weaning with fruit and vegetable purees and plain rice or barley cereals. Other cereals, especially wheat, can trigger allergies and are better left until later on.

Asian babies have been traditionally weaned on rice gruel, a practice which is now being adopted in the West. The reason for this is that, unlike wheat, rice rarely causes any allergy; some Western babies have coeliac disease, a genetic intolerance to wheat.

If there is history of allergies in your family, do not give your baby egg until he is six months old and then give him only the yolk until he is about a year old, as the white is more likely to trigger an allergy.

3. Easy to swallow and digest

Baby's first foods should be semi-solid to the point of being runny. In order not to tax baby's digestive system, very small amounts should be given and the food should be prepared without oil, butter or margarine as fat is more difficult to digest than other nutrients.

The weaning guide on pages 64 and 65 and the following step-by-step weaning charts show samples of how weaning may be carried out during baby's first year. The ages are meant only as a rough guide; more importantly is the developmental stage of the child, some children develop earlier or later than others.

The suggested serving sizes are also meant only as a guide, and parents must be attuned to information coming from the baby about timing, amount and preferences. It is good for the infant to feel he is capable of conveying what he wants and that he can trust someone to provide it for him. Otherwise, if parents are always wrong in guessing when he wants to eat, and are domineering and forceful about feeding, he may become anxious and confused about his needs, and it may reduce his independence and initiative.

Tips on introducing solids

1. If starting from six months, introduce a little food on the spoon before a milk feed when baby is alert and hungry. If starting earlier, it is better to give the food after the milk feed, as otherwise baby's appetite may be spoilt and he will not take adequate milk. Solids before six months are more to satisfy baby's curiosity rather than being nutritionally essential.

2. Introduce one new food at a time. Wait a few days (at least four) before introducing another new food. This gives baby adequate time to get used to and accept the new food. Also, any allergic reaction should surface by then and can be pinpointed to that particular food.

3. If introducing new textures and flavours, start with a small quantity (¼–½ tsp). If baby does not like it, try diluting the new food with familiar ones such as milk or rice porridge. You can then progress to the food alone later.

4. Give baby a chance to taste individual foods. Do not fall into the habit of always serving rice porridge with the ingredients mixed in. Learning how each food tastes will help baby accept the foods better when they are given separately in the toddler stage.

5. Present each new food in as many forms as possible. Baby may not take to a particular food in one form but may enjoy it better when it is prepared differently.

6. Do not omit foods because you do not like them. Parents tend to avoid giving foods they dislike but children should be free to develop their own likes and dislikes.

7. Do not force baby to take something he refuses. Baby may suddenly refuse a food that he had previously enjoyed. No one food is essential, and there are always alternatives. Remember, battles at mealtimes are best avoided.

Table 1a: Weaning Guide—Complementary Foods for a Day

Age in Months[a]		0–4	4–6	6–7
MILK		Breast (or bottle 90–150 ml) 6–8 times	Breast (or bottle 150–180 ml) 6–7 times	Breast (or bottle 180–210 ml) 4–5 times
			+	+
Food Groups	Foods		1–2 servings of those suggested (optional)	1–2 servings from each group daily
FRUIT & VEGETABLES	Fruit juice		Diluted, strained orange or others 3–4	Diluted, strained orange or others 2
	Fruit		Scraped or sieved banana, papaya or apple ½–1	Scraped or sieved banana, papaya, soft pear 2–3
	Vegetables		Boiled mixed vegetable stock 3–4	Cooked & sieved carrot, greens or peas 2–3
CEREALS & STARCHY FOODS	Rice			Milled or unmilled ground rice gruel ¼–½
	Others		Boiled barley water in place of water feed	Ground barley or mashed potato 2–3
PROTEIN-RICH FOODS	Egg			Cooked yolk only ¼
	Small dried fish			Toasted, ground *ikan bilis* or whitebait ¼
	Fresh fish			
	Liver			
	Pulses			Cooked & sieved lentils or beans 2
	Bean curd			Mashed bean curd 2–3
	Meat			
	Cheese			
	Yoghurt			

[a] Your baby may start each stage earlier or later depending on his rate of growth and development. If in doubt, consult your doctor.

 teaspoon    chinese spoon   rice bowl   cup

Table 1b: Weaning Guide—Complementary Foods for a Day

Age in Months		7–8	8–10	10–12
MILK		Breast (or bottle 210 ml) 3–4 times	Breast (or bottle 210–240 ml) 3 times	Breast (or bottle 240–240 ml) 3 times
		+	+	+
Food Groups	Foods	2–3 servings from each group daily	3 servings from each group daily	3–4 servings from each group daily
FRUIT & VEGETABLES	Fruit juice	Semi-diluted, strained orange/others 2–3	Strained 4	Strained 4–5
	Fruit	Mashed or finely chopped soft fruit, grated apple 3–4	Cut up soft fruit as finger fruit 2	Cut up 2–3
	Vegetables	Cooked or sieved or mashed carrot, peas greens, pumpkin 1	Cooked & finely chopped 1–2	Cooked & coarsely chopped 2
CEREALS & STARCHY FOODS	Rice	Porridge ½–¾	Porridge ¾–1	Porridge 1 or very soft rice ½
	Others	Pureed oatmeal, 3–4 barley or wheat cereal, mashed potato	Cooked cereal or softened weetbix or muesli 4 Bread ½ slice	Cooked cereal or noodle 2 Bread 1 slice Plain biscuit 1–2 pcs
PROTEIN-RICH FOODS	Egg	Cooked ½ yolk only	Yolk ½–1 Try cooked white ¼	Whole egg if white tolerated 1
	Small dried fish	Toasted & ground ¼	Toasted & ground or cooked, finely chopped ½	Toasted, ground ikan bilis or whitebait ½
	Fresh fish	Cooked, soft mashed white fish 2	Cooked & mashed or flaked 1-2	Cooked & flaked 1–2
	Liver	Cooked & pureed pig, calf, lamb or chicken liver 2	Cooked & mashed 1	Cooked & chopped 1–2
	Pulses	Cooked & sieved lentils or dried beans 3	Cooked & mashed 1–2	Cooked & mashed 1–2
	Bean curd	Mashed bean curd 2–3 Unsweetened soyabean milk ½	Soft beancurd 1–2 Soyabean milk ½	Bean curd 2 Soyabean milk ¾
	Meat		Scraped & cooked chicken, pork, lamb or beef 1–2	Minced or finely chopped & cooked 1–2
	Cheese		Soft, low-fat cottage cheese 2–3	Soft cheese or grated hard cheese or cut up as finger food 3
	Yoghurt			Plain yoghurt 4–6

Table 2a: Step-by-step Weaning (4–6 months—Preparing for Weaning [optional])

Baby's Developmental Stage	Sample Weaning Schedule		Notes
1. Rapid weight gain during first 3 months. Usually has added ⅔ of birth weight.	6–7 am	Milk feed	• Do not force if baby refuses the first introductory liquids. Give time for baby to acquire the taste.
2. Can suck small quantity of semi-liquid food from spoon.	9 am	🥛 or 🍊	• Barley or rice water can be given in place of one water feed.
3. Intestinal function still not fully mature; risk of allergies if weaning started too early.	10–11 am	Milk feed	• ½–1 tsp pureed fruit or vegetable or thin rice gruel can be given if baby is keenly seeking food. Give after a milk feed.
	2–3 pm	Milk feed	• Some babies will begin to sleep through the night by 2 months.
	4 pm	💧 or 🥄	
	6–7 pm	Milk feed	
	10–11 pm	Milk feed	
	Night feed if required	Milk feed	

 diluted, strained fruit juice   strained vegetable stock   water

Table 2b: Step-by-step Weaning (6–7 months—Early Weaning)

Baby's Developmental Stage	Sample Weaning Schedule		Notes
1. Can sit with back support and control grip with finger.	6–7 am	Milk feed	• It does not matter which milk feed is complemented or replaced with solids. Choose the times when baby is alert and happy. It is frustrating to feed a sleepy, grouchy little baby!
2. By 6 months, weight should have doubled. Growth is slower from now onwards.	9 am	(spoon) or (fruit)	
3. Better digestion capability (with increased secretion of intestinal enzymes).	10–11 am	Milk feed	• The consistency should be liquid paste at first, progressing to semi-solid.
	2–3 pm	Milk feed	• Expressed breast milk, kept in the refrigerator, can be mixed with introductory foods (as can infant formula milk).
4. Early teethers will begin to cut lower two front teeth.	4 pm	(drop) or (drop)	
	6–7 pm	Milk + (spoon)	• You can gradually bring the 10–11 pm milk feed earlier so that it eventually replaces the 6–7 pm feed.
	10–11 pm	Milk feed	

Sample Menu:

Morning
Pureed papaya or pureed vegetable broth
[see Food Preparation for Baby's First Year on pages 71–75]

Evening
Ground rice porridge mixed with ¼ cooked egg yolk
or ¼ teaspoon toasted, ground *ikan bilis*

Table 2c: Step-by-step Weaning (7–8 months)

Baby's Developmental Stage	Sample Weaning Schedule		Notes
1. Can sit well without support.	6–7 am	Milk feed	• About 30% of baby's calories are now derived from solids. Although milk feeds are reduced, milk can be used in baby's food.
2. Good mouth and tongue control. Able to chew soft food.	8–9 am	Breakfast +	
3. Can self-feed with fingers. May refuse food by pushing with hand.	11–12noon	Lunch + Milk	• Before progressing to finger foods, give baby semi-solid food with some lumps.
4. Two lower front teeth complete.	3–4 pm	Milk feed	• Teething rusk may be given.
	6–7 pm	Dinner +	• Give adequate fluid (150 ml/kg body weight each day including milk) to prevent constipation.
	9–10 pm	Milk feed	• Keep a record of food intake. This may help if an allergy is suspected and is also useful in planning meals.

Sample Menu:

Breakfast
Oatmeal, softened and pureed with milk
Mashed banana

Lunch
Steamed fish (mashed) with white sauce (see recipe on page 142)
Boiled and sieved peas with mashed potato

Dinner
Liver and carrot congee (see recipe on page 134)

Table 2d: Step-by-step Weaning (8–10 months)

Baby's Developmental Stage	Sample Weaning Schedule		Notes
1. Crawls well and can stand without support. 2. Can hold well with hand and begins to drink from cup. 3. Shows interest in what goes on at family table. 4. Growth of two upper teeth.	6–7 am	Milk feed	• Allow infant to join family table and finger-feed himself, albeit messy! • Most Asian mothers still cook separately for their babies but some foods can be taken by the baby from the family meal (before salt, soya sauce or chilli is added). Avoid oily or deep-fried foods. • Ideally, adjust baby's mealtime to fit in with family meal—otherwise, baby will tend to fill up on "nibbles" from adult food causing a loss of appetite when his own mealtime approaches.
	9 am	Breakfast +	
	12–1 pm	Lunch +	
	3–4 pm	Milk feed	
	6 pm	Dinner +	
	8–9 pm	Milk feed	

Sample Menu:

Breakfast
Wheat cereal in milk or baby's French toast (see recipe on page 137) with soaked chopped raisins or prunes

Lunch
Bean curd and French bean congee (see recipe on page 134)

Dinner
Tasty chicken stew (see recipe on page 136)
Chopped fruit (kiwi, soft pear, papaya or apple)

Table 2e: Step-by-step Weaning (10–12 months)

Baby's Developmental Stage	Sample Weaning Schedule		Notes
1. Has reached roughly three times birth weight by 12 months. 2. Has about eight teeth and can chew quite well. 3. Able to attempt self-feeding with spoon and drinks well from cup. 4. Can form single syllables and walk with or without support.	7–8 am*	Breakfast + Milk	• Food can be adapted entirely from family meals but with mild seasoning. • A little oil is acceptable now so mode of cooking can be more versatile. • In order to leave room for the other foods needed for growth, do not give baby more than four 240 ml feeds of milk daily. • Avoid urging baby to eat when interest lags—this could set the stage for future mealtime battles!
	11–12 noon	Lunch +	
	3 pm	Snack + Milk	
	5–6 pm	Dinner +	
	8–9 pm	Milk feed	

* The 6–7 am milk feed can be given if baby wakes up early. In this case, give the breakfast a little later and omit the milk with breakfast.

Sample Menu:

Breakfast: Lightly boiled egg (whole if white is tolerated)
Toast fingers for dipping
Chopped orange segments

Lunch: Fish macaroni (see recipe on page 135)

Snack: Small hard cheese finger and digestive biscuit or fruit (e.g. mango) with custard or yoghurt

Dinner: Thick congee or soft rice
Tender stuffed hairy gourd (see recipe on page 139)
Tasty apple dessert or fruit juice jelly (see recipes on page 140)

Food preparation for baby's first year

The following section is a guide on how to prepare foods for early weaning. As can be seen, a blender is useful, but there is really no need for special baby food grinders or other special equipment.

For foods which take a longer time to cook, e.g. carrots, lentils and beans, it is a good idea to cook a larger quantity than needed. Keep the balance in the refrigerator for use within the next 24 hours or freeze in individual portions labelled with the name of the food and the date, and use within a month.

Food	Preparation Guide
Baby's thirst quenchers	
Orange juice	Take one slice of orange and squeeze. Dilute with at least an equal amount of cooled boiled water. Later, when a greater quantity is required, use a citrus squeezer. The juice would still need to be strained before it is given to your baby.
Starfruit juice	Peel and place a few cut pieces in double muslin (an unused baby nappy will serve this purpose well). Hold the two ends of the muslin together and press with a metal spoon, squeezing against the side of the bowl or cup. Dilute the juice if necessary.
Tomato juice	Dip the tomato in boiling water for a few minutes. Remove it, rinse in cold water and peel off the skin. Press the flesh of the tomato through a fine sieve or follow the method used for the starfruit.
Unsweetened juices in bottle, tin or carton, e.g. grape, apple, prune, etc.	Once opened, pour the remainder into a bottle with a tight-fitting lid and keep it refrigerated. Be sure to dilute the juice before feeding. Do not keep any leftovers for longer than two days.
Vitamin C-enriched syrups, e.g. blackcurrant or rosehip	Dilute syrup according to the instructions on the label. These are useful as a standby when fresh fruits are not readily on hand or available. They are also convenient to pack when travelling.
Barley water	Boil 2 Chinese spoons of pearl barley in 1½–2 cups water for 10–15 minutes. Give this to your baby occasionally in place of water. If the barley water is lightly sweetened, add a squeeze of lemon juice.

Fruit

Babies love the natural sweetness of fruit so let them try as many as possible by their first year.

Banana, apple, ripe pear	Squeeze a little lemon or lime juice over the peeled pieces of fruits to prevent browning. Scrape with a spoon and feed directly or grate finely and then serve. Choose ripe fruit only.
Papaya, honeydew melon, kiwi, chiku, mango, watermelon and other soft fruit	Scrape, sieve or puree fruit. Small soft pieces can be given to baby when he is slightly older.

Vegetables

Vegetable stock	Wash and chop mixed vegetables such as onion, carrot, celery, tomato, cabbage or spinach. Simmer in water for 10–15 minutes and strain. The stock can be used to cook tasty rice porridge. Any excess can be frozen in an ice cube tray. When frozen, pop out the cubes and keep them in sealed bags for use later.
Pureed vegetable broth	Puree single or mixed boiled vegetables with some stock and milk*. Blend puree to the desired consistency (remove onion and celery from the stock if it is for very young babies).
Carrots, potatoes, tomatoes	Cut these into small pieces and boil or steam them till they are soft. Sieve the vegetables and mix with a little milk if desired. Remove the skin and seeds if using tomatoes.
Leafy greens, e.g. cabbage, spinach, *chye sim*, etc.	Wash leaves thoroughly. Chop the leaves finely and add to soups and porridge just before serving. Blanch spinach before use** then discard cooking liquid.
Other greens and gourds, e.g. French beans, broccoli, snowpeas, yellow/hairy gourds	Wash and chop them. These can be cooked in a small amount of water or in porridge. Alternatively, they can also be steamed till they are tender and soft.

* During early weaning, any milk used in food preparation should be made from expressed breast milk or baby's own formula milk. Ordinary cow's milk should not be introduced until one year of age.

** This is to reduce the oxalic acid content of the spinach, which interferes with the absorption of minerals such as iron and calcium.

Unmilled rice gruel	Wash about ½–1 kg of unmilled rice and dry it thoroughly. Grind the rice into a powder and store in an airtight container in the refrigerator. Before serving, mix the required amount of powder with water until a fairly liquid paste is formed. Cook this for a few minutes stirring constantly. You can add milk or more water to obtain the desired consistency of gruel. Add ¼ teaspoon ground toasted *ikan bilis*, and serve with pureed vegetables.
Rice congee	When baby is 6–7 months old, soft rice congee (unmilled or milled, or a mixture of both) can be given to him. Double boiling in a small pot over a gentle fire or using a mini crockpot will be suitable for cooking a small quantity. Alternatively, boil cooked fresh rice in 3–4 times more amount of water until soft. Use vegetable stock for added nutrients and flavour or cook with vegetables, e.g. carrot. Meat and fish can be added nearer the end of the cooking time or can also be served separately.
Pre-cooked infant cereals	Add water or milk according to the directions on the pack. It is best to store the dried cereals in the refrigerator.
Barley	If cooked until soft, the barley used to make barley water can be pureed or mashed and added into soups.

Ikan bilis	Buy the cleanest fish. Remove the head and entrails if this has not already been done but keep the bones. Wash, dry and toast the fish. Pound or grind it finely and store in an airtight container.
Egg yolk	Soft boil the egg. Remove the white and feed only the yolk to the baby. Alternatively, you could separate the egg and add the yolk to porridge or pureed vegetables while these are being cooked. Hard boiled egg yolk can be mixed with a little milk and served. This might be a bit cloying so be sure to give baby some water after every few spoonfuls of egg.
Bean curd	Rinse or blanch with hot water and add to food just before serving. The packaged silken type can be served cold, together with pureed vegetable or fruit sauce if desired.

Peas	Use frozen ones and not the tinned variety. Boil until soft. The peas can then be pressed through a sieve or pureed. For slightly older infants, the peas can be broken up with the back of a spoon.

Later cereal foods

Oats, wheat	Give this as a breakfast cereal, cooked with milk or mixed with fruit. Instant varieties are available and should be made up according to the manufacturers' instructions.
Rusks	You can make your own by simply drying some bread in a very slow oven (120°C). Rusks are ideal finger foods for teething babies.
Bread	Fresh soft bread can be dipped in soft boiled egg yolk or soup and given to baby. After 10 months, baby can be fed with bread thinly spread with unsaturated margarine or peanut butter.
Muesli	Buy the unsweetened, preservative-free, commercial variety. The muesli can be ground to a powder for younger babies, or the bigger bits can be chopped up and the whole mixture softened in milk for the older infant.
Soft rice	Besides thick congee, soft rice can be given to baby by 11 months of age to encourage chewing. You can use either white rice or a mixture of white and unmilled rice which has been cooked until very soft.
Noodles and pasta	*Bee hoon*, macaroni, and the like, can be boiled until soft and then mashed or chopped into small pieces to serve. Avoid using noodles with colouring or preservatives. Fresh noodles can be made quite easily at home. You can make them plain or with pureed vegetables (see recipes on page 159).

Later protein-rich foods

Liver	Boil liver and sieve or mash. Chicken liver is smoother in texture and less strong-smelling. If you are giving pig's liver in chopped pieces to an older infant, do not overcook it as it will toughen. Give liver no more than three times a week as it is high in vitamin A and too much of this vitamin can be harmful.

Chicken	Remove the skin before cooking. Scrape or mince the meat, then cook or boil it. You can puree it after this if it is to be given to a young infant. Chopped or shredded chicken can be given to older infants.
Fish	Cook fish and mash. To start with, choose low fat fish, e.g. *kurau, merah* or pomfret. Chopped small fresh whitebait is also suitable for babies.
Pork, beef, mutton	Use lean and tender cuts. Scrape or finely mince the meat then cook it. Small thinly sliced pieces can be given to baby later.
Yoghurt	Buy the plain, unsweetened type. You can sweeten this yourself with pureed fruit. If the fruit-flavoured variety is used, choose one without any preservatives, colouring, flavouring and added starch. Home-made yoghurt is also suitable for babies (see recipe on page 228).
Cheese e.g. cottage	Blend or sieve the cheese for smooth consistency if so required. Add this to mashed vegetables or fruit to enrich them. Later on, the cheese can be spread thinly on bread or biscuits. Select brands that are free of additives. Hard cheeses can be given as finger food occasionally for older infants.
Whole egg	Introduce egg white slowly only after baby reaches 10 months. If no allergy is encountered, whole egg can be given boiled, scrambled, poached or as a custard. If there is a family history of allergies, eczema or asthma, wait until the child is 1½–2 years before attempting to introduce egg white.

Do's and don'ts of weaning

Prepare food hygienically

Improper and unhygienic handling of food can lead to contamination. Bacteria multiply rapidly once they are introduced to food.

Here are some simple rules to prevent bacterial contamination of food:

1. Wash hands before handling food.
2. Do not allow raw food to come into contact with cooked food.
3. Always cook meat thoroughly to ensure all the bacteria in it is destroyed.
4. Reheating of food must be done thoroughly. If liquids are involved, make sure that the food is brought to a rolling boil—some bacteria will survive unless temperatures are sufficiently hot.
5. Do not leave food standing for long periods of time at room temperature. As soon as leftover food has cooled, keep it in the refrigerator. Always cover food containers properly before putting them in the refrigerator
6. Do not keep unfinished foods once they have been served. Food gets contaminated once it is mixed with saliva and will spoil quickly afterwards.

Pay attention to fluid requirements

When weaning gets underway after the age of six months, it is important to give enough fluids to baby in the form of water, juices and soups. About 150 ml of fluid is required for every kilogram of the baby's weight daily. An 8 kg baby, for example, would require at least 1200 ml per day, which could be given as four 240 ml feeds plus two 100 ml drinks of water or diluted fruit juice.

Nutritional do's and don'ts

1. Do not give fried foods before 10 months.
2. Do not add salt or other salty seasonings and sauces to baby's weaning food. You should not judge the taste of the food by adult standards. Food naturally contains enough salt for baby's needs. Added salt can place a strain on a baby's kidneys which are still not fully mature.
3. Avoid adding sugar to baby's food. Sugar increases the calories in food without increasing the other nutrients. This can lead to the baby becoming overweight and may give him a sweet tooth so that he will demand more sweet things later with disastrous results to his teeth.

To have is to hold

Food is a major part of a young child's environment and, once he begins to gain some control of his fingers and can grasp and hold objects, he will love the chance to handle his own food. These early attempts at self-feeding should be encouraged. You can expect a mess, so lay newspaper or a large plastic sheet on the floor beneath baby's chair to help make cleaning up easier. Baby's first "finger foods" should be very soft such as small slices of banana or papaya. Later, when baby starts teething, harder foods can be given for him to work on with his gums. Besides teething biscuits, you can try toast or bread that has been hardened in the oven for 15 to 20 minutes, or plain biscuits such as crackers and digestives.

The hard core of a pineapple or a peeled apple will also give baby many happy hours of gnawing. Once baby can bite, however, there is a danger of choking on a small piece that has been bitten off, so never leave the baby alone with food.

Once baby has some teeth, his mealtimes should include pieces of soft cooked food that can be picked up with fingers or a plastic fork. Carrot pieces, tiny minced-meat balls, tender chicken strips and pieces of hard-boiled egg are all suitable. Cooked sweet potato, pitted watermelon in bite-sized pieces, peeled and halved grapes and pieces of pitted dried prunes will provide further interesting textures and colours for baby.

Safety in feeding

When infants graduate to eating lumpy foods and whole pieces of food, the danger of choking becomes greater. If food goes down the wrong way and is inhaled into the airways it can cut off the air supply.

We strongly recommended that parents and caregivers learn coronary pulmonary resuscitation (CPR) from a recognised course provider, in order to be able to deal with any choking emergency that may arise.

Take the following precautions to help prevent any incidence of choking in your baby:

1. Make sure feeding is appropriate to the child's capabilities.
2. Avoid foods that are particularly difficult to control in the mouth, such as nuts, raw carrots or hard sweets.
3. Modify some foods to prevent the risk of choking. Cooked meat can be shredded or crumbled, grapes cut into halves or quarters, and sausages cut into small slices. Pieces of other foods such as apple should be cut so that they are too big to swallow. However, keep an eye on baby to see that he does not bite off a smaller piece and swallow that whole.
4. Always be with your child when he is eating.
5. See that the child sits down to eat. Many choking incidences are due to eating "on the run".
6. Make sure the environment at feeding time is calm. Fighting, excitement or hilarity can make a child catch his breath and inhale food.
7. Spread peanut butter thinly. It can block the airways as it is so thick and sticky.
8. Remove small seeds from grapes and guava. They can be inhaled into the airways and may later trigger pneumonia.

Pros and cons of commercial baby foods

A visit to any supermarket will reveal an amazing array of baby foods in cute little bottles, jars and boxes — juices, purees, powders, strained meat or vegetables and even complete strained meals.

Commercial baby foods do have their uses as stand-bys if you really do not have the time to prepare something for baby or if you are travelling with baby. They are hygienic, usually prepared without any added salt and the ready-to-feed types can be heated up and served straight from the jar. A jar of baby food also ensures a decent meal for baby if he is temporarily in the care of someone else. It is advisable to get baby used to one or two varieties in advance so that when the time comes to use them there will be no problem with acceptance.

Convenient though they are, there are drawbacks to relying solely on commercial baby foods:

1. Expense—baby foods usually work out to be double or more the cost of making the food yourself at home.
2. Baby may not be able to finish all of one jar and it may be wasted.
3. Baby foods are often thickened with starch which reduces the amount of other more nutritious ingredients.
4. With the complete dinners, baby does not get a chance to try individual foods and experience their different textures.
5. Local foods are not emphasised, and many of the varieties will not be foods that baby can expect to be served once he reaches the toddler stage. This may lead to poor acceptance of the family's food, and a toddler who demands to continue having his own baby food.

Do not be concerned that commercial foods are often fortified with vitamins and minerals, whereas your home food is not. There is absolutely no need for baby to have fortified foods, provided he is taking a good variety of natural foods. Only for infants who are slow to wean, however, may supplementation, particularly of iron, be necessary. In such a case, the iron-fortified infant cereals will be useful.

When baby is in someone else's care

If you are a working mum and unable to prepare baby's food yourself, it can often be a source of worry wondering if your baby is eating well in your absence. If you have a maid or someone else in your household to look after baby, this is not so much of a problem as you can show by example how to prepare baby's foods and can leave instructions each day on what to give. It is a good idea to ask, on your return each day, what baby ate. Perhaps, for a week or so, you could keep a written record. This will help reassure you that baby is eating enough or alert you if he is eating poorly. You will then be in a good position to suggest alternatives and revise directions when necessary.

If baby is looked after by a babysitter outside your home, you should enquire at the end of each day about baby's meals. If you are not happy with what you hear, it is most likely to be because the babysitter gives the same thing, day after day, with no variety. Do not be too hard on the babysitter; many mums fall into the same routine too. When your baby likes a particular type of porridge it is very tempting to go on serving this every day as acceptance is guaranteed, but even babies will grow tired of the same tastes if served too often. However, the main reason for varying his diet is to provide a more complete range of nutrients. So, explain this to your babysitter and suggest alternatives that you know baby likes. If you are still concerned, you may want to bring baby's food with you on some days for the babysitter to heat up before serving. It is always a good idea to stipulate at the outset what your expectations are regarding meals and reach a good understanding with the babysitter on this before engaging her services.

A note on baby's growth

Checking baby's weight regularly and plotting it on the chart provided in baby's health book (fortnightly or monthly) is a good way of assessing if his growth is normal. The actual weight of your baby is not as important as whether or not he is gaining weight at a reasonable rate. So, your baby may start out below the average weight, but if his weight steadily increases parallel to the standard curve, you should not worry. The growth rate should not slow down too much, however. If it drops below the curve it has been following for more than two consecutive weighings then you should consult your doctor as to the possible reasons.

Overweight babies

There is usually no cause to be concerned if your baby is overweight during the first year. It was formerly believed that fat babies became fat adults, but this is now known to be not necessarily so.

Chubby babies usually lose their extra weight once they become more active and gain height in the toddler years. Having said this, however, it is not good to overfeed your baby as you are taxing his digestive system. If you think you may be overfeeding your baby, make a note of what you give him over a three-to-four day period and show it to your doctor or a dietitian who can then advise you accordingly. If you have a plump baby who is also quite underactive, it would be good to encourage more physical activity. Use baby chairs and playpens as little as possible as they restrict movement. Obesity in toddlers and later childhood is discussed more fully in Chapter 6.

Travelling with babies

Parents with babies are often reluctant to go out or go on holiday because of having to prepare food and drinks to take along for baby. The thought of feeding baby anywhere but in the convenience of your own home can be a bit daunting. But with a little planning beforehand, you will be surprised how easy it is to organise yourself for a trip, be it just an afternoon at the park or a week by the sea.

Many parents also believe their baby may be upset by travelling, but babies travel much easier than we think. They do not suffer from travel sickness, are usually able to sleep anywhere and, in fact, will enjoy the experience of new sights and sounds. Nevertheless, it is true that new foods or a different water or inability to keep baby's food and milk as safe in terms of hygiene as it is at home, can pose potential problems for the baby.

Young babies

If baby is less than six months and not yet on solids, all he needs is milk, with supplementary drinks of boiled water and juice. If you are breastfeeding, this can be very simple indeed but a word about breastfeeding in public is appropriate here. It is still not a common sight in this part of the world to see a mother suckling her baby in public, and many breastfeeding mothers avoid travelling with their babies for this reason.

There are places, however, where you can breastfeed in relative privacy. If going by car, you can breastfeed in the car provided you are travelling with your own family. In airports, there may be an infant feeding/changing room where you can feed comfortably. In the plane itself, you have relative privacy in your seat and can usually feed discreetly without feeling self-conscious. For more privacy in trains, avoid seats which face each other.

Since you cannot be sure if breastfeeding will be practical when the time comes, it is best to take along milk powder (pre-measured for convenience), boiled water and sterile bottles and teats, just in case. Remember to take baby's pacifier if he uses one—it can be useful should you have to delay his feed slightly. In this hot climate of ours even a short time spent outside makes us very thirsty. So always take a bottle or two of water or juice for your baby.

Items to take on a holiday

1. Sterilising container (any large container will do)
2. Sterilising tablets (or rely on boiling).
3. Bottle and teat brushes and some washing-up liquid.
4. A plastic jug with a lid for cool, boiled water will be useful.
5. A plastic "tray" bib will reduce the amount of washing. You can even use disposable bibs.
6. Lots of tissue paper, pre-moistened baby wipes, and several little face towels to wipe baby after meals.

Older babies

For babies on solids, jars of baby foods are ideal. To avoid wastage, however, take the smallest size jars as once opened, the contents cannot be kept beyond one mealtime. A baby under nine months does not need to have meat and vegetable dinners more than once a day. For the other meals, take a few varieties of dried pre-cooked infant cereals in airtight containers. Fruit and freshly squeezed fruit juices can usually be obtained at any time of the day from

Encourage your child to handle his own food and feed himself.

hotels for direct feeding to baby. If you are diluting them, however, use only boiled water.

If baby is taking egg, this can be fed at one meal a day. The hotel can usually prepare it in whatever way your baby likes. For babies over nine months, other menu items may be suitable: porridge, potato, soft-cooked fish, soft-cooked carrots which can be finely mashed. Ask for minimal seasoning to be used if possible and do not feed baby anything tough, fried or oily. Do try to take along at least some foods that are familiar to baby in order to minimise the number of new foods you have to feed him. These new foods may not be well accepted and may cause an upset tummy.

05 Feeding Your Toddler and Preschooler

- What food does my child need?
- Feeding a toddler
- Food refusal
- Increasing your child's interest in food
- Picnics and holidays with toddlers

After his first birthday, your child should have settled down to three meals a day, plus two to three milk feeds. He will have a good number of teeth and so can handle lumpy textures. He will enjoy most of the family's food and, rather than focusing on how much the child eats, see that he eats a good variety of foods. Take advantage of your child's curiosity—he will enjoy trying many new foods with different flavours, colours and textures. Also, experiment with different ways of preparing and presenting the same food. ●○○●●

Although children should be encouraged to feed themselves from as early as possible, they need help and supervision, particularly if their food is taken from the family's portion. Your little one might sit and devour a bowl of plain rice with a little gravy and no one might even notice that he did not eat any meat or vegetable!

A high chair is an excellent way of allowing your toddler (up to 18 months or so) to join in the family meals at the dining table. Later on, you can seat him at his own little kiddy-sized table for his meals, which will make him feel very independent! Even if your child has already had his meal, he may enjoy sitting at the dining table while you eat, watching, listening and, more often than not, enjoying tidbits from your plate. This is a good way of introducing him to adult food.

This is the formative period when food habits are being developed. Therefore, it is important for you to follow good food habits and, in so doing, teach your child by example. Use every opportunity to inculcate awareness in your child of the role food plays in health. Children learn quickly and are good at reasoning, so if you tell them milk will help them grow big and strong because it helps their bones to grow, they will be much more likely to drink their daily quota than if you just give them a flat order to drink it.

Having said this, however, some children do go through phases when, no matter how hard you try, you cannot get them to eat well. This problem will be dealt with in a subsequent section.

What food does my child need?

The rate of growth slows down somewhat after the baby's first birthday and a previously ravenous baby may become a finicky toddler who only picks at his food. A reduced appetite is no cause for alarm so long as the food taken is nutritious and varied. Table 1 on page 85 shows the foods required for the one- to three-year age group and the preschool group of three to five years.

Note that at least two cups of milk (240 ml each) should be taken daily. A child does not outgrow his need for milk. Milk remains an excellent food and a valuable source of calcium right throughout the growing years. If your child begins to refuse milk, try flavouring it or give the equivalent amount in the form of custards, yoghurt, cheese and ice cream.

On the next page (see Table 2) is a daily menu which will give you an idea of suitable meals for your toddler/preschooler. In addition to the main meals listed, most children enjoy some fruit juice at least once a day, either with breakfast or between meals. It is also a good idea to offer plain water a few times each day, say with lunch and dinner. Get your child used to this important thirst quencher right from babyhood. Otherwise, you may find your child refusing to drink anything but sweetened drinks.

Table 1: A Food Plan to Supply Daily Nutrient Needs for a Toddler/Preschooler

Food Group	Amounts of Food for a Day	
	1–3 years	3–5 years
Milk	2–3 cups	2 cups
Protein-rich foods	3–4 Ch sp meat[a]	4–5 Ch sp meat[a]
Cereals and starchy foods[b]	1 bowl rice or noodles + 1 slice bread + ½ cup ready-to-eat cereal	1–1½ bowls rice or noodles + 1 slice bread + 1 cup ready-to-eat cereal
Fruit and vegetables	½–1 piece fruit + 2–3 Ch sp vegetables including at least 2 types of dark green leafy or red/yellow fruit and vegetables	1–2 pieces fruit + 3–4 Ch sp vegetables including at least 2 types of dark green leafy or red/yellow fruit and vegetables
Fats and oils	1 Ch sp	1–1½ Ch sp

[a] or alternatives, for example 1 Ch sp meat = 1 egg or 1 slice cheese or ¼ large square bean curd.
[b] extra carbohydrate, including snacks such as biscuits, may be included depending on activity level and appetite.

Table 2: Sample Daily Menu for a Toddler/Preschooler[a]

Breakfast	½ cup unsweetened orange juice ½ cup wholegrain breakfast cereal with ½ cup milk 1 slice cheese or 1 scrambled egg
Morning snack	1 digestive biscuit ½ cup milk
Lunch	¾ bowl of *mee tai mak* soup 2 Ch sp prawns or fish cake 2 Ch sp chopped *chye sim* and carrots 1 small banana
Afternoon snack	1 carrot bran muffin (see recipe on page 248) ½ cup milk
Dinner	½ bowl "vitamin soup" (see recipe on page 219) ¾ bowl rice 2 Ch sp baked lemon chicken (see recipe on page 186) ½ slice papaya
Bedtime	1 cup milky drink
Oils and fats for the day: 1–1½ Ch sp	

[a] Serving sizes will vary depending on the child's age, size, appetite and activity level. Make use of recipe sections for more ideas and variety.

Feeding a toddler

Meat and fish

For a toddler to enjoy meat, make sure it is tender enough to enable him to chew it with his few teeth. It is advisable to mince the meat and make patties or balls or cut the meat into small pieces. Fish and chicken are less of a problem texture-wise and can be given more often. Slow cookers are handy for rendering tougher cuts of red meat soft.

if you are worried that your child does not eat much meat, continuing to use iron-fortified cereal once a day (infant or adult ones) will safeguard him against iron deficiency.

Fruit and vegetables

It is very important to expose young children to a wide variety of fruit and vegetables because they provide the necessary vitamins and minerals needed by the body. Despite their interesting colours, shapes and texture, however, a lot of youngsters are reluctant to eat them.

To solve this problem of convincing children to eat fruits and vegetables, many mothers resort to force feeding their children. But if the aim is to encourage a child to develop a liking for fruit and vegetables, then forcing him to eat them is not a good option.

A more successful method of introducing vegetables to children is through stories or by creatively cutting the vegetables into nice shapes. Vegetables with texture are usually better received than the soft types. For example, a child may reject mushy chopped spinach but enjoy picking up and feeding himself green peas one by one. Similarly, cauliflower and broccoli florets, baby sweetcorns, sliced green beans, carrot cubes and celery slices may go down better with your child than cabbage. If your child is not keen on vegetables, disguise them in soups or liquidise them in stews.

Instead of serving fresh fruits, you can make them into juices, mousses, jellies and ice-lollies. You can also add freshly cut fruit pieces—in different shapes and sizes—to fruit juices to make them more interesting.

If you are really worried that your child is not eating much vegetable or fruit, you can supplement with a daily multivitamin/mineral tablet as a temporary measure. However, always consult your child's doctor before starting a supplement and make sure you give the correct dose. Note that you should avoid giving chewable vitamin C tablets to children—these are acidic and can cause erosion of the tooth enamel.

Suitable snacks

If a child is hungry between meals, he can be offered one of the following snacks:

- a slice of banana and prune bread (see recipe on page 249)
- a portion of fruit
- a plain biscuit
- some yoghurt
- a piece of cheese
- a small sandwich.

You will find more ideas on suitable snacks for your child in the "Teatime Munch" section of the recipes from page 241 to page 256.

Food refusal

You should distinguish between a variable appetite and food refusal. After all, these are days when you are less hungry than others depending on how preoccupied you are with other things. So respect your toddler if there are days when he does not want to finish all his food. Do not jump to the conclusion that he is being naughty and stubborn or is seeking attention. There may be a number of reasons why your child is refusing to eat.

Following are some of the common ones, and what you can do to prevent them:

- Not hungry—Avoid giving your child snacks and nibbles between meals if he does not eat much at his main meals. Give only a drink of juice or milk but not too close to the mealtimes. The child will then be more hungry at his proper mealtimes.

- Distracted with an activity— Minimise distractions such as toys or the television during a meal.

- Too tired—There may be no choice here but to give the child milk and let him have his nap. Try as far as possible to have regular nap times so that the child will not be tired at mealtimes.

- Not keen on the particular food served—Just like us, kids have their likes and dislikes. It is pointless to pressure a child to eat a certain food. There will always be alternatives you can try which are just as nourishing, e.g. instead of liver give meat or egg; instead of spinach give broccoli; instead of orange juice give apple juice. If a child refuses a food which he usually enjoys, perhaps he could be tired of it. This could be the case if you have been giving it to him very often. So, leave a break of at least a week before serving the food again. It will probably be enjoyed once again after this time.

- Demanding a particular food instead of the one served—Toddlers will often have a penchant for a particular food, e.g. banana, or jelly and custard, for a period of time. They will eat that food at every meal, to the exclusion of all others. Expressing food likes and dislikes may be partly psychological, as little one enjoys his independence at being able to influence what mum gives him to eat. This independence should be encouraged to an extent. Parents who always dictate what their child must eat often end up with a child

refusing food. So you should give in partly to his favourite whims; he will tire of them eventually. Draw the line, however, by only allowing the favourite food at one meal a day. This way, you can still ensure that a wide variety of foods is taken at the other meals.

Is food refusal harmful?

These yo-yo periods are short-lived and do not affect the child's overall nutritional status and health. Food refusal that excludes most foods over a period longer than three days, however, should give rise to some concern. It is not uncommon and the reasons are not fully known. In some families, food refusal has been linked with the arrival of the second baby and is usually considered a form of attention-seeking—even if the attention given is punishment. The way to deal with this is to be calm and simply remove the food after 20 to 30 minutes. Although it may seem that he is not eating hardly anything, he may be getting quite enough, particularly if he is still drinking milk.

Ask yourself if you have been giving your little one the attention he needs and try to give more in other ways which are not related to food—more kisses and cuddles, reading, spending time playing with your child on the floor with his toys or taking him out for a walk. There are some other points that you might like to note on dealing with food refusal and avoiding it in the first place:

1. Try to avoid bribing your child into eating. ("If you eat this I'll give you that.") This may create a negative situation where the child uses eating as a tactic to manipulate the parent.

2. Do not become anxious at mealtimes. Tension kills whatever appetite may be present.

3. Do not expect too much from your toddler. Serve small portions and then give seconds if required. Do not overwhelm him by serving him a huge plate of food.

4. If possible, have your toddler's mealtime coincide with your own. Seeing you eat and sensing the pleasant relaxed atmosphere at the dinner table will encourage your little one to take part in this grown-up activity. Help him to feed himself, but do not make him the focus of all your attention. This is much better than feeding him "on the run", trailing all over the house behind him with his bowl of food in hand, or feeding him when you are in the middle of preparing the family's meal with one eye on the oven. If you have two or more children, eating their meals all together makes for a better appetite.

5. Keep mealtimes regular and always associate eating with one place—the dining table, breakfast bar or kid's dining corner.

6. Give your child a choice of two alternatives for each category of food, e.g. rice or pasta, chicken or beef, peas or carrots. This encourages their independence and gives them some control.

Increasing your child's interest in food

Teach him the names of foods through picture books.
Recognising and naming the foods he has seen in the book on his plate can be fun.

Use attractive serving plates, bowls, and cutlery.
There is a wide variety of children's crockery sets available in the stores. While some are impractical and expensive, there are other very attractive non-breakable ranges.

There are numerous plates, trays, bowls, cups and spoons of different sizes to choose from. Think of what will suit the type of meals you prepare and your child's appetite and buy accordingly. One bowl for cereal, one plate or tray, and perhaps a smaller bowl for desserts is usually sufficient, with appropriately-sized cutlery. A tray with separate compartments is usually preferable to a plate, as most toddlers like to see each item of their food separately.

Encourage kitchen play.
Children are usually fascinated with the kitchen and will amuse themselves for hours with your pots and pans and other cooking utensils. This helps create an interest in food and you can develop this interest further by buying playdough, plastic food, utensils and tea-sets for your child to play with. You can even allow him to help make real food, for example, spreading butter and jam on a piece of bread (with a plastic

knife of course), stirring ingredients for a cake or biscuit mixture, or rolling and cutting biscuit dough.

Bring your child to the supermarket.
Most children enjoy shopping trips. Let your child choose some items he likes and explain why you are choosing certain foods. On reaching home, allow your child to help put away the provisions.

Make up funny names for your child's favourite dishes.
Your child might like "Carebear's honey bread" or "Ah Meng's banana delight".

Have meals outdoors sometimes.
Food, eaten outside—even if it is just on the balcony—always seems to taste better! A picnic lunch at the park or seaside will be a welcome change from the usual lunch eaten indoors.

Picnics and holidays with toddlers

Picnicking with toddlers

Picnics are fun and in our lovely climate, we can have a picnic practically any day of the year. Picnics require planning but once you have organised a few, you will soon not have to think twice about it! To help, here is a list of useful things to bring along:

- a few large mats or large plastic sheeting
- a plastic tablecloth
- a roll of kitchen towel or soft paper serviettes for spills
- wet tissues (for everything from wiping sticky hands to cleaning up after a dirtied nappy)
- a vacuum flask of hot water
- a bottle or two of boiled water
- a cooler for items which need to be kept cold

- disposable plates, cups and cutlery.

For young children, a bowl is easier to manipulate than a plate. Buy the plastic rather than the paper ones—plastic bowls are more expensive but, if handled with care, they can be washed and re-used.

In a picnic, all the food is brought ready to eat from home. Barbecues are a popular variation, however, when the food is cooked then and there. As a barbecue consists mainly of meat which may be too tough for small children, you must bring along complementary dishes for them.

Avoid bringing foods that are easily perishable, such as curry with coconut milk.

Picnic ideas

> sandwiches
> homebaked cakes—avoid fresh cream fillings
> biscuits, scones, muffins
> fruits and fruit juice
> fried rice, *bee hoon*, spaghetti— cook just before the picnic if to be taken warm
> corn-on the-cob
> pizza, quiche, pies and meat-loaf —bake, cool and wrap. Keep in cooler.

(See also school lunch box ideas on page 97 in Chapter 6).

Travelling with toddlers
Some tips for the journey

1. While younger babies rarely get travel-sick, toddlers often do and so it is best not to overfeed them en route but to keep food and milk to a minimum. Carry one or two changes of clothing for both toddler and yourself just in case! It is also handy to carry a few spare plastic bags (particularly the variety that can be zipped shut) to catch whatever is thrown up.

2. Avoid dried and salted snacks which cause thirst. A few boiled sweets or mints are pleasant to suck and relieve monotony. Ration these, however, as they may cause sickness if taken in excess.

3. Take your own food with you as far as possible, as there may not be any suitable restaurants to bring your child to. See the section on picnics on page 89 for ideas on what foods should to bring when travellling.

Meals at your holiday destination

If you are staying in a hotel, your toddler will take great delight in choosing from the menu. Do not worry if he does not eat as much as normal—he will make up for it when he gets back home. You can allow him to drink more milk than usual, which will ensure he does not go hungry. Bring along some packets of his favourite cereal and biscuits which he can have for breakfast or as snacks throughout the day.

For children over a year, there is no longer any need to boil the water in your home if your supply is safe and the adults in the family drink it unboiled. However, if you are travelling to a country where the water supply is not one hundred per cent safe, always request boiled water for your child or buy bottled mineral water (the still type and not the aerated ones).

Constipation is a common complaint of travellers, and babies and toddlers are no exceptions. Thus, it is a good idea to bring along individual-sized jars of prune juice or dried prunes which are available from most supermarkets. Some hotels do provide prune juice as a menu item.

Safety of prepared foods

When relying on outside foods, protect your child from the risk of food poisoning by avoiding:

1. Foods which may have been prepared many hours earlier and kept sitting outside at room temperature for a long period.
2. Uncovered food.
3. Foods which are handled with bare hands.
4. Food sold in dirty or untidy surroundings.

Take advantage of your child's curiosity to introduce her to new foods with different flavours, colours and textures.

06 Food and the School-going Child

- Nutritional needs of your school-going child
- Eating through a school-child's day
- Eating out—hawker and fast food
- Obesity in the young

The diet of young school-going children (we are talking only of the early schoolers from six to ten years of age) is often given less attention by parents, as the children are assumed to be able to meet their nutritional requirements from whatever they care to eat! This may stem from the fact that their visible growth rate is much slower than the very young and they have not yet reached the spectacular growth spurt which occurs during adolescence. The truth is, their nutritional needs continue to be significant. ●●●●

Nutritional needs of your school-going child

The need for proper nutrition

Nutrition is important during childhood for the following reasons:

1. To provide nutrients and energy for continuing growth.
2. To meet energy and nutrient needs for vigorous physical and mental activities.
3. To help maintain resistance to infections.
4. To build up body stores of nutrients to meet the coming demands of the growth spurts of puberty and adolescence.

It has been shown that children of this age group tend to have lower than recommended intakes of calcium and iron, especially non-milk drinkers and poor meat-eaters.

Furthermore, mealtimes tend to be less organised due to numerous outside activities for both adults and children. Quick snacks often replace proper meals during the day with more reliance on outside convenience foods. There is thus a tendency to consume more foods that are high in calories but otherwise, low in nutritive value. Parents should therefore supervise their children's diet to ensure that their child is well-nourished.

Supervising your school-going child's nutrition

1. Check and be aware of the foods your child is consuming during the entire day, including snacks eaten in school. Refer to Table 1 below for a guide as to the amounts of different foods he should be having.

Table 1: A Food Plan to Supply Daily Nutrient Needs for a Young School-going Child

Food Group	Amounts of food for a day	
	5–7 years	7–10 years
Milk	2 cups	2 cups
Protein-rich foods	6 Ch sp meat[a]	7–8 Ch sp meat[a]
Cereals and starchy foods[b]	1½–2 bowls rice or noodles + 1 cup ready-to-eat cereal	2 bowls rice or noodles + 2 slices bread + 1 cup ready-to-eat cereal
Fruit and vegetables	2 pieces fruit + 2 serving vegetables (3 Ch sp each) including at least 2 from the dark green leafy or red/yellow fruits and vegetables	2 pieces fruit + 2 servings vegetables (3 Ch sp each) including at least 2 from the dark green leafy or red/yellow fruits and vegetables
Fats and oils	1½–2 Ch sp	2 Ch sp

[a] or alternatives, for example 1 Ch sp meat = 1 egg, 1 slice cheese or ¼ large square bean curd
[b] extra carbohydrate, including snacks such as biscuits, may be included depending on activity level and appetite.

2. Make an effort to plan or supervise at least two organised meals at home each day, e.g. breakfast and dinner. You can refer to Table 2 below for ideas on suitable meals. For these meals, create a warm and sociable family environment whenever possible to build on the good nutritional habits developed in the earlier years.

3. To help your child balance his energy intake with energy expenditure, establish regular physical activities, preferably those that can be enjoyed by the entire family. This will help in maintaining desirable weight as well as build good muscle tone.

Table 2: Sample Daily Menu for a Young School-going Child[a]

Breakfast	1 soft-boiled egg ½ cup enriched cereal or fruits ¾ cup milk
Morning Snack (suitable for packing)	½ cup soyabean milk 1 wholemeal sardine or tomato sandwich ½ apple
Lunch	1 bowls *yong tau foo bee hoon* soup ½ cup unsweetened orange juice 1 slice watermelon
Afternoon Snack	½ cup yoghurt or milk 1 slice banana and prune bread (see recipe on page 249)
Dinner	½ bowl spinach and *ikan bilis* soup 1 bowl rice 1 portion minced chicken patties (see recipe on page 186) 3 Ch sp broccoli and baby corn with liver (see recipe on page 201) Sliced pear
Bedtime	1 cup milk or milky beverage
Oils and fats for the day: 1–2 Ch sp	

[a] Serving sizes will vary depending on the child's age, size, appetite and activity level. Make use of recipe section for more ideas and variety.

NB: Water should be offered throughout the day and to accompany meals.

Eating through a young school-child's day

Breakfast

Breakfast is often the most poorly planned and hastily prepared meal of the day. But it is a very important meal and one that should provide a reasonable proportion of the nutrients for the day—at least a quarter. Studies have shown that students who skip breakfast are more likely to be inattentive, careless and lacking in concentration powers. This may be due to hunger and a decreasing energy level by mid-morning. Mid-morning snacks, while useful, will only partially remove the disadvantage of going without breakfast.

Join your child at breakfast time to set an example as well as to encourage him to eat so early in the morning! This is also a nice opportunity to spend a little relaxed time with your child before you go your separate ways for the rest of the day. Your child will set off for school more cheerfully and start the school day brightly.

A good breakfast should contain some protein-rich food such as milk, egg, cheese or fish, and some carbohydrate and fibre food such as wholemeal bread, cereal, fruit or fruit juices. Besides providing all the essential nutrients, these foods are more substantial and your child will not feel hungry during his morning classes.

Of equal importance, a good breakfast should consist of food that the child will enjoy eating. Otherwise, your child may treat it as a chore and grow to dread this first meal of the day. So, be imaginative! There is more to breakfast than just instant cereals and boiled egg. Interesting sandwiches, leftover stews, or pancakes with fruit are a few of possibilities. Many of these tempting dishes can be pre-cooked and kept frozen, or partly prepared the night before and kept refrigerated.

Breakfast ideas

Following are some suggestions for breakfast. You will find recipes for many of the dishes in the second part of the book. All of these can also be used as snacks between meals.

Drinks:
- milk and milky beverages
- fruit juices
- tomato juice
- soyabean milk

Egg dishes:
- soft or hard-boiled, fried or scrambled
- omelette with tomato, ham or mushroom
- French toast
- various other varieties of toast
- Scotch egg
- savoury steamed egg custard

Meat and fish dishes:
- fish fingers
- tuna or sardine sandwiches
- congees
- hamburger meat patties with wholemeal bread bun
- chicken stew
- small pizza
- *pau or dim sum*
- chicken pie

Cereals:
- oatmeal with raisins
- ready-to-eat cereals with milk and fruit
- muesli
- banana bread
- pancake or muffin

Others:
- cheese on toast
- baked beans on toast
- peanut butter sandwich
- noodle soups

Lunch

A good lunch is essential, especially for those who miss out on an adequate breakfast. In our hot weather, a light meal during lunch will be better tolerated. Noodles, macaroni, potatoes or spaghetti can alternate with rice-based dishes. Others, such as *yong tau foo*, home-made burgers, chicken pie and *wontons* will add variety. All these can be pre-made and kept frozen, to be defrosted and cooked when needed. Remember to include some vegetables which could be in the form of a puree soup if your child is not keen on vegetables. Fresh fruit and fruit juices will be a refreshing and healthy addition to the meal.

Parents who are not at home to supervise their children's meals should discuss possible meals with them. If lunch is always taken at the hawker centre or fast-food restaurant, make sure your child can choose nutrient-rich foods and does not always end up with simply a plate of fried noodles or a packet of French fries and a soft drink.

Dinner

Dinner poses the least problem as it is usually the best thought out meal of the day. Dinnertime is an ideal opportunity for the child to learn and experience new foods and tastes. By now, your child will be ready for more highly seasoned and spiced foods and he will enjoy what is prepared for the rest of the family.

Avoid serving dinner in front of the television. Let mealtimes fulfil their social role of providing family members with opportunities to talk and share the experiences of the day, and not be merely occasions to fill empty stomachs.

Snacks

With a good breakfast, the mid-morning snack should be light and consist of a milk beverage, fruit or juice. If your child does not eat a substantial breakfast, nutritious mid-morning snacks are essential to fill a hungry stomach and provide needed nutrients. One good way of ensuring extra nutrient intake is to participate in the school milk programme, especially if little milk is consumed at home. A packed snack box may mean work at home, but it assures good snacks for your child.

A late evening meal may find a child eager for a more substantial afternoon snack. When possible, plan nourishing snacks that ease hunger but do not interfere too much with the child's appetite for dinner. Leave a sufficient time gap between the two.

Ideas for nutritious snacks

1. Home snacks
- soft bean curd dessert (*tau huay*)
- home-made soyabean milk
- milk-based drinks
- custard and other milky desserts
- yoghurt with fresh fruit
- home-made soup
- red or green bean soup
- peanut dessert
- barley and *gingko* nut soup
- yam *kuih*
- toast toppers
- home-made fruit ice-lollies or ice cream
- wholegrain cereals with milk and added fresh fruits
- cheese on toast
- plain wholewheat crackers or biscuits

Several of the above items can be found in the Recipe section.

2. Packed lunch box ideas
These are particularly suitable for a snack at recess or as part of a meal at lunchtime if the child has to stay back for extra-curricular activities.
- wholemeal sandwiches
- home-made biscuits, bread and cakes
- cheese with crackers
- red bean paste bun
- fresh fruit
- raw carrot or celery sticks with a cheesy dip
- fresh fruit juices

For meat sandwiches, prepare, wrap and freeze the night before and let them thaw during the time between breakfast and snacktime to prolong freshness and reduce the likelihood of spoilage. On very hot days, avoid using meat. Canned fish, eggs or cheese would be more suitable.

School canteens

If you prefer your child to select his snack from the school canteen rather than take along a packed box, it is wise for you to be familiar with the types of food being sold there. If possible, an "inspection" trip at the beginning of the school year will be of value. Note down the choices available for both the hot and cold items and compare their nutritive value. Your child needs to be guided as to which foods are suitable choices and which are best avoided.

Proper selection of food is especially important if little breakfast is taken or breakfast is skipped due to the early morning rush.

All in all, the nutritional value and quality of school canteen food is fairly good. There is also minimal availability of "junk" food and sweets. There are, however, still far too many fried and oily items. Moreover, it is possible for a child to choose tidbits, ice-lollies and potato chip-type snacks as opposed to more substantial snacks like fish ball noodles, red bean soup or meat porridge.

Casual conversation with your child after school will help shed light on what he has eaten in school earlier in the day and will provide a good opportunity for you to instil basic nutritional knowledge.

It has been shown that children between the ages of seven and ten are most vulnerable to becoming overweight—overeating and indiscriminate snacking on calorie-rich foods is the chief cause. Restricting your child's money allowance is one way of controlling excess spending on snacks. Providing your child with a water bottle is a good idea as it will avoid reliance on fizzy and sugar-laden drinks.

For variety and to keep up interest, arrange a packed snack two to three times a week and then give your child the freedom of choice from the canteen on the other days. This may be the best way of ensuring reasonably nutritive snacking.

Eating out

Hawker food

Hawker-style food is a regular part of many Singaporean children's diets. In many households, half or more of all meals are eaten outside. Traditional hawker food provides a quick and inexpensive meal and there is a great variety to choose from. Unfortunately, as with fast foods, many hawker dishes are high in calories, saturated fat and salt and low in dietary fibre and certain vitamins. It will benefit the whole family, and not just the children, if some thought is given to nutrition before you decide what to order from your favourite stalls.

A guide to healthy and not-so-healthy choices in hawker food is included in Table 3 on page 99.

Fast foods

Children are the number one fast food consumers in Singapore. Besides the Western fare of hamburgers, fried chicken, pizza and French fries, local favorites such as *satay* are adding to the expanding array of foods available in fast food outlets.

Table 3. Choosing Hawker Foods and Fast Foods

Poor Choices	Better Choices	Health Tips
Hawker Food		
Fried prawn *mee* or *kuay teow*	Soup noodles, e.g. prawn or *wonton* or *yong tau foo* with vegetables	Request for less oil, salt and no MSG or lard.
Roast pork rice or stewed belly pork	Lean fish or pork porridge or rice with lean meat and vegetables	Avoid adding extra soya sauce, duck sauce, etc.
Laksa or thick curries	*Mee siam*, *gado-gado* or *tauhoo goreng*	Remove poultry skin and visible fat.
Oyster omelette and carrot cake	Steam bun (*pau*), *chee cheong fun*, *poh piah*	
Chendol or *bubor cha cha*	Red bean or green bean soup, *tau huay*, *pulut hitam* (no coconut milk)	
Nasi briyani, *roti prata*	*Chapati*, *thosai*, *dhal* curry	
Fast Food		
French fries and ice cream sundae	Hamburger and milk	Scrape off excess mayonnaise.
Double cheeseburger and flavoured milkshake	Single cheeseburger and fresh orange juice	Limit use of ketchup and sauce.
Fried chicken and soft drink	Roast beef, lean ham or chicken sandwich with corn-on-the-cob & milk	Remove skin before eating fried chicken.
Burger, onion rings and apple pie	Pizza and salad	

The appeal of fast food restaurants is not limited to food. Atmosphere, colourful and imaginative decor, gifts, and, in some outlets, play corners, all add to the attraction. Air-conditioning and pop music are an additional draw for the older kids. Children's sense of independence is also given a boost as they are usually allowed to order for themselves.

Regular consumption of fast foods, however, gives rise to concern. Many fast food items are high in calories, saturated fat and salt which may contribute to heart disease in later life. Figure 1 on page 100 illustrates that a much higher-than-recommended proportion of energy (calories) in fast foods comes from fat. When fast foods are eaten between meals, the child's calorie intake is greatly increased. This may cause him to be overweight, especially if he is physically inactive. When fast foods are taken frequently instead of home meals, there is a likelihood of imbalance in the nutrient intake. This is because vegetables and fresh fruits are often lacking, hence the vitamin A and C intakes will be low, with practically no fibre.

Figure 1: Percentage of Energy from Fat, Protein and Carbohydrate —Fast Food versus Ideal

Composition of a fast food meal of double burger, French fries and a thick shake.

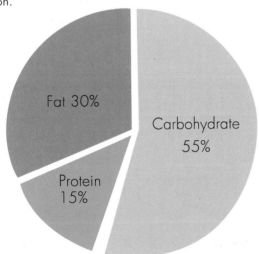

Fat 43%

Carbohydrate 39%

Protein 18%

Composition of an ideal meal for good nutrition.

Fat 30%

Carbohydrate 55%

Protein 15%

Taken occasionally, fast food meals pose no great harm. However, if your child eats them more than two to three times a week, you should help him to be more selective in his choices, and compensate for the missing nutrients during other meals in the day. See Table 3 on page 99 for healthier choices when eating at fast food restaurants.

Make your own fast food at home

Even away from the cheery atmosphere of fast food restaurants, children still enjoy fast food because it is fun and a change from their everyday meal. It is quite easy to adapt popular items and give your children a fast food treat in your own home. You can ensure nutritious ingredients are included and can cut down on salt and fat.

Examples:
- homestyle meat and lentil burger (see recipe on page 190)
- healthy burger companions:
  wholemeal bun
  melted grated cheese
  tomato and lettuce
  cucumber
  shredded coleslaw (see recipe on page 212)
  baked beans
  boiled egg slices
- baked or mashed potato
- corn on the cob
- easy pan pizza (see recipe on page 190)

Obesity in the young

Obesity is one of the most common nutritional problems not only in Singapore but also all over the developed world. Obesity in children is undesirable for the following reasons:

Long-term concerns

1. Likelihood of becoming an obese adult

About one-third of adult obesity originates in childhood or adolescence. Prevention during childhood is, therefore, important.

2. Increased risk of circulatory disorders, such as heart disease and stroke

Elevated levels of cholesterol in the blood have been found in obese children. Thus, there is an increased possibility that the obese child may develop atherosclerosis (hardening of the arteries) in adulthood, which is a major risk factor for developing coronary heart disease. High blood pressure is much more common in the obese than the non-obese and this is another risk factor for heart disease as well as for strokes and kidney disease.

3. Orthopaedic disorders

Carrying extra weight puts a strain on the bones and joints. Furthermore, because bones are strengthened by exercises, an inactive obese child's bones may grow relatively weak.

4. Respiratory problems

Extra fatty tissue can result in difficulty in breathing and the obese child may be prone to respiratory infections.

5. Diabetes

If obesity persists into adulthood, there is a higher chance of developing diabetes. A family history of diabetes further increases the risk.

More immediate concerns

1. Psychological problems

An obese child is often an unhappy one. Obese children often have a poor self-image. They feel inferior and rejected, feelings which often persist into adulthood.

2. Social discrimination

An obese child has low social status. Discrimination against the obese is often encountered in schools, among peers and, in the future, by employers.

Is your child obese?

Obesity occurs because of an excess accumulation of body fat. Being 20 per cent heavier than the desirable weight for a given height is usually taken as obesity. This is not a foolproof definition, however, since a child with heavy bones or more muscle mass than normal may be "overweight" for his height but may not have excess body fat. It is generally easy enough to see if a child is obese, although someone other than the parents will usually spot it first, as its gradual onset may not be noticed by those who see the child every day.

How can obesity be prevented?

The answer, of course, is to nip it in the bud. You can help ensure that your child does not become overweight by doing the following:

1. Ensure that you do not overfeed your child when young (see Chapter 4).
2. Offer nutrient-rich food only.
3. Refrain from having high-calorie snack foods in the house all the time.
4. Encourage your child to eat fruit or bread for a snack rather than sweets, chocolate, cakes or ice cream.
5. Encourage plenty of physical activity, such as sports and outdoor pursuits. You can join in too with activities such as swimming, cycling or jogging.
6. Inculcate in your child the importance of following regular

meal patterns rather than having him snack all day long.

7. Ban eating in any place other than the kitchen or dining table; just think how effective this would be for yourself as well!

8. Do not make food the panacea for your child's every whim and cry. Attention in other forms, such as taking an interest in the child's activities, playing with him, etc., will meet his emotional needs much better than food.

9. Do not use food as a form of bribery (e.g. "If you do your homework, I'll give you ice cream").

Helping your obese child

Since your child is still growing, the aim is not for him to lose weight but rather for him to gain weight at a slower rate. Any food restrictive treatment programme should be carried out under the supervision of a doctor and dietitian to ensure that it is safe and that the child is not deprived of essential nutrients.

Excess weight gain occurs when the calorie intake exceeds body energy expenditure. To curtail this, calorie intake must be reduced and, if possible, energy expenditure increased. To do this, here are some practical steps to take:

- Modify your eating habits as a family. This way, your child will not feel left out and there is a better chance of him keeping to his new meal plan. Best of all, the whole family will benefit too!

- Rid the house of all empty-calorie "junk" foods.

- Water and mildly sweetened home-made beverages such as soyabean milk or lemon-barley should be available to quench thirst rather than commercial soft drinks and syrups loaded with sugar.

- Avoid excess fat intake by reducing consumption of fried foods.

- Have sweet desserts served only occasionally and limit the portion sizes.

- Allow treats such as ice cream, *kuih* or a chocolate biscuit only occasionally, but ensure they are "rationed".

- A good breakfast will reduce the urgency of indiscriminate snacking during recess in school. Skipping breakfast is therefore a bad practice. If possible, give packed snacks or limit the money allowance for snacking in school.

Watching calories in your child's diet

Nutrient-rich foods

It is worthwhile consuming calories from nutrient-rich foods as these foods are also concentrated sources of nutrients. A list of nutrient-rich foods is given below. But watch the portion sizes of foods marked with an asterisk, though, as these are quite high in fat:

- *lean meat or poultry
- fish
- *egg
- *milk
- *cheese
- skimmed milk
- low fat yoghurt
- cottage cheese
- beans
- bean curd, soyabean milk
- rice, noodles, bread, potatoes
- plain or wheatmeal biscuits
- fruit, fruit juices
- vegetables—boiled in soup or steamed rather than fried
- salads—dilute the dressing

Foods that are "top-heavy" in calories

Compared to the nutrient-rich foods, these foods give your child too many calories in exchange for fewer nutrients and should be taken no

The nutritional needs of your school-going child continue to be significant.

more than twice a week:

- cakes, cream-filled or chocolate biscuits, *kuih*, butter cookies
- *kacang*—dried peas, roasted nuts, etc.
- *goreng pisang* and fried sweet potato
- cultured milk drinks
- ice cream
- sweetened milk shakes
- French fries
- condensed milk
- curry puffs
- fried rice
- fried noodles

Nutrient-empty foods

These are often termed "junk food". They provide calories but practically no other nutrients. Minimise your child's exposure to these but do not make a big fuss about banning them as it will only intrigue your child and increase his desire for them.

- sugar
- soft drinks and syrups
- commercial jellies and ice lollies
- chocolate
- candy and sweets
- jams, honey
- *keropok*, potato chips

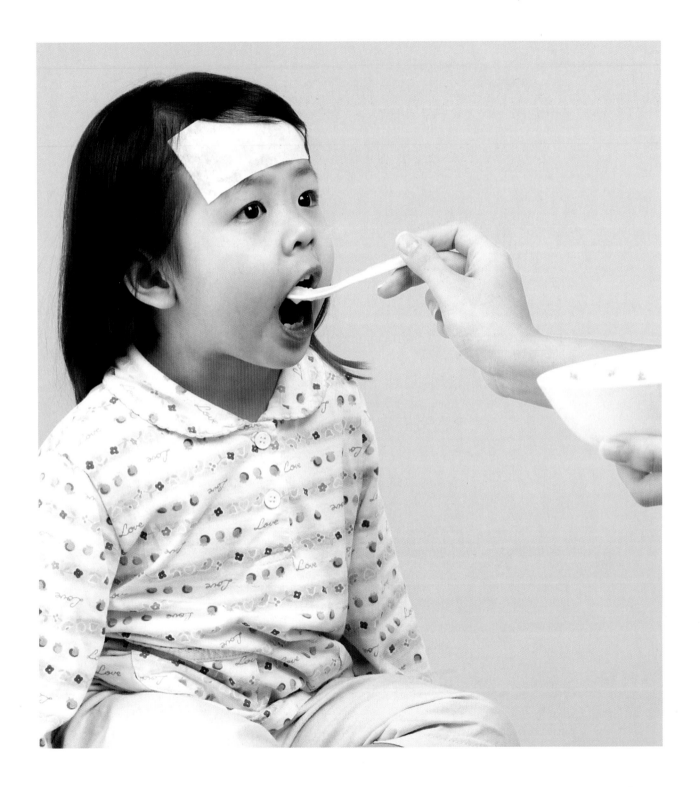

07 Diet in special Circumstances

- Food allergy
- Lactose intolerance
- G6PD deficiency
- Upset tummies, colds and fevers
- Easy-to-eat foods for a convalescing child

When children fall sick, parents are often at a loss as to what to feed them—food must not only be nourishing and speed up recovery, it must tempt a poor appetite. Other circumstances may arise in which children's diets have to be modified because of allergies or intolerance to certain foods. The information in this chapter is designed to better equip parents to cope in such situations. However, If your child's diet has to be restricted for any length of time, it is essential to seek a doctor's and a dietitian's advice regularly for individual counselling on your child's particular needs, which will change with his continuing growth.

Food allergy

Allergies to food occur perhaps more often than we think. Toddlers are more prone to food allergy than older children, but it is usually temporary and they may grow out of it by seven to eight years of age.

A food allergy is an adverse reaction of the immune system to food. It is not to be confused with food intolerance such as lactose intolerance, which is due to an inability to digest a particular food component.

The symptoms of allergy may include any of the following:

- persistent diarrhoea and vomiting
- weight loss
- abdominal pain
- wheezing due to asthma
- bronchitis
- eczema and rashes

As cow's milk is the most common allergy-provoking food, a good way of minimising the risk in infants is by breastfeeding. This is particularly important for those whose parents or siblings have a history of allergy.

Other foods which may provoke an allergic reaction include egg, fish, shellfish, wheat, chocolate, soyabean, fruit, tomato, nuts, meat, poultry, food colourings and preservatives.

What to do if you suspect a food allergy

If you notice an association between a particular food and a symptom, omit the food from the child's diet. Should the symptoms disappear, well and good. If they persist, you should consult a physician. This is so that you do not go to extremes in trying to eliminate many other foods, thus jeopardising your child's health. In any case, it is best to have a doctor confirm your suspicions by diagnosing the allergy. This is because all allergy-causing foods, if avoided for a time, can provoke a severe body reaction when reintroduced even in small quantities. This reaction is known as anaphylactic shock, and may be life-threatening.

Diagnostic tests are not always capable of confirming suspected food allergies. If the doctor is not able to confirm the allergy, you should go by your own observations and instincts, and avoid the aggravating food at least until the child is older. If the food is an important one, such as milk or egg, or if many foods are involved, do seek professional nutritional guidance from a dietitian on how to plan a healthy diet for your child.

A child's nutritional status may be compromised when dietary restrictions are prolonged, especially if the restrictions involve more nutrient-rich foods such as dairy foods. Appropriate vitamin or mineral supplements may therefore be needed. Always check with your doctor or dietitian regarding which ones should be taken by your child.

Lactose intolerance

Inability to digest the milk sugar lactose is termed "lactose intolerance". It results in symptoms of diarrhoea, wind and upset tummy. It is more common in some races than others. The Chinese, for example, have a particularly high incidence of it. The intolerance is caused by insufficiency of an enzyme called lactase, which is needed for the digestion of lactose. It is not certain whether this enzyme deficiency is inherited or occurs when a child begins to drink less milk. It seems that children who continue drinking a lot of milk do not usually suffer from lactose intolerance but those who stop milk and take it only occasionally are more likely to be intolerant. A very small number of babies are lactose intolerant from birth and require a special lactose-free formula.

There are two solutions to the problem of lactose intolerance—one is to use fortified soya milk formula and the other is to use low lactose or hydrolysed milk.

Avoiding milk entirely is not such a good idea for children as milk is an excellent food throughout the growing years and is our best source of calcium. Children with a mild lactose intolerance can usually take one glass of milk without any symptoms and this will help keep their levels of lactase up. You can also give milk in smaller quantities throughout the day, together with cheese and yoghurt, which are low in lactose.

If a child belongs to the severe lactose intolerant category you may have to watch out for hidden sources of lactose in other foods besides milk and milk products.

Milk products high in lactose

- fresh and powdered milk, full-cream and skimmed milk
- condensed and evaporated milk
- ice cream
- soft cream cheese
- cheese spreads
- fresh and sterilised creams.

Milk products low in lactose

- hard cheese—the lactose is broken down in the processing
- yoghurt and cultured milk drinks —the lactose is partly digested by the culture bacteria
- hydrolysed milk—milk in which the lactose has been predigested by addition of an enzyme.

Non-milk products which may contain lactose

Commercial breads, biscuits and cereals often have milk added and so do many instant desserts. Besides looking for milk or skimmed milk powder, cheese or whey on the list of ingredients, look out for the words "enriched", "fortified" or "high protein", as these are all indicators that milk may have been added. Lactose is used as a filler in some tablets and vitamin pills, so always check with your pharmacist to obtain a lactose-free medication.

Pay special attention to other calcium sources in your child's diet if he is not drinking much milk. These include bean curd, ikan bilis, nuts, beans and green leafy vegetables (see table on page 34).

Glucose-6-phosphate dehydrogenase (G6PD) deficiency

Glucose-6-phosphate dehydrogenase (G6PD) deficiency affects 3–4 per cent of male Singaporeans, and much fewer females. It is screened for at birth and so you will be told right away if your baby is G6PD-deficient.

The factor that is deficient is actually an enzyme which is important in protecting the red cells of the blood against damage (haemolysis) by certain compounds. These compounds incude many drugs and some Chinese herbs. Besides causing jaundice, too much damage to the red blood cells will cause anaemia, as these cells are responsible for carrying oxygen around the body to all the tissues.

In newborns there is an additional danger of mental damage if exposure to the damaging compounds occurs, and so G6PD-deficient babies are usually kept in hospital for two to three weeks until the critical period is over. Their jaundice is treated by phototherapy. They can be breastfed during this time and may need extra water to combat dehydration due to the phototherapy.

So long as the G6PD-deficient person avoids exposure to the damage-causing compounds there is no danger. Parents of G6PD-deficient children are given a list of medications and herbs to avoid. Mothballs are also to be avoided when storing your or baby's clothes.

In G6PD-deficiency, vitamin K in excessive doses can cause damage to the blood cells. vitamin C in very large doses may also cause complications in G6PD-deficiency. Therefore, parents should seek their doctor's advice before giving any vitamin supplement to their children.

In addition, G6PD-deficient people must not consume the fava bean or broad bean. Large and kidney-shaped, this bean is most often taken roasted and salted as a type of *kacang*. It is also sold in some supermarkets as tinned, cooked broad beans, or may be purchased dried for cooking. While breastfeeding a G6PD-deficient baby, you should not eat these beans or use herbs such as *chuan lian* and *san tze chze*. Even ginger has been suspected as a trigger for jaundice in G6PD-deficient babies, and so is best avoided.

Upset tummies, colds and fevers

it is usually very difficult to get a child to eat when he has an upset tummy or feels ill and weak due to influenza, infection or food poisoning. Yet nourishment is very important for his recovery. If the child is unable to eat one or two meals, there is no cause for concern. If he is off his food for more than a day, however, you should ensure that some fluids and light food are taken.

Tummy upsets

Tummy upsets are usually accompanied by vomiting and diarrhoea which can quickly lead to dehydration and loss of important salts from the body. If this happens, the first priority is to make sure your child drinks enough fluids. If there is severe vomiting, the child should be given only clear fluids such as:

- boiled water
- diluted fruit syrups
- honey or glucose drinks
- thin rice water or barley water
- clear soup with no fat
- meat or yeast extract drinks
- plain jelly

Clear fruit juices such as apple or strained orange may also be given. But keep this to a minimum if there is an onset of diarrhoea.

Besides replacing water, you need to replace salts lost from your child's body.

A simple rehydration drink can be made by dissolving 1½ Chinese spoons of sugar and ½ teaspoon of salt in a little hot water. Add cool boiled water to make up to one litre. When your child cannot retain any fluid due to severe vomiting, or if you suspect dehydration, you must take him to the doctor.

Always look out for the following signs of dehydration:

- dry mouth and lips
- white furry tongue
- skin which sags or wrinkles when pinched
- a deeper than usual fontanelle (soft spot on baby's head)
- no urine passed for six or more hours
- a child who is less active than usual

Once a bout of tummy upset has passed the acute stage and there is no more vomiting or diarrhoea, more nourishing liquids can be given, such as nutritious soups and congees. It is best to avoid milk for a day or two as it sometimes makes diarrhoea worse.

When adding milk to the diet again, make it diluted at first (half-strength). Feed more often, say six small feeds through the day.

Getting back to solid foods

Your child himself will probably let you know when he is ready to have something solid again. Plain dry biscuits, breakfast cereals, bread and egg are a good start. It is usually wise to avoid very fatty or fried food as a delicate stomach will have difficulty digesting fat.

Colds and fevers

Any infection, such as an ear infection, can cause a fever but the most common cause is the influenza virus which all of us seem to succumb to now and then. During a fever, taking plenty of fluids is again the golden rule. They help keep the body cool and the throat moist.

Easy-to-eat foods for a convalescing child

Foods for a convalescing child

Here is a list of food you can give your child on his way to recovery from an illness.

Milk

Milk in any form is suitable during recovery from illnesses. Ice cream, custards and milk shakes or milk-based desserts will be particularly popular.

Eggs

Easy to digest and a valuable source of protein, iron and other nutrients, eggs can be incorporated into custards, or added to soups such as egg-flower soup. Egg can also be mashed into potatoes if your child likes mashed potato. Try to include at least one a day.

Cereals

infant cereals mixed with milk or liquidised oats are ideal.

Porridge and noodle soups

Congee, macaroni, *mee sua*, etc., cooked in clear soups, are easy to digest and help to boost fluid and energy intakes. Cook with a little minced meat or tender chicken or fish and chopped or grated vegetables to give extra taste and nutrients.

Fruit

This excellent source of vitamin C should be given to your child at least once a day. vitamin C aids recovery and wound-healing. Freshly squeezed orange juice is usually quite popular and sweetening slightly with sugar or glucose will provide extra energy.

Meat and fish

Lightly cooked liver, chicken or fish can be sieved or blended and added to soups or stews.

Soups

Plain stock can be enriched by adding vegetables or meat purees and some milk.

When your child has been off his food for a long time, it may be advisable to give him a vitamin/mineral supplement, which your doctor can prescribe.

Practical tips for feeding a sick child

1. Use familiar and well-liked foods —this is not the time to be trying new foods!

2. Use differently coloured foods and pretty dishes to make the food look attractive. Serve fish, for example, in a little tomato sauce. Two or three small servings of different coloured vegetables look nicer than one large serving of the same vegetable. Foods can be cut into nice shapes, e.g. heart-shaped sandwiches.

3. Serve only very small portions. Individual portions may be more attractive to a child than taking food from the family dish.

4. Straws make milk-drinking fun and also help prevent spillages —handy if you are feeding the child in bed.

Offer your convalescing child familiar and well-liked foods and present them in an attractive manner.

5. Serve food in convenient bite-sized pieces to avoid the child having to bite or cut. Toast, for example, can be cut into small fingers ideal for dipping into a soft-boiled egg. A boiled egg scooped out of the shell and beaten up in a cup with a little soya sauce or salt and pepper is easier for a child to eat than one served in its shell in an egg-cup.

08 Traditional Food Beliefs and Vegetarian Diets

- Food in traditional medicine
- Food beliefs in pregnancy and confinement
- Traditional dietary advice in lactation
- Traditional dietary beliefs in infancy and childhood
- Vegetarianism

F ood beliefs pervade all Asian cultures and obviously, these influence the foods eaten. One category of food beliefs widespread in Asia includes those which are a component of Asian traditional medicine. This means that many foods are taken or avoided for health reasons. While people may not pay much attention to these beliefs on an everyday basis, they tend to be followed more closely during those times when health is of special concern, for example during pregnancy, confinement and infancy. ● ● ●

Besides health-related beliefs, there are other food beliefs based on religion, certain foods being viewed sacred or unclean. Islam, for example, prohibits the eating of pork. Hinduism and certain Buddhist sects prohibit the eating of beef. Furthermore, devoted Buddhists, Hindus and Sikhs are likely to be vegetarians. Fasting is another aspect of religious dietary practice, particularly for Muslims who fast during the month of Ramadan.

Vegetarianism will be discussed in the second part of the chapter. First, however, we will take a look at the local health-related food beliefs and their significance in relation to the nutritional intakes of the Asian mother and child.

Food in traditional medicine

Principles behind traditional food beliefs

Dietetics, or food therapy, is an inseparable component of traditional Chinese medicine. Many people have only a limited knowledge of food therapy beliefs, which are usually handed down orally through the generations. As a result, sometimes people may follow the principles more rigorously than is recommended. We therefore feel it would be useful to briefly describe the principles behind the traditional Chinese food beliefs.

In China, as from 770 B.C., there existed a group of court officials who were trained "food physicians". They developed royal court menus and were responsible for the royalty's nutritional maintenance. Tsun Sze Miao, a renowned monk physician during the Tang dynasty (A.D. 619-907), who wrote many invaluable medical works throughout his 101 years, had this to say in his famous *T'sien Chin Fang* (Thousand Golden Prescriptions):

"All therapy should begin with dietary treatment, only failing which should drug medication be sought."

He divided food into four groups—grains, vegetables, fruit and animal products—and discussed at length the nutritional functions of each. For example, he recorded the use of seaweed for treating goitre, and used liver to treat night blindness. This coincides with our present-day knowledge of the properties of iodine and vitamin A, of which seaweed and liver, respectively, are excellent sources.

The *yin-yang* principle

Many of the beliefs about food in traditional medicine are based on the theory of *yin* and *yang. Yin* and *yang* are idealised states; neither of them can exist solely, only in relativity to the other. The theory says that the healthy body is balanced with respect to *yin* and *yang*; once the *yin* and *yang* are out of balance the body will become sick. The forces of *yin* and *yang* are thus believed to govern and determine one's state of health and any therapeutic measure undertaken in sickness is done in order to restore the balance of the two forces.

Foods considered to have *yin* properties are termed "cold" and "cooling" foods, while *yang* foods are the "warm" and "heating" varieties (see Table 1). A balanced intake of *yin* and *yang* within the two groups is believed to maintain one's good health within the constraints of our physical environment. For example, *yu char kuay* (deep fried dough sticks), a heating food, is thought best accompanied by *tau nee* (soyabean

Table 1: Some Examples of the *Yin-Yang* Properties Attributed to Various Foods

Property*	Animal Foods	Non-Animal Foods
Warm/heating	Deep fried, roasted and toasted food Mutton, beef, ham, goose, turkey, pig's liver and stomach, venison Hen's egg yolk Abalone, prawn, sea-cucumber, sea-crab Eel, hairtail, silver-carp, octopus	Wheat, yeast, raw and brown sugar Ginger, chilli, onion, spices Wine, spirits, vinegar Soyabean and sesame oils Longan (fresh and dried), lychee, durian, mango, *rambutan*, dates, pomegranate, prunes, peach, *kumquat* Cocoa, chocolate and chocolate beverages Brinjal, chestnut
Neutral/mild	Pork, pig's kidney, blood, heart, lung, spleen Chicken Sheep's heart and lung Milk Pigeon, quail, frog-meat Threadfin (*ikan kurau*), *ikan bilis*, pomfret, squid	Rice, barley, sweetcorn, black beans, red bean, soya bean, broad bean, lentils *Taro*, sweet potato, potato *Kangkong*, lettuce, *chye sim*, carrot, *kai-lan*, cauliflower Black Jew's ear, mushrooms, cooked lotus root, nuts, sesame seeds (whole) Apples, banana (*pisang mas* and *tali*), starfruit, papaya Soyabean paste, honey
Cooling/cold	Pig's brain and intestine Duck, duck egg Lard Snakehead fish (*shen-yu*), turtle, clams, cockles, mussels, snails	Green bean (mung bean), yam, bamboo shoot, water chestnut, sugar cane, white and rock sugar Chinese cabbage, watercress, mustard green, angle gourd, cucumber, bitter gourd, wintermelon, tomato, white radish, water pear Banana (green skin and wild variety), orange, persimmon, mangosteen, pomelo, pineapple, coconut water, tea, *agar-agar*, salt

* The degree of coolness and hotness is said to vary between individual items in each group, and to be relative to the individual's physical condition and susceptibility.

milk), a cooling food; durian (heating) and mangosteen (cooling) are likewise complementary. Water chestnut and sugar cane drinks or barley water (cooling) are believed to be suitable during hot, dry spells or for a fever of a "heaty" nature. Boiled ginger water (heating) is usually taken after getting soaked in heavy rain or sometimes during menstruation to prevent penetration of "external coldness".

A person believed to have a *yin* constitution is advised to refrain from too much cooling foods which might result in elevated "humidity" and "dampness", an undesirable state which is said to be a precursor to ill-health. Likewise, a person with a *yang*-based body constitution is warned that he may find himself with a sore throat and constipation after an excess of fried, spicy or toasted ("heating") food.

The *yin-yang* laws say that the intrinsic value of a *yin* or *yang* food can be altered during cooking or processing. For example, raw lotus root is considered "cooling", while the cooked form is not; adding ginger to a cooling food will also lessen or neutralise its coolness.

It is held that the five tastes of food (sweet, sour, salty, bitter and spicy-hot) also affect the balance of *yin* and *yang*, and any excess of the five is deemed undesirable. Spicy-hot foods such as chilli or pepper belong in the *yang* category while the bitter and sour usually come from the *yin* group, e.g. bitter gourds and pomeloes. Both salt and sugar are considered to be *yin*.

"The five caveats of eating" (*wu jin*) in traditional medical theory warn against eating habits alleged to cause nutrition and health problems. As can be seen, these five provisos offer sound advice, even by modern nutritional standards. Let us have a look.

The five caveats of eating

1. Avoid excesses of the five tastes.
2. Refrain from a monotonous diet.
3. Refrain from overeating.
4. Avoid over-indulgence in alcoholic beverages.
5. Avoid unhygienic and unfamiliar foods (those likely to cause poisoning or allergy).

Food beliefs in pregnancy and confinement

Pregnancy and the period following childbirth are considered vulnerable states and the *yin-yang* laws are often followed more strictly at this time, particularly by the Chinese and Malays. The act of giving birth is believed to deplete a woman's body of the "hot" element (blood) and inner energy ("*chi*"). This places her in a "cold" state for a period of around 40 days (which is the assumed period needed for the womb to heal). During this time, it is said her body must be restored by the addition of the depleted elements, both internally (through "hot" foods and tonics) and externally (e.g. by lying over a heated platform whilst receiving a body massage, a Malay practice known as "*berserdiang dan bertungku*", or by the Chinese prohibition of hair-washing and bathing except in water boiled with ginger and herbs.)

As can be seen from Table 2, the main foods which are prohibited during this time are "cold" or "sharp" vegetables and fruit and some seafoods. The danger lies with taking the prohibitions to extremes and avoiding all fruit and vegetables, which would then result in lowered intakes of vitamins C and A, iron, folic acid and calcium. Fibre intake would also be very much reduced, which could result in constipation, already a common problem in pregnancy.

In practice, it is still possible to observe some of the food taboos and yet have a balanced diet. Nutritive fruit and vegetables such as papaya, starfruit, apple, banana, *kangkong*, *kai-lan*, spinach, medlar seeds (*kei chi*) and carrot are among the foods permitted. While some seafood is taboo, there are plenty of permitted

alternatives. Mild-flavoured white fish, for example, is considered nourishing.

With the frequent inclusion of liver, kidney and chicken in the Chinese woman's diet after childbirth, (see Table 3 on page 117), protein and iron are not likely to be lacking. The practice of taking sesame and other seeds, beans and nuts is, in fact, to be encouraged as these foods are good sources of calcium, iron and fibre as well as protein. Avoiding tea is also a good practice as tea inhibits the absorption of iron.

Table 2: Traditional Dietary Prohibitions During Pregnancy, Confinement and Lactation

Classification	Food Items	Reasons for Avoidance	
		Pregnancy	Confinement/Lactation
"Cold" foods	Iced or cold drinks, coconut water, "cold" varieties of vegetables and fruit, tea	Poor blood circulation	Poor blood circulation Stomach ache in the nursing baby
"Sharp" or *tajam* foods	Pineapple, mango, limes, sour orange, *assam*, *tapai* (fermented tapioca rice), concentrated coconut milk	Threatened miscarriage or bleeding	Increased bleeding Diarrhoea in the nursing baby
"Hot" foods	Excess chilli, pepper, spices, "tonics", spirits, medicines	Headache, "heatiness"	Diarrhoea in susceptible nursing baby
"Poisonous" or *bisa* foods	Certain seafoods, e.g. *keli*, *puyu*, *sembilang*, *sepat*, prawns, cockles, crabs	Stomach upset and vomiting	Delayed wound healing Allergy and eczema in nursing baby
"Windy" foods	Jackfruit, tapioca, pumpkin, onions	Indigestion	Colic pain in the nursing baby

Table 3: Foods Frequently Included in Chinese Women's Diet During Pregnancy and After Childbirth

Meat Products	Vegetable Products	Others (Confinement/Lactation Only)
Pig's stomach, kidney, liver Chicken (especially black chicken) Beef tendon Fish, fish broth* Bone soup Eggs Pig's trotters*	Sesame seeds*, sesame oil Spinach, lettuce* Seaweeds Soyabean products Longan (dried), red dates, *gingko* nuts, lotus seeds, red beans*, black beans Groundnuts (fresh) Papaya* (semi-ripe) for cooking Medlar seeds (*kei-chi*), *wei-san*, ginger, vinegar in cooking	Rice wine Herbal liqueurs or wine *Tang kwei* (*Angelica sinensis*) Ginseng (Korean and Chinese) *Tang seng* *Sou-wu* (*Polygonum multiflorum*) Essence of chicken

* These are considered helpful in stimulating milk flow.

Combinations of items from the three groups, or from the meat and vegetable groups only, form the basis of common traditional dishes eaten during confinement.

NB: The use of ginger, sesame oil and herbs should be avoided in cases of jaundiced infants and those with G6PD deficiency.

Herbs and tonics in pregnancy

Of more concern is the traditional practice of taking herbs and tonics during pregnancy and confinement. Mildly heating foods and tonics ("pu") are traditionally taken during early pregnancy and occasionally during the ensuing months as they are believed to strengthen the mother. Herbs and tonics, including alcoholic wines, are considered even more important during confinement, when they are said to help prevent the loss of body heat.

Today, herbal preparations are less frequently relied upon during pregnancy due to the well-publicised health warnings given by the health authorities—some herbs may cause abnormal foetal development, as do a variety of Western medical drugs.

The best advice to give on this is if in doubt do not take, and always seek your doctor's opinion.

Traditional dietary advice for lactation

Advice on how to increase milk flow in breastfeeding mothers probably exists in all cultures of the world. Some traditional recipes said to help improve milk supply are given in Table 4. As can be seen from the recipes described, the emphasis is on soups and porridge, which will help to ensure that the mother has an adequate fluid intake.

Since blood and chi are regarded as the essential sources of a mother's milk, it is believed that the post-partum practices to restore these two elements in the body will also promote lactation. Thus, the common practice of taking heating herbs and tonics, ginger and wine during confinement is designed not only to strengthen the mother, but to stimulate milk production. Malays also emphasise some spice extracts (akar kayu and air rempah).

In recent years, however, local research has associated the practice of taking these substances, particularly ginger, with the high incidence of jaundice among Chinese breastfed babies. This is of special concern in G6PD-deficient infants, where haemolysis may be triggered (see Chapter 7). Therefore, breastfeeding mothers should avoid taking these substances in order to avoid unnecessary risks.

As alcohol can cross into breast milk from the mother's bloodstream, it is also advisable not to follow too closely the tradition of taking wine or liqueur during confinement if breastfeeding. A little alcohol (½ standard measure) taken occasionally is acceptable, however, and may in fact be helpful to some breastfeeding mothers as it has a relaxing effect and therefore helps promote the let-down reflex. We are not, however, recommending the use of alcohol especially for this purpose. A little wine used in cooking is not considered harmful as the alcohol evaporates off during the cooking process.

Certain restrictions on the lactating woman's diet are followed in order to prevent the supposed transmission of harmful properties of foods to the infant. Thus "cold" foods are avoided as they might cause colicky pain and, similarly, "poisonous" foods are avoided to prevent possible itching or eczema.

These restrictions are no cause for concern so long as they are not carried to extremes. Taking a variety of "mildly cool" or "neutral" fruit and vegetables will help ensure that the breast milk is not deficient in water-soluble vitamins.

Table 4: Some Traditional Chinese Recipes Believed to Improve Milk Flow in Lactation

Pig's Trotters and Groundnut Soup or Porridge 1 pair pig's trotters 200 g fresh groundnuts (with skin) 1 Ch sp vinegar *Clean and slit pig's trotters. Boil and simmer with groundnuts in water.* *Add a pinch of salt and vinegar. Cook till soft. Rice can be added to make rice porridge.*
Fish and Papaya Soup 200 g semi-ripe papaya 1 whole fish, e.g. carp, snakehead, sea-bream, pomfret or *kurau* fillet Few slices of ginger *Scale and clean fish. Simmer together with papaya pieces and ginger for ½ hour or till soft. Remove bones before serving.*
Kidney Fried with Lily Flower 200 g kidney, cleaned and sliced 20 g dried lily flower ("golden needles") Few slices of ginger Vegetable oil Dash of rice wine *Stir fry kidney slices in oil with ginger. Add lily flower and adjust seasoning.*
Black Sesame Seed and Rice Pudding or Porridge 25 g black sesame seeds 30 g rice or as desired Rock sugar *Pudding: Blend soaked rice and sesame seeds into paste. Cook into thin gruel with sufficient water.* *Porridge: Cook rice porridge. Blend sesame seeds and add to rice. Add rock sugar to taste.*
Wei-san and Groundnut Porridge 20 g fresh groundnuts 30 g unmilled rice 20 g *wei-san* *Cook ingredients together as rice porridge. Meat bones can be added for extra flavour.*
Lettuce with Rice Wine 200 g lettuce leaves 1 Ch sp rice wine Meat stock *Cook lettuce briefly in a little soup. Add salt and rice wine. Eat both soup and lettuce.*
Longan and Red Date Tea 10 pieces dried longan flesh 6–8 dried red dates (seeds removed) 4–5 g tang-kwei (Angelica sinensis) optional *Boil and simmer ingredients in 3–4 cups water for 30 to 45 minutes until liquid is fragrant and tasty. Drink throughout the day.*

Traditional dietary beliefs in infancy and childhood

Just as in modern medicine, paediatrics constitutes a specialised field in traditional medicine. Dietary remedies are used in conjunction with other types of treatment, their role being supportive and to aid in convalescence. Many of the ancient prescriptions are still available today in literature, with others being handed down from experience by generations of traditional physicians. Table 5 gives a few examples of traditional food recipes for childhood ailments.

Table 5: Examples of Traditional Food Recipes for Childhood Ailments

Ailments	Food	Beliefs
Sore throat and "heaty" cough/phlegm	2–3 Chinese pears simmered with 20 sweet Chinese almonds, 5–10 bitter almonds, 2 dried figs and 2 cups water for ½–1 hour. Drink 2–3 times a day for a few days.	Considered valuable in reducing internal "heat" and "fire".
Fever	Green beans (50 g) and *sio pai tsai* (1–2 stalks) boiled in water to a soft porridge consistency. Serve a few times throughout illness. **Alternatives:** Green bean and rice congee; boiled barley and preserved wintermelon drink; water chestnut and black sugar cane drink.	Considered "cooling" and best for "heaty" fever, as a result of mumps, tonsilitis and other infectious diseases.
Constipation	500 ml soyabean milk cooked with rice as congee; or ground black sesame seeds (30 g) and ground walnut (50 g) soup or paste.	Clearing the intestines is considered essential in maintaining good health.
Diarrhoea, ringworm	Chinese black olives (10–20 g flesh), boiled to extract juice and cooked with 50 g unpolished rice as congee. Areca (*pinang*) may be used in place of olives.	There are various other remedies recommended for these complaints, Chinese tea being one.
Failure to thrive or malnourishment	Unmilled rice, black and red beans in 8:1:1 proportion, cooked as for rice; or Cow's or breast milk congee (cook rice with minimum water and add milk when almost done); or Thick soyabean milk and egg rice congee.	Recorded for use since Ming dynasty in convalescence and infant malnourishment.
Indigestion, general malabsorption	30–40 g dried *haw* fruit boiled to extract juice and cooked with rice as congee.	Considered "tonifying" for spleen and stomach functions.
Smallpox, measles	Wheatgerm, dried figs and carrot soup.	Considered helpful in the post-eruptive healing stage.

While most of these food recipes are nutritionally sound, their effectiveness as remedies is not well-established. Therefore, if a young child does not find them appetising, it is unreasonable to insist that he should take them. When a child is sick and his appetite is poor it is important to coax him to eat and this is best achieved by the use of familiar, favourite foods in an easily digestible form, as discussed in Chapter 7.

Some foods are traditionally considered to be of potential harm to the child who is suffering from a particular illness, and are accordingly avoided. Most of these which we have listed in Table 6 are quite appropriate and would probably be followed by mums all over the world as they appeal to common sense. For example, it is advised that chilli, coconut and sour fruits be avoided during a bout of stomach ache. Cold drinks should be steered clear of during a cough and sweets avoided during diarrhoea. Once again, these prohibitions in themselves will not affect the nutritional quality of the diet. If, however, a mother tries to be too restrictive in the foods she gives her child, it might result in deficiency of some nutrients. It will also hinder the recovery process if the child's appetite is not improved due to a limitation of choice.

The main danger with traditional dietary remedies for sick children is that they may be followed as an alternative to seeking medical attention. **Delay in taking a sick child to the doctor could have disastrous consequences, and traditional food practices should take only a supportive role.**

Table 6: Traditional Food Prohibitions for Sick Children

Food Items	Complications
Mango, lime, guava, pineapple, chilli, spices, coconut	Stomach ache
Certain fish, e.g. *kembong*, *kayu*, *keli* Guava, groundnut, coconut Fresh water chestnut	Worms
Mango, *rambutan*, *langsat*, sweets, unboiled water	Diarrhoea
Cold food, ice cream, chocolates, sweets, unboiled water	Cough

Vegetarianism

Being a vegetarian is not just a matter of doing without meat or fish. Any individual on a vegetarian diet or thinking of embarking on a change to a vegetarian diet pattern should first learn the principles of vegetarian food selection so as to meet nutritional needs adequately. It is generally the case that communities who are vegetarian as a way of life—in Asia this is usually as part of religion, for example Hinduism and Buddhism—have evolved a very sound vegetarian diet pattern, taking the right combinations of foods for nutritional adequacy. People turning to vegetarianism for the first time, however, particularly those who have not been exposed much to vegetarian concepts, are a source of concern. Moreover, a dietary regimen which may be adequate for the average person may become inadequate for the pregnant or lactating woman. Children who are being raised as vegetarians are also at risk, unless the principles of vegetarianism are well-understood by the parents.

There are three types of vegetarians:

1. Lacto-ovo vegetarians—exclude all meat, fish and poultry from their diets but include milk and eggs.
2. Lacto-vegetarians—take milk and dairy foods, but exclude all meat, fish, poultry and eggs.
3. Vegans—exclude all animal products.

Planning a nutritionally sound vegetarian diet

In order to ensure that a vegetarian diet is nutritionally sound, there are three main points to consider:

1. Plant proteins are not as complete as animal proteins.
2. Plant foods are lower in energy than animal foods.
3. Plant foods are low in certain vitamins and minerals.

1. Plant proteins are not as complete as animal proteins.

Plant sources of protein (see Table 7) are incomplete because they are lacking in some of the essential amino acids (see page 16 in Chapter 1). This means they are also less efficiently used by the body than animal proteins. Carefully combining different plant proteins, however, makes them more complete. The low level of an essential amino acid in one protein will be compensated for by the higher amount found in another protein. Cereals, for example (which are low in the amino acid lysine but high in methionine), can be combined with pulses (high in lysine but low in methionine). Note that the cereals, not usually considered protein foods, do contain sufficient proteins when combined and, as Table 8 on page 123 shows, can contribute importantly to providing "complete" proteins in the vegetarian diet.

2. Plant foods are lower in energy than animal foods.

Since plant foods are usually lower in energy than animal foods, the

Table 7: Protein-containing Foods for Vegetarian Diet

Food Group	Examples
Cereals	rice, wheat, barley, oats, corn (maize), millet, rye, gluten
Pulses	black beans, peas, soya beans, red beans, kidney beans, chick peas, broad beans, mung beans, "baked" beans, lima beans, lentils
Nuts	groundnuts, cashews, walnuts, Brazil nuts, almonds, pistachio, pecans, macadamia, coconut, hazelnuts, pine nuts
Seeds	pumpkin, sesame, sunflower, watermelon

Table 8: Food Combinations that Provide "Complete" Proteins

Combinations	Examples
Beans or peas with cereal	beans on toast; red bean and rice soup
Lentils with cereal	*dhal* and *chapati*; *idli*, *thosai*; spaghetti with lentils
Bean curd and cereal	vegetarian *bee hoon* containing *tau kwa* and "*mock char siew*"; *yu char kuay* with soyabean milk
Nuts and cereal	peanut butter sandwich; *ketupat* with *satay* sauce
Cheese or egg and cereal	cheese on toast; French toast; fried rice with egg
Nuts and bean curd	*gado gado* with peanut sauce

diet may be more bulky as relatively more food has to be consumed to meet energy needs. This may pose a problem for children with small appetites. Fats and oils must therefore be used slightly more liberally than in non-vegetarian diets, as fat is a concentrated source of calories. It is especially important that the food eaten supplies enough energy for growth in children and during pregnancy, as well as for maintenance of weight in adults.

3. Plant foods are low in certain vitamins and minerals.

Vitamin B$_{12}$

Since vitamin B$_{12}$ is not normally found in plant foods, a vegan diet usually needs B$_{12}$ supplements. Small amounts of B$_{12}$ may be found in some plant foods as a result of its manufacture by bacteria. However, when requirements increase during pregnancy and also when growth is critical as during infancy and childhood, supplements are essential. vitamin B$_{12}$ supplements may be obtained either through a doctor's prescription or from fortified foods, e.g. fortified infant soya milk formula, or fortified breakfast cereals. Yeast extracts are also good sources but this is suitable only for children above two as they are very salty.

Vitamin B$_2$ and calcium

Milk and milk products are major sources of calcium and vitamin B$_2$. Therefore, if they are not included in the diet, other sources of calcium (bean curd, dark green vegetables and some nuts, especially almonds) and vitamin B$_2$ (mostly in whole grain or enriched breads and cereal products) should be emphasised. Fortified soyabean milk is a desirable alternative, particularly for the pregnant and nursing mother and for children.

Iron

Even lacto-vegetarians are at risk of having low iron intake, as the best sources of iron are meats and egg, with very little being found in milk. Iron is found in moderate amounts in pulses, vegetables, particularly dark green leafy ones, and in dried fruit, nuts, cocoa and wheatgerm. Foods fortified with iron are good sources, e.g. breakfast cereals, enriched breads, and infant cereals. Iron from vegetables is not as well-absorbed as that from meats, but including a vitamin C-rich food at each meal will help enhance the absorption of the iron.

If symptoms of anaemia occur, such as tiredness, it is wise to have your serum iron level checked and take the supplements prescribed by the doctor.

Vegetarianism in pregnancy and lactation

During pregnancy and lactation, when requirements for protein, calcium, iron and vitamins increase, it is important that the vegetarian mother-to-be pays careful attention to her diet and takes supplements if necessary, particularly of calcium if she does not drink milk. She should also take supplements of iron, vitamin B_{12} and possibly zinc if advised to do so by a doctor or dietitian. The same precautions must be followed during lactation. Table 9 illustrates a balanced day's meals for a pregnant or lactating vegetarian woman.

Table 9: Sample Daily Menu for a Vegetarian Pregnant/Lactating Woman

Breakfast	½ cup unsweetened orange juice 2 Ch sp baked beans 1 slice wholemeal bread 1 tsp margarine ½ cup milk*
Morning Snack	½ cup yoghurt* 1 slice wholemeal bread 1 tsp peanut butter

Lunch	1 bowl rice
	vegetable curry with:
	  1 cake *tau kwa*
	  2 Ch sp cabbage
	  2 Ch sp long beans
	or gado-gado with extra *tau kwa*
	1 slice papaya

Afternoon Snack	1 bowl red bean and rice soup ½ cup milk*

Dinner	1 bowl seaweed soup
	1 bowl rice
	3 Ch sp stir-fried *kai-lan*
	2 Ch sp gluten (e.g. mock duck)
	⅓ large square bean curd fried with
	  2 Ch sp mixed vegetables and
	  ½ Ch sp black mushroom
	1 slice honeydew melon

Bedtime	1 cup milk* 2 plain crackers 2 slices cheese or 1 tsp yeast extract

* or fortified soyabean milk

Vegetarianism in infancy and childhood

For vegan infants, it is desirable that they be breastfed for as long as possible and later introduced to fortified soyabean milk and not simply local fresh soyabean milk. The calcium content is quite low in the latter, and it cannot be used as an alternative for cow's milk in the growing child.

Special attention must be given to the nutritional content of vegetarian weaning food. Iron intake will be a problem for all vegetarian infants unless the mother uses iron-fortified milks, cereals and other fortified foods. The vegetarian mother should consult her doctor about the use of supplements for her baby. Tables 10 and 11 give examples of balanced meal plans for vegetarian babies and toddlers.

Table 10: Sample Meal Plan for Vegetarian Baby of Approximately 8 months

Meal	Sample menu
Early morning and three other feeds during day	Milk (breast milk, cow's milk infant formula or soya based infant formula)
Breakfast	Fortifed infant cereal with a little milk Unsweetened fruit juice
Lunch	Lentils cooked with tomato, carrot and rice porridge Plain water
Dinner	Brown rice flour cooked with water or milk* Bean curd cubes with pureed pumpkin Custard with pureed raisin and pear

* or soya based infant formula

Table 11: Sample Vegetarian Menu for a Toddler/Preschooler[a]

Meal	Sample Menu
Breakfast	½ cup unsweetened orange juice 1 egg or 2 Ch sp baked beans with ½ tsp yeast extract 1 slice wholemeal bread 1 tsp peanut butter
Morning Snack (if needed)	1 flaky oatmeal cookie (see recipe on page 246) ½ cup milk*

Lunch	½ bowl soup with 1 Ch sp spinach
	2 Ch sp cooked lentils
	cooked with:
	   1 medium potato
	   1 medium tomato
	   3 tsp grated cheese or cashew nuts
	½ slice papaya

Afternoon Snack	¾ bowl *tau suan* with *yu char kuay* ½ cup milk*

Dinner	½ bowl corn soup with 2 Ch sp cream style corn
	¾ bowl rice
	¼ large square bean curd
	fried with:
	   ½ Ch sp carrot
	   ½ Ch sp mushroom
	   1 Ch sp French beans
	½ orange

Bedtime	1 cup milky drink*
Oils and fats for the day: 2 Ch sp	

* or fortified soyabean milk
[a] Serving sizes will vary depending on the child's age, size, appetite and activity level. Make use of recipe section for more ideas and variety.

An understanding of the reasons behind food beliefs and principles behind vegetarian diets will help you make a more informed decision with regard to your child's diet.

Part II
Recipes

09 Notes on the Recipes and Kitchen Hints

Notes on the recipes

The first section of the Recipes, "Treats for Tiny Tots", consists of recipes for the weaning period (approximately six months to one year). Quantities stated are for a single baby, although the amount eaten at one meal will vary greatly. Quantities in the subsequent "potpourri" of adapted family recipes are for a family of two adults and two children unless otherwise specified. If you are cooking specially for a child, adjust to the child's needs which will depend on age and appetite. The recommended intakes of each food group can be referred to.

Our emphasis is on fresh natural ingredients, using a minimum of commercial products so as to minimise the amount of additives and artificial colouring or flavouring eaten. Our intention is to provide you with a greater variety of healthy recipes which your family will enjoy and benefit from. Traditional recipes have been modified to use less sugar and saturated fats and incorporate more fibre and nutrients.

Rice
To avoid repetition, we do not state each time that you will have to wash and rinse the rice three or four times before cooking.

Oil
We recommend that unsaturated oil (such as olive, canola and soya) and unsaturated margarine be used generally. The occasional use of pure groundnut oil, with small quantities of sesame oil as a seasoning, is acceptable. Using a non-stick pan will minimise the amount of oil needed for frying.

Salt
Salt in recipes should be minimal and we have stated "dash of salt" or "salt to taste" in the recipes to encourage you to use your discretion and gradually become accustomed to less salty food. In some recipes where soya sauce or other salty ingredients such as cheese and ham are used, we suggest omitting salt or using a minimum.

Meat
We have avoided the use of pork in many recipes to accommodate Muslim readers. For many of the recipes, however, chicken can be substituted with pork.

Nutritional analysis of recipes
For your information and reference, we have analysed the nutritional content of the adapted family recipes (using food composition values in published food tables). The nutrient content of a single portion is given, assuming a portion to be a quarter of the total recipe unless

otherwise stated. Obviously, a child may eat less than the analysed portion and an adult smore, hence the analysis serves only as a guide to the nutritional value of the recipes. The energy content in kilocalories (kcal), protein, fat and fibre in grams (g) and cholesterol in milligrams (mg) are given. For those recipes that can be used as "meals on their own" we also show the percentage of energy from fat. As can be seen, in most cases it lies within the recommended 20–30 per cent.

For the other key nutrients, we have indicated which recipes are good sources by a star system as follows:

*   supplies between 30–50 per cent of the recommended daily intake
**   supplies between 50–70 per cent of the recommended daily intake
*** supplies 70 per cent or more of the recommended daily intake

(The star rating is based on requirements for an average 5–7 year old child, according to the Recommended Daily Dietary Allowances for Singaporeans. The star rating highlights only instances where there is a particularly high level of a nutrient in a dish. Recipes without stars still, however, provide significant amounts of nutrients and make a valuable contribution to our overall diet.)

For vitamin C in cooked dishes, we have taken into account vitamin losses due to cooking. In recipes using plain yoghurt, the analysis has been based on the low fat type.

Guide to weights and measures used in the book

1 cup	= 240 ml
1 Ch sp (Chinese spoon)	= 18 ml
1 tsp (teaspoon)	= 5 ml
1 Ch sp oil	= 14 g

Note that in our recipes, we have preferred to use the Chinese spoon as a measuring standard instead of the more conventional tablespoon as, in practice, not many households have the American standard-sized measuring spoons. The Chinese spoon, which is often used for drinking soup, is usually of a standard size and holds slightly more than the tablespoon.

Abbreviations used

kg	=	kilogram
g	=	gram
mg	=	milligram
ml	=	millilitre
kcal	=	kilocalorie
Ch sp	=	Chinese spoon
tsp	=	teaspoon

Oven temperatures

°C	°F	Gas Mark
140	275	1
150	300	2
170	325	3
180	350	4
190	375	5
200	400	6
220	425	7
230	450	8
240	475	9

Kitchen hints

Useful cooking aids and equipment

Nowadays, most homes have an array of gadgets, both manual and electric, that make home cooking so much easier to cope with. Amidst all this, only a few pieces are really essential when you have a baby to cook for. The other pieces of equipment are useful to have around for speeding up food preparation, but there is no necessity to acquire them all just for that purpose.

Crockpot

A crockpot is a slow cooker and is available in varying sizes. It is quite useful, particularly for working mothers since it involves slow simmering but without the fear of the food drying up or burning. The food can be left to cook overnight for a delicious, hot breakfast the next morning. You can also set the crockpot cooking just before you leave for work so that baby's food is ready by lunchtime or the family's meal is ready by dinnertime.

The crockpot is especially useful for cooking dishes like stews, soups or congees. Ingredients such as greens and fish, however, should be added shortly before serving as they are easily cooked and also to retain their vitamins.

Double boiler

A double boiler uses indirect heat for cooking. It is similar to a crockpot, in that it is designed for slow, gentle cooking.

Egg beater or cake mixer

If you bake or plan to make home goodies, a beater is quite indispensable. The electric hand-held ones or the more complete mixer sets would be welcome presents! Otherwise, a simple hand-mixer or wire egg whisk will serve quite adequately. It is unnecessary to buy a baby mixer exclusively for baby's food.

Electric blender and grinder

An electric blender and grinder is one of the most useful sets of modern kitchen equipment. Anyone who spends time and enjoys cooking for the family should invest in one if possible. It is a useful replacement for the pestle and mortar, especially when large quantities are involved. It is particularly handy for pureeing larger quantities of food or fruit. It is unnecessary to buy a special baby food grinder.

Grater

A grater is indispensable for grating fruit and vegetables or cheese. One with a few different hole sizes for varying degrees of coarseness will be best.

Mesh sieve

A mesh sieve is a great help when pureeing small quantities of food for your baby such as vegetables or meat. Choose a small mesh sieve that can be held conveniently over a bowl and keep it solely for baby's food if possible.

Microwave oven

A microwave oven is the ultimate gadget in modern kitchen convenience. With it, you only need to spend a few minutes in the kitchen to rustle up a meal. Cooking, defrosting and reheating can all be done at the touch of a few buttons. Microwave cooking can be healthier too since many deep fried dishes can be adapted to cook in a microwave oven with a minimum use of oil. A word of caution though—to avoid scalding or burning, always check the temperature of the food before serving to your child. For those who do not miss the aroma of a busy kitchen, happy "microwaving"!

Muslin

A clean, unused baby's nappy (muslin cloth) can be cut up and sewn to the desired size for straining juices and other home-made drinks. A traditional cloth coffee strainer can be an alternative to muslin cloth although it can make the straining process rather slow if larger quantities of liquid are involved (for example for soyabean milk).

Pressure cooker

Some families swear by the pressure cooker. A pressure cooker speeds up cooking of the tougher cuts of meat and pulses. It is quite unnecessary, however, if it is to be used solely for baby's food.

Useful items to have in stock

In the refrigerator

1. Yoghurt, cottage cheese and a hard cheese (e.g. cheddar) for grating.
2. Milk, soft bean curd and other bean curd products.
3. Fresh vegetables and greens, wrapped well and used within three days (this especially applies to leafy greens).
4. Fresh and dried fruit (e.g. prunes).
5. Lean ham and cooked meat, used within two days unless kept frozen.
6. Home-made sauces, kept in covered containers and used within two to three days. For sauces that have been bought off the shelves, such as dressing, buy the healthier choices, e.g. calorie-reduced mayonnaise and low sodium tomato sauce.
7. Unsaturated margarine or butter; jam or preserves, peanut butter and the like.
8. Eggs.
9. Water.

In the freezer

1. Meat and fish (fresh or cooked). The keeping duration will depend on the size and efficiency of your freezer. For better efficiency, do not jam-pack and overload a freezer.
2. Cooked soup stocks and sauces (in the form of frozen cubes or otherwise) in plastic bags or containers.
3. Ice cream and frozen yoghurt in tubs and shaped trays, or as lollies —home-made if possible.
4. Frozen peas, mixed vegetables and sweetcorn.
5. Bread, home-made pancakes, muffins and the like.
6. Frozen fresh yeast, for baking purposes.

Date all the items so that you can check and update weekly to prevent over-keeping.

In baskets or an airy dry corner

1. Onions, garlic, shallots and ginger.
2. Potatoes and sweet potatoes.
3. Spices (peppercorns, cinnamon bark, cloves, etc.) in airtight bottles.

Cooking corner

1. Unsaturated cooking oil
2. Seasoning ingredients, for example salt, soya sauce, pepper, herbs, etc.
3. Cornflour, in an airtight container
4. Cooking wine

Note that cooking oil should not be reused more than about twice. With repeated heating, changes occur in the oil and undesirable flavours and compounds develop. Do not allow oil to smoke excessively. If it does, or if it turns dark and cloudy looking, or if it foams upon adding foods for frying, discard it.

In the cupboard or larder

1. Bottled baby foods—Keep a few handy for outings and the occasional standby meal.
2. Dry baby cereals—If you make use of these, check the list of ingredients and whenever possible, get the unsweetened ones whenever possible. Once the packet has been opened, keep the cereal in an airtight container.
3. Other dry cereals—These include rice, oatmeal, rolled oats, muesli, wheat flour, barley, semolina, sago, etc. Use unpolished and wholemeal as much as possible and keep them in airtight containers.
4. Pasta, dry noodles, *bee hoon* and vermicelli (*mee sua*) are handy

to have around. It is best to keep *mee sua* refrigerated once the box is opened to prevent them from turning mouldy.

5. Dry beans, lentils, sesame seeds, groundnuts, raisins, etc.—keep airtight.

6. Canned meat and fish—Sardines, tuna, mackerel, salmon, luncheon meat, etc. Drain off excess oil before use by standing the fish or meat in a mesh sieve over a bowl. If available, buy the water-packed variety. Use luncheon meat only very occasionally since most processed meats are not as nutritious as fresh meat and are high in fat.

7. Canned vegetables—Sweetcorn, baked beans, red kidney beans, etc. The kidney beans make nice additions to salads, minced meat stews, or *chilli con carne*. It is also useful to keep a few tins of tomato puree or paste handy. Try to buy the unsalted variety.

8. Canned fruit—Avoid those in heavy syrup and use only if you run out of fresh fruit or the needed fresh variety is unavailable.

9. Others—Skimmed milk powder, gelatine, agar agar powder/strips, baking powder, etc. will come in handy at times.

Plan ahead for healthy meals

"Menu planning" means thinking and selecting what foods to eat together for a meal, a day or even a week ahead. There are many advantages to planning meals:

1. Saving time and cost—Needed items will be on hand, thus avoiding numerous shopping trips and impulsive buying.

2. Increasing the variety—More new recipes can be tried out instead of falling back on the same old dishes. You will be more inclined to make the meals interesting and attractive too.

3. Improving nutritional value— A little effort spent on combining complementary dishes and choosing recipes and cooking methods which cut down on fat, sodium and sugar will ensure a healthier diet for all the family.

Keep a notebook handy in the kitchen and write down your day's or week's menu plan. This will not only guide you in drawing up your shopping list, but will be a useful reference if you run out of ideas later on.

Nutritious meals can be fun

Novel presentations will increase a child's enjoyment of food. Make use of cookie cutters and moulds in the shape of animals and alphabets to prepare sandwiches, and serve other types of food in bowls or plates of different shapes and sizes. An ordinary bowl of oatmeal porridge can be livened up by a smiling face of raisin eyes and cherry mouth. Likewise, decorate a mound of rice (obtained by up-turning a bowl packed with rice on to a plate) with peas, diced carrot and shredded seaweed (for hair) and see it all disappear! You can also turn a scoop of ice cream into a butterfly by adding triangular wafers.

It really only takes a few minutes of thought and preparation to whet a child's appetite. Remember, we are the ones who decide what our children will eat. Besides the responsibility of providing for our children's nutritional needs, we must also provide a conducive eating environment so that our children can develop healthy eating habits to last a lifetime.

10 Treats for Tiny Tots

Recipes for Weaning

The recipes in this section are for the weaning period of 6–12 months. For guidance on the introduction and consistency of weaning foods refer to Chapter 4, particularly the Weaning Charts on pages 64–70 and the section on "Food preparation for baby's first year" on pages 71–75. For the earlier weaning period the recipes should be pureed by sieving or blending. Later, soft mashed or chopped foods can be given to encourage chewing. Quantities in the recipes are for ease of preparation and they are not meant to be adhered to rigidly when feeding. A young baby, for example, may eat only a few teaspoons whereas an older baby may take much more. The light seasonings used in some recipes should be included only from 10 months onwards. For the rice porridge and congee recipes, allow approximately 7 Ch sp liquid for 1 Ch sp rice.

Liver and carrot congee

1 Ch sp rice
½ a small pair of chicken liver, cleaned
1 Ch sp cubed carrot
vegetable stock

Cook the rice and the carrot with the vegetable stock. Add cleaned chicken liver and simmer until cooked. Remove liver and carrot and strain through a sieve or puree. Return to the congee and boil briefly, or serve liver and carrot separately with the congee. For a slightly older infant, chop the liver and carrot before cooking and serve without mashing. When feeding, you might need to break up some of the larger lumps by pressing them with your spoon. Scraped or minced meat can also be used instead of liver.

Bean curd and French bean congee

¾–1 Ch sp bean curd, diced
¾ Ch sp thinly sliced tender French beans (remove string first)
1 Ch sp rice
vegetable stock

Cook the rice with the vegetable stock. Toward the end of the cooking time, add the sliced beans and boil till tender and soft. Add the diced bean curd just before turning off the heat. Cool and serve (pureed if necessary). Add shredded carrots for variation. Other greens, e.g. broccoli florets, can be used too.

Steamed fish with peas over rice

1½ Ch sp rice
1 Ch sp white fish fillet, thinly sliced
1 Ch sp frozen green peas

Seasoning for fish:
2 tsp infant formula milk or breast milk
¼ tsp cornflour
a few drops of light soya sauce
a few grains of mild pepper (optional)
1 thin slice of ginger

The fish slices may be lightly seasoned as given. Briefly boil the peas and press (sieve if they are big). When the rice is almost ready but still slightly wet and steamy, spread the fish and pea mixture over the surface of the rice evenly. Cover and steam for 3–5 more minutes over slow heat. Serve this dish with a soup and some mashed potato. Soft rice given to an older weaning baby will encourage chewing and prevent "lazy" eating habits.

1 Ch sp white fish fillet
1 Cp sp uncooked macaroni
or 1 small bundle *mee sua*
  (vermicelli)
1 Ch sp finely chopped tender
  chye sim or spinach
vegetable or bone stock

Light seasoning for fish:
a little dissolved cornflour
a few drops light soya sauce

Fish macaroni

Prepare the vegetable or bone stock. Boil the macaroni or vermicelli in a separate pot of water, then drain and rinse with cold water. This stops the cooking process and keeps the macaroni from sticking together. If you are using vermicelli, check to make sure that it is not salty. Cook the chopped vegetable briefly in the stock until tender. Add in the fish slices to cook just prior to serving. Pour the soup over the macaroni or vermicelli in a bowl, cool slightly and serve.

*If you are using spinach, remember to blanch first before adding to the soup.

3 Ch sp fresh, soft *kuay teow*,
  chopped
1 Ch sp minced lean meat,
  e.g. chicken, pork, beef
½ Ch sp chopped tomato,
  skin and seeds removed*
2 tsp broccoli florets (or green
  cabbage), chopped
vegetable or bone stock

Light seasoning for meat:
a few drops light soya sauce
a few grains pepper
a little dissolved cornflour

Kuay teow with minced meat and tomato

Wash the chopped *kuay teow* in boiling water and drain. Add the chopped tomato, minced meat and chopped greens to the boiling stock. When the meat is cooked and the vegetables are tender, pour this stock over the kuay teow in a bowl. Cool slightly and serve.

*To remove the skin, first scald the tomato in boiling water.

1 Ch sp tender whole kernel
  corn (frozen variety)
1 Ch sp minced chicken breast
30 ml infant formula milk or
  breast milk
¼ tsp cornflour, dissolved in
  a little water
1 tsp egg yolk (optional)
1½ Ch sp oatmeal or rolled oats
a few cooked peas

Minced chicken and sweetcorn oatmeal porridge

Cook the oats by boiling with ½ cup water. Puree the corn with a little water. Heat the pureed corn in a small pan with the milk for a short while and then add the minced chicken, stirring to break up the lumps. Adjust the consistency of the sauce with water, thickening it slightly with the cornflour and egg yolk if necessary. Serve the sauce over the oat porridge and garnish with a few sieved cooked peas.

Oat and fruit porridge

1½ Ch sp oatmeal or rolled oats
½ cup infant formula milk or
  breast milk
1 Ch sp soaked and chopped
  dried fruit (e.g. prunes,
  sultanas) or mashed/chopped
  fresh fruit (e.g. apple, banana
  or pear)

Cook the oatmeal in ½ cup water and, when the mixture begins to boil, lower the flame and simmer until the porridge is thick and soft. Add the milk and fruit and cook a further one minute. Cool and serve.

Quick savoury oat porridge

1½ Ch sp oatmeal or rolled oats
1 Ch sp chopped or minced
  meat
½ Ch sp diced *tau kwa*
½ Ch sp chopped greens
  (e.g. *chye sim*)
¼ cup infant formula milk or
  breast milk
water or vegetable stock

Cook the oatmeal in ½ cup water or stock. When the mixture begins to boil, lower the flame and allow to simmer for a while. Add the milk and other ingredients and cook to the desired consistency. Add a little extra water or stock if necessary.

This is a quick-to-fix nutritious meal and a good alternative to congee or rice.

Steamed fish with white sauce

1 Ch sp white fish fillet (e.g. *kurau*)
2 Ch sp white sauce (see recipe
  on page 142)
dash of lemon juice or thin slice
  of ginger

Steam the fish on a small plate with a dash of lemon juice or a slice of ginger to remove the fishy smell. Flake the fish when it is cooked and pour the white sauce over it. Serve this with mashed potato and mashed vegetables, e.g. peas.

Tasty chicken stew

3 pieces chicken on the bone
  (e.g. chopped from one thigh
  or drumstick)*
1 medium potato, finely diced
½ medium carrot, chopped
1 small tomato, skinned and
  seeded
½ Ch sp chopped onion
a little plain flour
1 cup water

Remove the skin from the chicken and roll the pieces in flour. Place all the ingredients in a saucepan with 1 cup water and boil. Once the mixture boils, cover the saucepan, lower the flame and simmer until the vegetables are soft. Remove the bone from the chicken and cut the meat into small pieces, or puree the ingredients together for a younger infant.

* Use a sufficiently sharp and heavy chopper to make clean breaks in the bones. Otherwise the bones may splinter and you may have a hard time removing the little bits from the meat and the stew.

Sunset lentil puree

4 Ch sp orange lentil (dhal),
   washed
1–2 small shallots, skinned and
   chopped
1 medium tomato, skinned

Boil the lentil in sufficient water to just cover it. Add more water if necessary while the lentil is cooking. After 10 minutes, add tomato and onion. Cook until the lentil is soft. If you are preparing this for a young baby, strain the whole mixture through a sieve or blend before serving. You can freeze any extra portions in an ice cube tray for later use. Add milk and mix with a little soft rice or mashed potato for a complete baby's meal.

Egg yolk custard

1 egg yolk
60 ml infant formula milk
   or breast milk
½ tsp sugar or honey
   (if for dessert)

Beat the yolk with the water and milk. Add the sugar or honey if it is for dessert. Place this in a small cup and steam over low heat until set. The custard will not be smooth if the heat is high. The custard is done when a tooth pick inserted in the middle of the custard comes out clean. The custard can be served with pureed fruit. Alternatively, if it is done without sugar, you can serve it with vegetables as part of a meal.

Tiny tot's trifle

1 rusk or piece of steamed
   sponge cake
⅓ cup fresh fruit juice
   (or a mixture of apple juice
   and diluted blackcurrant
   syrup)
½ tsp gelatine, dissolved in
   1 Ch sp water
egg yolk custard (see previous
   recipe)

Place the rusk in a small dish. Dissolve the gelatine in a little boiling water and add to the fruit juice. Pour over the rusk and chill in the refrigerator until set. Make the custard, omitting the sugar (as rusk and jelly are sweet), and pour over the jelly. Chill again until the custard is firm. For an older baby, chop some soft pear or banana and add to the jelly.

Baby's French toast

1 egg yolk
30 ml infant formula milk
   or beast milk
30 ml water
1 slice bread, crust removed

Beat the egg yolk together with the milk. Dip the bread into the mixture so that it coats both sides. Toast under a grill until slightly brown. Cut into strips and serve. A good finger food for a nine- to 10-month old baby.

Tiny shepherd's pie

- 1½ Ch sp lean meat (e.g. beef, pork, lamb), minced or scraped
- 1 medium potato, boiled and mashed together with 2 Ch sp infant formula milk or breast milk
- ½ Ch sp chopped onion
- 1 Ch sp peas and diced carrot
- ½ Ch sp grated cheese
- ½ tsp cornflour, dissolved in a little water

Simmer the onions, peas, carrot cubes and meat in a little water until cooked. Thicken slightly by simmering with the cornflour for a few minutes. Place this in a small individual souffle dish and spread mashed potato on top. Sprinkle with grated cheese if it is for an older infant and place under the grill for a few minutes until it is slightly brown.

Tender stuffed gourd

- 1 piece (4-cm thick) sliced hairy gourd, skinned with centre pulp removed
- 1½ Ch sp minced meat, e.g. pork or chicken
- 1 tsp chopped onion
- vegetable stock

Seasoning for meat:
- ½ tsp cornflour
- a few drops light soya sauce

Mix the onion with the minced meat. Add the cornflour and a few drops of light soya sauce. Stuff this mixture into the middle of the gourd piece and place it in a small saucepan. Add sufficient vegetable stock to cover the gourd. Boil this and simmer gently until the gourd is tender and soft. Serve with soft rice.

Steamed bean curd cup

- ¼ square piece of bean curd
- 1 large egg yolk, beaten together with some water
- 1 Ch sp chopped carrot and tomato
- 1–2 leaves spinach, blanched and chopped

Mash the bean curd with a fork. Add the bean curd and the vegetables to the beaten egg yolk. Place in a cup or small bowl and steam for 20 minutes over low heat. The bean curd mixture is cooked if a knife which is dipped into it comes out clean, without any traces of the egg yolk. Turn out the cup and serve with soft rice.

Bean curd medallion dinner

- 1 Ch sp sieved liver (or scraped/minced meat)
- 2 pieces (4-cm thick) bean curd slice (from roll)
- 1 Ch sp cooked mashed carrot or pumpkin

Place the bean curd slices on a small plate. Place a layer of sieved liver on top and pile the carrot/pumpkin over the liver. Steam this for 3 to 4 minutes. Serve with rice porridge or soft mashed potato.

Tasty apple dessert

1 red apple, skinned, cored and sliced
½ tsp finely grated orange rind (optional, but if used, wash the skin thoroughly before grating)
2 tsp plain yoghurt

Squeeze a little lemon juice over the apples to prevent them from turning brown. In a small saucepan, cover the apple and orange rind with ¼–½ cup of water. Simmer until soft. Mash or blend it and then stir in the yoghurt. You can adjust the consistency with a little milk if necessary. Other fruit, such as banana or pear, can be used too.

Fruit sauce (for custard or soft bean curd)

¼–½ cup fresh fruit, e.g. mango, soft pear, apple, papaya, banana, honeydew, etc.
water or fruit juice for blending

Chop the fruit and squeeze a little lemon juice over it to prevent browning. Puree in a blender, adding a little water or fresh juice until the sauce is of pouring consistency. For apple or pear, simmer in a little water for 10 minutes until soft before blending. Add a little milk in place of part of the water if a milky fruit sauce is required.

Infant tomato sauce

3 medium ripe tomatoes
¼ small onion or 1 shallot, sliced
¼ clove garlic, pounded
¼ tsp sugar (optional)

Scald the tomatoes in boiling water and remove the skins. Dice them and boil together with the other ingredients in a little water to cover. Simmer over low heat until soft. Sieve or blend. This is great for dipping bread into, or you could add it to a little soft cooked rice and fish. It is also useful as a base for stews. Milk can be added to thin the sauce into a soup.

Fruit juice jelly

⅓ cup fresh/carton/bottled unsweetened fruit juice
½ tsp gelatine powder

Dissolve the gelatine in a little hot water. Add this to the fruit and pour the mixture into a cup. Chill this in the refrigerator to set it. One good way of serving this to an older baby is with egg custard or chopped fresh fruit.

Variation: Add 2 tsp soft chopped fruit to the jelly before allowing it to set and serve this as a fruit jelly mould.

Ground red/green bean dessert

2 Ch sp dry red or green beans, soaked for ½ hour before cooking, then drained
a few strips of orange rind, washed thoroughly
a little milk and sugar to taste

Boil the beans in water until well expanded and soft. Remove the orange rind. Blend or puree the beans with a little milk for added smoothness and taste.

White sauce

White sauce, although Western in origin, makes an interesting change in texture and taste for baby. Served occasionally with plain boiled vegetables or fish, it is well liked by children. There are many variations which mums can imaginatively employ.

3 scoops infant formula milk powder
⅓ cup (80–90 ml) water
   (or 90 ml breast milk)
2 tsp cornflour

Simple method

Blend the cornflour with the milk, stir and simmer until it is slightly thickened. Serve this with chopped or pureed vegetables or over fish/chicken.

1 Ch sp plain flour
1 level Ch sp unsaturated margarine
1 cup milk

Traditional method (not suitable for young children under one year of age due to higher fat content)

Melt the margarine and add in the flour. Mix well, stir and cook very gently until it bubbles and looks grainy (roux). Remove from the heat and gradually add the milk, stirring continuously to make it smooth. Return to the heat, stir gently until it boils. Simmer gently for one minute.

Variations of basic white sauce

1. Egg
   Raw egg yolk can be added to the sauce when almost cooked. Stir well.
2. Cheese
   ½–1 tsp grated cheese can be added for the older infant. Stir cheese into the hot sauce. Do not boil.
3. Yoghurt
   Diluted plain yoghurt can replace part of the milk.
4. Vegetables
   A little pureed vegetable mixed into the sauce gives it more texture. Add a dash of pepper for extra taste and serve with scraped cooked meat or liver.

11 Family Recipes Adapted for Young Children

A Meal on Its Own (light luncheons)

For a busy mum (and which mum is not?), a simple, no-fuss lunch to prepare is most welcome. A light one-dish meal that is nutritionally sound and yet appetising provides the answer. This can be in the form of rice, congee or noodles (in this section) or even sandwiches and soups (see later sections). A variety of ingredients and novel visual presentations can be used to improve a child's interest in these basic dishes. We have given a few examples of one-dish meals, but you can easily add to the list by adapting other recipes or inventing your own.

Quantities are for two adults and two children unless otherwise stated.

RICE

The staple throughout most of Asia, the versatility of rice is often underestimated and it is taken for granted as "plain old rice". Most ethnic groups in Asia have their own ways of dressing up this "Cinderella" of food; all that is needed is a little innovation to provide that magic touch. To avoid repetition, we do not describe in each recipe how to cook the rice but, in general, 1½–2 cups water is required to cook 1 cup rice.

1 cup rice
100 g white fish fillet, sliced thinly
100 g medium prawn, shelled and deveined
2–3 pieces scallop (optional)
a few fresh mussels, cleaned (optional)
1 egg white
2–3 garden lettuce leaves, washed
1 Ch sp unsaturated oil
2–3 slices ginger
1–2 cloves garlic, finely chopped
1 tsp cornflour, dissolved in a little water
1 sheet crispy Japanese seaweed*, cut in small strips
½ medium carrot, grated

Seasoning for fish:
½ tsp rice wine
½ tsp cornflour
¼ tsp sesame oil
dash of salt and pepper

Fisherman's rice

Cook rice. Season fish. Stir-fry ginger and garlic in oil and add in fish, prawn, then scallops and mussels (if used). Add a little water and blend in dissolved cornflour. Stir in the egg white and simmer for a few minutes.

Serve seafood mixture over rice on lettuce leaves (as boats), with mussel shells on top (as sails). Garnish each seafood boat with the seaweed strips and grated carrot. This is a fun meal that will stir up any toddler's interest!

*Crispy seaweed is available at Japanese specialty supermarkets and at the Japanese counters of most supermarkets. Choose the variety that is not salted or highly seasoned.

Portion analysis	
energy	: 287 kcals
protein	: 13 g
fat	: 7 g
% energy from fat	: 23 %
fibre	: 1.6 g
cholesterol	: 72 mg
vitamin A	: ★ ★

Tomato rice with beef and onions

1 cup rice
250 g tender cut of beef
  (e.g. striploin), thinly
  sliced
1 cup tomato juice
  (low salt if possible)
½ cup water
1 medium onion, sliced
2 tomatoes, chopped
2 cloves garlic, pounded
2 slices ginger
½ Ch sp unsaturated oil
dash of salt, sugar and
  pepper

Cook the rice. Fry garlic, ginger and onion briefly. Add in chopped tomato, tomato juice and seasoning. Simmer until onion is tender, then add beef slices. Take care not to overcook the beef so as to retain its tenderness. Serve beef over rice, accompanied by vegetable of choice, for example lady's fingers.

Portion analysis	
energy	: 323 kcals
protein	: 16 g
fat	: 7 g
% energy from fat	: 18 %
fibre	: 2.5 g
cholesterol	: 37 mg
iron	: ★★
vitamin B$_1$	: ★★★

Crispy crackling rice cakes

2 bowls cooked glutinous
  rice
100 g sliced chicken or
  other meat
150 g shelled prawns
3 Ch sp peas
3 medium tomatoes
1 Ch sp tomato puree
3 cups chicken stock
dash of salt, sugar and
  pepper
1 Ch sp cornflour
unsaturated oil for frying

Spread the cooked glutinous rice while still hot on a tray. Cool it and cut into thin 8-cm by 5-cm rectangles. Do not compress the rice too much. Lightly fry the chicken and prawn. Boil the chicken stock with the tomatoes until the latter turns to pulp. Thicken this sauce with dissolved cornflour; add peas and other ingredients. Simmer briefly and adjust seasoning. Meanwhile, deep-fry glutinous rice cake until slightly golden and crispy. Drain and soak up excess oil on kitchen paper and place in a large serving bowl.

When you are ready to serve the meal, pour the boiling sauce mixture over the rice pieces. The crackling, sizzling sound made when the sauce is poured over the rice never fails to delight children and the combination of taste and texture is a winner. Serve this as an occasional treat. For best results, do not pack the rice too tightly to allow for air spaces. Also be sure to cool the rice cakes completely before frying.

Portion analysis	
energy	: 295 kcals
protein	: 19 g
fat	: 5 g
% energy from fat	: 15 %
fibre	: 3.6 g
cholesterol	: 99 mg
iron	: ★
vitamin A	: ★
vitamin B$_1$	: ★★
vitamin B$_2$	: ★★
niacin	: ★

Stuffed lotus or cabbage leaves

2-3 large dry lotus leaves* or fresh cabbage leaves

3 bowls cooked rice (use the glutinous variety if desired)

100 g lean roast pork (*char siew*), diced

½ cup shelled cooked prawns

3-4 pieces (30 g) Chinese mushrooms, softened in hot water and diced

3 Ch sp cooked carrot, diced

2 tsp light soya sauce

2-3 drops sesame oil

salt and pepper to taste

Wash the lotus or cabbage leaves and wipe dry. Cut in half and brush with a little oil. Mix the cooked meat with the rice and seasoning. Place a little of the rice mixture on to the middle of a lotus leaf and wrap it into a square package. Secure this with a wooden toothpick. When all the rice has been wrapped, steam the packages for 10–15 minutes and serve hot. If cabbage leaves are used instead, dip them briefly in hot water to soften, and drain away the water before use.

The fragrance of lotus leaves gives the rice a special flavour. Children will enjoy unwrapping and eating the rice from the little packages which will be a welcome change from the usual rice on a plate or bowl.

*Dry lotus leaves are available from most Chinese medicine shops. Using cabbage leaves will provide extra fibre and nutrients. Serve with sautéed cabbage if using lotus leaves.

Portion analysis

energy	: 315 kcals
protein	: 16 g
fat	: 5 g
% energy from fat	: 15 %
fibre	: 2.1 g
cholesterol	: 75 mg
iron	: ★
vitamin A	: ★ ★

Beef and sweetcorn over rice

1 cup rice

250 g lean tender beef, thinly sliced

1 egg

½ can (250 g) cream-style corn

1 cup water or stock

1-2 cloves garlic, finely chopped

1 small shallot, thinly sliced

½ Ch sp unsaturated oil

salt to taste

Seasoning for meat:

¼ tsp pepper

Cook the rice. Marinate the beef slices with the pepper and the egg. When almost ready to serve, heat the oil in a frying pan, lightly fry the garlic and shallot until fragrant. Add in the sweetcorn and water or stock. Bring to the boil, then add in the beef slices (separate the pieces first to avoid clumping) and turn off the heat once the colour of the meat changes. Season to taste. Do not overcook as the meat may toughen. Serve over a plate of rice with some green vegetables.

This is a quick and easy meal to prepare and most children will like the combined taste of corn and meat.

Portion analysis

energy	: 342 kcals
protein	: 18 g
fat	: 8 g
% energy from fat	: 22 %
fibre	: 1.1 g
cholesterol	: 93 mg
iron	: ★
vitamin B_2	: ★
niacin	: ★

1 cup rice
3–4 pcs dried
  mushrooms, soaked
½ cup hot (but not
  boiling) water
100 g chicken meat
  (or pork tenderloin),
  diced
½ medium carrot,
  cut into strips and
  parboiled in ½ cup
  water
1 pc bean curd cake
  (*tau kwa*), cut into
  strips (1 cm x 4 cm)
1 cup chicken stock
1 clove garlic, finely
  chopped
2 tsp light soya sauce
2 tsp *Hua Tiao* (Chinese
  wine)
a few pieces crispy
  Japanese seaweed,
  cut into strips
salt and pepper to taste
1 Ch sp unsaturated oil

Tasty meat and vegetable rice

Soak the dried mushrooms in the half cup of hot water for about 15 minutes. Remove the mushrooms from the water and cut them into strips. Set aside the remaining water for use as stock later. Similarly, set aside the water used for parboiling the carrot.

Heat the oil and sauté the garlic till fragrant. Pour in the wine and add in the chicken. Stir fry until the colour of the chicken changes. Add the carrot, *tau kwa* and mushroom strips and stir briefly to mix well. Next, add the seasonings and the chicken, mushroom and carrot stocks. Cover the mixture with the reserved stock and boil it for 5–10 minutes. Drain off the stock into a pot and set aside the meat mixture. Use the stock (add extra water if needed) to cook the rice. When this is cooked, fold in the meat and vegetables to mix evenly with the rice. Add in the seaweed strips just before serving. Some fried omelette strips can also be mixed in to add colour and variety. Serve this dish with a soup.

Vegetarian variation:
Substitute the meat with half a cup of mock meat (gluten; available in cans from most supermarkets) and add 1–2 Ch sp of halved cashew nuts.

This is a healthier alternative to fried rice. For young children, the rice can be pressed into round or fluted jelly moulds and then turned out on to a plate when ready to serve. This makes eating much more fun!

Portion analysis

energy	: 281 kcals
protein	: 14 g
fat	: 7 g
% energy from fat	: 24 %
fibre	: 1.8 g
cholesterol	: 24 mg
iron	: *
vitamin A	: *

1 cup rice

500 g chicken (approx ½ a medium chicken), chopped into bite-sized pieces

3–4 pcs Chinese mushrooms, soaked and sliced

1 pc Chinese sausage (optional), boiled briefly and sliced thinly

dash of sugar and pepper to taste

½ Ch sp spring onion, chopped

Seasoning:

1 tsp ginger juice

¼ tsp sesame oil

1 tsp *Hua Tiao* (Chinese wine)

2 tsp dark soya sauce

1 tsp light soya sauce

1 tsp cornflour

Claypot rice

Marinate the chicken in the seasoning ingredients. Cook the rice in a medium-sized claypot. When the rice is half cooked but still steaming, spread the chicken, mushroom and Chinese sausage evenly over the rice and cook for another 10 minutes or so. Turn off the heat and let the rice sit for a further 5 minutes. Serve with a soup and a vegetable dish.

Do not give Chinese sausage to very young children as it has a very high fat content. For older children, however, eating a little Chinese sausage occasionally will be of little harm. Furthermore, the sausage adds a special taste to the rice which is very appetising for fussy eaters. Cooking and serving food in a claypot adds novelty and interest to the meal.

Portion analysis

energy	: 365 kcals
protein	: 30 g
fat	: 9 g
% energy from fat	: 23 %
fibre	: 1.2 g
cholesterol	: 85 mg
iron	: ★
vitamin B$_2$	: ★
niacin	: ★ ★

Assorted sushi rice rolls

1 ¼ cups rice, short grain or stickier variety
100 g grilled fish meat, flaked
100 g roast meat (e.g. chicken), shredded
2 medium eggs, cooked as a thin omelette and cut into strips
½ medium carrot, boiled and cut into thin strips
½ small cucumber, cut in thin strips
a few sheets of Japanese seaweed (variety used for sushi)
1 Ch sp roasted sesame seeds (optional)

Seasoning for rice:
1 Ch sp rice vinegar
1½ tsp fine sugar
dash of salt

Cook rice. When done, stir in rice seasoning. Place in shallow container and cool quickly by fanning to make rice shiny. Prepare other ingredients. Place a clean, damp cloth over a fine bamboo "chick" scroll or table mat. Spread a layer of cooled rice over the cloth; wet your hand to prevent rice from sticking. Place a sheet of seaweed on top of the rice together with strips of egg and vegetables, roll up and press tightly. Remove from scroll and cut into 2.5-cm rolls. Sprinkle with sesame seeds if desired. Do likewise for fish and meat filling. Arrange cut rolls nicely and serve with bean curd and vegetable soup. A more authentic but trickier way is to roll the rice inside the seaweed sheet (without using the damp towel): the seaweed will be crispier in this case.

Sushi rolls are fun, nutritious and a novel way of eating rice. Older children will enjoy helping with the preparation of the sushi and eating the fruits of their labour. Experiment and adapt them to your own family's particular tastes.

Portion analysis	
energy	: 363 kcals
protein	: 19 g
fat	: 9 g
% energy from fat	: 24 %
fibre	: 2.6 g
cholesterol	: 156 mg
iron	: ★
vitamin A	: ★ ★
niacin	: ★

1 cup rice
1 cup thin coconut milk
    (second squeezed)*
1 cup water
3–4 *pandan* leaves

For each child:
1 Ch sp dried silver
    whitebait, washed
    and dried
½ egg
1 Ch sp spinach, chopped
1 tsp unsaturated oil
dash of salt and pepper
1 Ch sp home-made
    tomato sauce (see
    recipe on page 140)
    or a little ketchup

*Or ½ cup skimmed
    milk and ½ cup thin
    coconut milk.

Children's nasi lemak

Cook the rice with coconut milk and water together with the *pandan* leaves. Fry silver whitebait in oil until slightly crispy or toast it in the oven. Season the egg and whisk until the yolk and egg white are well mixed. Fry the egg with the spinach as an omelette and serve with rice, whitebait and tomato sauce.

For adults and older children, the traditional crispy *ikan bilis* with groundnuts, deep-fried *ikan kuning* and plain egg omelette can be served with the rice, together with sliced cucumber and chilli *sambal*. Serve only occasionally as the fat content of the combined meal is rather high.

Thick coconut milk is not suitable for young children as it contains a high level of a particular type of fat (known as short-chain). This fat is absorbed rather quickly into the bloodstream and abdominal discomfort may result. Older children and adults should also avoid taking coconut milk often as it is high in saturated fat.

Portion analysis

energy	: 388 kcals
protein	: 21 g
fat	: 16 g
% energy from fat	: 37 %
fibre	: 2.4 g
cholesterol	: 125 mg
calcium	: ★★★
iron	: ★★★
vitamin C	: ★★

Banana leaf rice

The traditional Indian style of eating rice from a banana leaf is fun and colourful. Any combination of a meat or lentil dish with two contrasting coloured vegetable dishes form the basis of this meal. For example:

1. Plain rice
2. Mild mutton curry (see recipe on page 195)
3. Spinach with pumpkin (see recipe on page 212)
4. Saffron potatoes (see recipe on page 208)
5. Papadums*
6. Plain yoghurt

*Papadums may be purchased in small packets, ready for quick frying, from any Indian provision shop. Children will love their crispy texture. Their consumption should be limited, however, as they are fried in oil and can also be quite salty.

CONGEES

These nourishing meals in a bowl are easily eaten, especially on occasions when appetite is poor, such as during illness or in the case of a child when teething or after some dental treatment. Congees are prepared without oil and it is therefore in the interest of health to include congee as a regular feature of your child's diet.

The congee may be prepared in the rice cooker or over a stove, generally allowing approximately 6–7 cups liquid per 1 cup of rice. In the recipes that follow, we shall not be including the amount of water to use as preferences differ regarding how dilute or thick the congee should be.

Besides providing a tasty and convenient lunch, congees are also a welcome change for breakfast. They can be put to cook in a slow cooker overnight so that the family awakes to a tasty, ready-to-eat, hot breakfast in the morning.

Beef and egg congee

¾ cup rice
200 g lean tendercut beef, thinly sliced
100 g Chinese cabbage, shredded
2–3 slices ginger
1 egg per person, beaten (optional)
1 Ch sp chopped spring onion
6–8 cups beef stock
dash of salt and pepper

Boil rice with the beef stock and ginger on slow fire. When cooked add shredded cabbage and simmer for another 10 minutes. Add the beef and simmer for another few minutes. Switch off heat and immediately stir in beaten eggs. Adjust seasoning and serve garnished with chopped spring onion.

There is minimum preparation for this dish, especially if ready sliced *shabu shabu* beef (available from most supermarkets) is used. This particular congee provides a well-balanced and convenient meal for both busy mums and children.

Portion analysis	
energy	: 279 kcals
protein	: 19 g
fat	: 10 g
% energy from fat	: 31 %
fibre	: 1.2 g
cholesterol	: 254 mg
iron	: ★★
vitamin A	: ★
vitamin B$_1$	: ★★
vitamin B$_2$	: ★
niacin	: ★

Rainbow congee

¾ cup rice
½ medium chicken,
  boiled and shredded
1 small carrot, grated
2 Ch sp green peas or
  snow peas (shredded)
1 small sweet potato
  (yellow flesh), coarsely
  grated
salt and pepper to taste

Rainbow congee

Boil the chicken in the water for 15 minutes or until the chicken is cooked. Remove the chicken from the water and discard the skin. When cooled slightly, shred the meat. Skim off any excess fat from the stock and return the chicken bones to it. Boil the rice in this stock for the congee. When the congee is of the right consistency, remove the bones and add the vegetables 10 minutes before serving. When the vegetables are sufficiently soft, mix in the shredded chicken, then adjust the seasoning and serve. To retain the colourful shreds of vegetable, take care not to over-boil.

Portion analysis

energy	: 277 kcals
protein	: 21 g
fat	: 5 g
% energy from fat	: 16 %
fibre	: 2.5 g
cholesterol	: 59 mg
vitamin A	: ★★★
niacin	: ★

¾ cup rice
200 g roast or braised
  duck meat
4–5 Ch sp braised duck
  sauce, fat skimmed off
duck or chicken bones
1 rice bowl finely
  shredded garden
  lettuce
1 Ch sp finely chopped
  spring onion

Roast or braised duck congee

Remove all skin and fat and shred the duck meat. Marinate in duck sauce (both meat and sauce can be bought from the roast meat stall in the market or hawker centre). Cook the congee with duck or chicken bones until rice is very soft and smooth (this congee is usually made more watery). Add marinated duck and lettuce; stir and boil briefly. Serve garnished with chopped spring onion. If desired, break an egg into each bowl immediately and stir thoroughly with the very hot congee.

Duck is quite an oily meat. For those who love duck porridge but find the ones sold in restaurants too oily, this home-made version offers a better choice. Even so, it is best served only occasionally.

Portion analysis

energy	: 223 kcals
protein	: 15 g
fat	: 5 g
% energy from fat	: 21 %
fibre	: 1.1 g
cholesterol	: 80 mg
iron	: ★
vitamin B_1	: ★
vitamin B_2	: ★

Seafood congee

¾ cup rice
100 g white fish, thinly sliced
100 g prawns, shelled and deveined
2 dried scallops, soaked briefly
2 Ch sp chopped coriander leaves
2 slices young ginger
dash of salt and pepper

Seasoning for fish:
1 tsp light soya sauce
1 tsp cornflour
dash of pepper and salt

Boil dried scallops in water or fish stock with the ginger for 5 minutes. Add the rice and cook until porridge is smooth and soft. When ready to serve, add seasoned fish and prawn. Turn off heat after a few minutes and adjust seasoning. Garnish with chopped coriander leaves. The natural sweetness of fresh seafood is hard to beat and over-seasoning will mask the delicate flavours.

Portion analysis	
energy	: 204 kcals
protein	: 14 g
fat	: 3 g
% energy from fat	: 15 %
fibre	: 0.8 g
cholesterol	: 74 mg

Mixed liver and fish congee

¾ cup rice
200 g liver, thinly sliced
150 g white fish fillet, e.g. *kurau* or *garoupa*, thinly sliced
50 g carrot or spinach (optional)
3 slices ginger
2 small shallots, thinly sliced and fried
1 Ch sp chopped spring onion
dash of salt and pepper

Seasoning for liver:
1½ tsp light soya sauce
1 tsp cornflour
1 tsp *Hua Tiao* (Ch wine)

Seasoning for fish:
1 tsp sesame oil
1 tsp Chinese wine
1½ tsp light soya sauce
1 tsp cornflour
½ tsp ginger juice

Cook rice with ginger to desired consistency. Stir in liver and fish shortly before turning off the heat. Serve garnished with chopped spring onion. When using carrot cut it into small cubes and cook with the rice for 20 minutes before serving. If spinach is used, chop it up and add 10 minutes before serving.

Variation:
Substitute liver with minced chicken or pork.

Portion analysis	
energy	: 278 kcals
protein	: 18 g
fat	: 8 g
% energy from fat	: 25 %
fibre	: 1.3 g
cholesterol	: 160 mg
iron	: ★★★
vitamin A	: ★★★
vitamin B$_2$	: ★★★
niacin	: ★★★

Groundnut and spare ribs congee

¾ cup unmilled rice
   (*cho bee*)
60 g raw groundnuts,
   with skin
250 g meaty pork spare
   ribs
1 Ch sp chopped
   coriander leaves, for
   garnishing
1 Ch sp shallots, sliced
   thinly and fried
dash of salt and pepper

Wash groundnuts and spare ribs and simmer with the rice until soft. Season and garnish with the coriander leaves and shallots. This congee is best cooked slowly, if time permits, to maximise the flavours. For the child's portion, break up the nuts and remove the bones. For those who dislike the coarse texture of unmilled rice, it will come as a surprise how smooth this congee is!

Portion analysis	
energy	: 306 kcals
protein	: 17 g
fat	: 14 g
% energy from fat	: 40 %
fibre	: 2.5 g
cholesterol	: 34 mg
iron	: ★★★
vitamin B₁	: ★★★
niacin	: ★

Sweet potato congee

¾ cup rice
1 medium yellow sweet
   potato, peeled and
   cubed

Choose the fragrant, yellow, loose-textured sweet potato. Boil the sweet potato with the rice in 6 cups of water for about 20 minutes or until the rice grains have swollen, but do not overboil. Cover and let the congee sit for more than 10 minutes before serving, as is the Fujien practice. This congee is usually eaten plain, served with separate meat or fish dishes and vegetables as desired. Minced pork cooked with soya sauce and pickled *chye sim* is one of the favourite accompanying dishes. The sweet potato adds considerable vitamin A to this congee.

Portion analysis	
energy	: 162 kcals
protein	: 5 g
fat	: 0.4 g
% energy from fat	: 2 %
fibre	: 1.7 g
cholesterol	: 0
vitamin A	: ★

Bean congee

½ cup rice
2 Ch sp red beans
2 Ch sp green (mung)
   beans (washed and
   soaked for 1–2 hours)
250 g meaty pork spare ribs
salt and pepper to taste

Cook the soaked beans with the rice and spare ribs until soft. Serve with vegetables of choice. This bean and meat congee is usually enjoyed at breakfast time or as a snack, and is nourishing for all ages. As well as being high in protein, the beans are a good source of fibre which is lacking in plain white rice.

Portion analysis	
energy	: 301 kcals
protein	: 19 g
fat	: 10 g
% energy from fat	: 29 %
fibre	: 4.9 g
cholesterol	: 34 mg
iron	: ★★★
vitamin B₁	: ★★

NOODLES

It is amazing to count the variety of noodles available in the market, both plain and coloured (from added vegetables) and in all shapes and sizes. Most children love noodles and seldom tire of eating them, but many parents often opt for the quick "instant" commercial products for a lack of ideas or time. Otherwise, it seems equally simple to buy takeaway cooked noodles from nearby hawker centres. Unfortunately, these are often very high in fat and lack adequate vegetables and are therefore undesirable on a regular basis. Making nourishing noodle dishes is relatively easy with ready pre-made fresh noodles or the dried variety, such as spaghetti or *bee hoon*. When you have an occasional free morning or afternoon, why not have fun with the children by making home-made dough noodles. It is very educational and the children will delight in playing with real dough that can be popped into the mouth later, after cooking.

400 g *kuay teow*
150 g tender beef slices
20 beef balls
1½ litres beef bone stock
1 Ch sp thinly shredded
   Sichuan vegetable*
2 medium tomatoes,
   skinned and quartered
50 g beansprouts, boiled
   briefly to cook
2 slices ginger
2 cloves garlic, crushed
1 tsp cornflour
salt and pepper to taste
½ tsp *Hua Tiao* (Chinese
   wine)
1 Ch sp unsaturated oil

Kuay teow soup with beef balls

Boil the *kuay teow* briefly in boiling water, apportion into bowls and add bean sprouts. Heat beef stock and add in beef balls (beef balls are available from supermarkets and most big wet markets). Fry ginger and garlic in heated oil, add wine and beef and sauté briefly. Add *Sichuan* vegetable, if used, and tomatoes. Stir in dissolved cornflour and adjust seasoning. Serve the beef mixture and soup over the *kuay teow*.

* Chilli is one of the ingredients used in pickling this vegetable, so use it sparingly when cooking for children. Soak to remove the chilli and the excess saltiness.

Portion analysis	
energy	: 333 kcals
protein	: 23 g
fat	: 10 g
% energy from fat	: 28 %
fibre	: 3.4 g
cholesterol	: 57 mg
iron	: ★ ★ ★
vitamin B$_2$	: ★
niacin	: ★ ★

300 g plain flour, sifted
1 medium egg
½ cup water

Home-made egg noodle

Place the sifted flour in a mixing bowl, add in the egg and stir with a wooden spoon to mix. Add water a little at a time until all the flour is incorporated. Knead with the hand to form a dry dough. You may need to sprinkle with flour occasionally. When the dough no longer sticks to the sides of the mixing bowl, shape it into a ball, cover the bowl with a dry towel and allow the dough to rest for 10 minutes. Separate it into three parts and roll each out on a floured surface. Cut into strips or finely with a noodle machine if available. Otherwise, roll each portion of dough out thinly and use a sharp knife to cut into thin, long strips (oil the knife to prevent the dough from sticking to it). Another way is to liberally sprinkle both sides of the rolled out dough with flour and then roll it up. The flour helps prevent the dough from sticking together. You then cut the roll into thin strips. When the cutting is complete, shake the noodles loose. Cook the noodles in a pot of boiling water (add a few drops of oil and a dash of salt to the water). When done, rinse the noodles in cold water to stop the cooking and to prevent the noodles from sticking together.

Variation:

Coral and jade noodles

Puree the boiled vegetables separately. Divide the flour into two portions and mix each half with one of the pureed vegetables. Work into a dough as with the egg variety and make into noodles. Use them separately or mix to form nutritious and colourful noodles.

Tomato noodles can be made by using 1–2 Chinese spoonfuls of tomato puree with the dough.

This recipe is for the adventurous or for those who want to keep the little children amused on a rainy afternoon! If, however, you are short of time, carrot and spinach pasta (spaghetti, macaroni, etc) can be bought from most leading supermarkets.

200 g plain flour, sifted
100 g carrot, diced,
    boiled and drained
100 g spinach, boiled,
    drained and chopped
a little water for mixing
    if necessary

Portion analysis	
energy	: 293 kcals
protein	: 8 g
fat	: 2 g
% energy from fat	: 7 %
fibre	: 2.5 g
cholesterol	: 56 mg

Portion analysis	
energy	: 196 kcals
protein	: 5 g
fat	: 0.6 g
% energy from fat	: 3 %
fibre	: 4.0 g
cholesterol	: 0
vitamin A	: ★★★
vitamin C	: ★★

40 pieces *wonton* skins
(3x3 inch)
¾ cup shelled prawns,
chopped
100 g minced meat
3 pieces water chestnut,
chopped
1 Ch sp chopped spring
onion
1 tsp dark soya sauce
2 tsp light soya sauce
3 drops sesame oil
1 tsp *Hua Tiao* (Ch wine)
½ tsp cornflour
salt, pepper and sugar
to taste
200 g cooked noodles

For noodle soup:
4 stalks *chye sim*
1½ litres bone and
prawn shell stock

Wonton noodle soup
(makes approximately 40 wontons)

Season the minced meat and prawn. Mix this with the water chestnut and spring onion. Wrap one heaped teaspoonful of the mixture with each *wonton* skin and shape into a dumpling. Place in boiling water just before it is time to serve. When cooked, the *wontons* will float to the surface. Drain and serve with the noodles and soup or as a soup on its own. Small bean curd cubes can be added to the *wonton* noodle soup to add further interest and nutritional value. Deep-fried *wontons* also make delicious snacks but offer them only occasionally.

Portion analysis	
energy	: 230 kcals
protein	: 12 g
fat	: 5 g
% energy from fat	: 20 %
fibre	: 3.4 g
cholesterol	: 47 mg
iron	: ★
vitamin B$_2$	: ★★
niacin	: ★

350 g spaghetti noodles

300 g lean minced beef
    or mutton

½ large onion, chopped

1 medium carrot, diced

100 g button mushroom,
    sliced or diced

1 stick imported celery,
    finely chopped

1 can tinned whole
    tomatoes

2 Ch sp tomato puree

2 cloves garlic, crushed

2 bay leaves

½ tsp paprika

dash of oregano or
    Italian mixed herbs, salt
    and pepper

1 Ch sp unsaturated oil

1 Ch sp grated Parmesan
    cheese (optional)

Tasty spaghetti

Boil the spaghetti until it is cooked but not too soft. Meanwhile, fry the garlic and onion in heated oil, add in vegetables then the minced beef and stir-fry briefly. Add the canned tomatoes, tomato puree, bay leaves, seasoning and sufficient water to cover the mixture. Simmer, with the lid on, for 30 minutes or more until the vegetables are soft and the sauce thick. Season and serve with the hot spaghetti. Garnish with grated cheese if desired.

Variation:

Asian vegetarian spaghetti

Instead of beef, use 200 g bean curd and 1 brinjal.

Portion analysis	
energy	: 441 kcals
protein	: 25 g
fat	: 13 g
% energy from fat	: 28 %
fibre	: 4.8 g
cholesterol	: 61 mg
iron	: ★★
vitamin A	: ★★★
vitamin C	: ★★★
niacin	: ★

Liver and kidney mee sua

50 g lean meat (chicken or pork)
100 g pig's liver, sliced thinly
100 g pig's kidneys, soaked, cleaned and scored with a criss-cross pattern
6 bundles dry *mee sua*
100 g lettuce, shredded
1½ litres chicken or pork bone stock
1 tsp light soya sauce
½ tsp dark soya sauce
2–3 slices ginger
1 tsp Chinese wine
salt and pepper to taste
1 tsp cornflour, dissolved in a little water
1 Ch sp unsaturated oil

Season the meat and liver with soya sauce, pepper and cornflour. Boil the stock and only add in the lettuce to cook briefly before serving. Boil the *mee sua* separately in a pot of boiling water, drain and apportion into serving bowls.

Heat the oil and lightly fry the ginger and garlic. Add in the wine and then sauté the pork, liver and kidney. Divide this between the bowls of *mee sua*, add in the vegetable and soup, and serve. This is a delightful way of serving liver and kidney which are normally not well liked by children.

Variation:
Alternatively, a sliced fish and minced meat combination can be used. These do not need to be fried. All you have to do is season the fish and meat beforehand and merely boil them in the stock shortly before serving the *mee sua*. This is a light and easily digestible meal suitable even during a bout of fever or while convalescing from an illness.

Portion analysis	
energy	: 290 kcals
protein	: 16 g
fat	: 7 g
% energy from fat	: 22 %
fibre	: 2.4 g
cholesterol	: 179 mg
iron	: ★★★
vitamin A	: ★★★
vitamin B₁	: ★
vitamin B₂	: ★★★

Seafood mee tai mak

400 g *mee tai mak*
150 g white fish fillet, thinly sliced
½ cup shelled prawns, deveined
3 stalks *chye sim*
2 litres chicken or prawn shell stock
salt and pepper to taste
1 Ch sp chopped spring onion

Seasoning for the fish:
1 egg white
½ tsp rice wine
½ tsp cornflour, dissolved in little water
½ tsp unsaturated oil

Season the fish slices. Prepare and boil the stock. In a separate saucepan, bring one bowl of water to the boil. Once it has boiled, briefly cook the *mee tai mak* in it, drain and apportion into bowls. Cook the vegetable in the boiling stock, add in the seasoned fish slices and prawns. Adjust the seasoning to taste, pour the soup over the *mee tai mak* and serve.

Fish balls and shredded chicken or other meat combinations can also be used for variety.

Portion analysis	
energy	: 285 kcals
protein	: 15 g
fat	: 5 g
% energy from fat	: 18 %
fibre	: 3.0 g
cholesterol	: 80 mg
iron	: ★

Yong tau foo soup

For the yong tau foo:
250 g fish meat filling
(see recipe for fishballs
   on page 173)
4 pieces bean curd
   cake (tau kwa)
4 lady's fingers, slit
   lengthwise and
   remove seeds
100 g spinach*, boiled
4 thick round slices of
   brinjal
200 g dry bee hoon,
   soaked

For the soup:
6-8 cups water
2 Ch sp dried local
   ikan bilis, cleaned and
   washed
fish bones or prawn
   shells, if available
2 Ch sp dried soya
   beans (optional),
   soaked for
   a few hours
salt and pepper to taste

Garnishing:
fried sliced shallot
chopped spring onion

*This replaces the usual
   kangkong (water
   convolvulus) which
   may not go down well
   with young children.
   However, you may still
   use kangkong if you so
   desire.

Prepare the stock by boiling the soup ingredients for 1–1½ hours, straining and seasoning to taste. Halve the bean curd cakes and scoop out a little of the centre of each half. Cross-sectionally slit half-way through each slice of brinjal. Stuff the assorted yong tau foo pieces with the fish meat filling (about 1–2 heaped tsp each). The remainder of the filling can be made into fishballs. Arrange all the pieces on a plate and steam over high heat for 5–7 minutes. Boil the soaked bee hoon briefly and divide among the individual bowls. When ready to serve, add the assorted pieces of yong tau foo and the spinach, then pour the soup over. Garnish with a little fried shallot and chopped spring onion.

Yong tau foo is one of the most nutritious local favourites. This home-made version may be more time-consuming, but wholesome ingredients are ensured for those who do not find the preparation a deterrent. Otherwise, the ready-stuffed yong tau foo in the markets still provides a good alternative if items are chosen carefully. Avoid an excessive number of fried items and go easy on the sauces, especially if you are eating out at a hawker centre.

Portion analysis

energy	: 230 kcals
protein	: 14 g
fat	: 5 g
% energy from fat	: 19 %
fibre	: 5.0 g
cholesterol	: 7 mg
iron	: ★★
calcium	: ★
vitamin A	: ★
vitamin C	: ★★

Tiny shell soup

2 pcs chicken thigh and
   drumstick
400 g noodle dough
   (see recipe on page
   160), or 200 g small
   pasta shells
1 slice ham
50 g carrot, diced or cut
   in shapes
2 Ch sp frozen peas,
   boiled briefly
2–3 pcs Chinese
   mushroom, softened in
   hot water
salt and pepper to taste
2–2½ litres water for stock

Tiny shell soup

Boil the chicken in the water until cooked and tender. Remove the skin and shred the meat. Skim off any excess fat from the stock. Make the noodle dough; either plain or with vegetables.

Roll the dough into long, pencil-like strips and cut them into 1–1½ cm pieces. Press these bits of dough with the thumb to shape them like shells. You could also mould them on the back of small shells if available. Cook the dough shells in boiling water with a few drops of oil. When cooked, remove them from the boiling water and immerse them in cold water to prevent them from sticking together. Drain and apportion.

Meanwhile, boil the carrots and mushroom in the chicken stock, and add the chopped ham, peas and shredded chicken. Adjust the seasoning and serve by pouring the stock over the "tiny shells". If a mixture of egg, spinach and carrot dough is used, this will make a tempting and colourful meal for young children.

Once again, enlist your child's help to make the shells and you are guaranteed a heightened interest when he eats his own creation.

Portion analysis

energy	: 314 kcals
protein	: 23 g
fat	: 5 g
% energy from fat	: 15 %
fibre	: 3.5 g
cholesterol	: 50 mg
iron	: ★
vitamin A	: ★★
niacin	: ★

200 g chicken meat,
    sliced
4–5 pieces dry Chinese
    mushrooms, softened
    and sliced
1 Ch sp dry lily flower,
    washed and singly
    knotted
3–4 cloves garlic, thinly
    sliced
2–3 shallots, thinly sliced
1–1½ litres chicken bone
    stock
2 medium tomatoes,
    quartered
1 tsp light soya sauce
1 tsp cornflour, dissolved
    in a little water
1 tsp Hua Tiao (Chinese
    wine)
salt and pepper to taste
250 g dry bee hoon,
    soaked
1 Ch sp chopped spring
    onion
1 Ch sp unsaturated oil

Seasoning for chicken
    meat:
½ tsp cornflour
½ tsp Hua Tiao (Chinese
    wine)
salt and pepper to taste
a few drops of sesame oil

Chicken bee hoon soup

Season the chicken. Boil the stock, add in tomatoes and adjust seasoning. Heat the oil in the pan, fry the garlic and the shallots. Add in the wine, then the mushrooms, lily flower and chicken pieces. Sauté briefly. Add in the dissolved cornflour, light soya sauce and pepper and simmer briefly. Boil the bee hoon separately in water and apportion into bowls. Add the chicken mixture over the noodles and add in some soup stock. Garnish with chopped spring onion and serve.

Portion analysis	
energy	: 320 kcals
protein	: 19 g
fat	: 8 g
% energy from fat	: 24 %
fibre	: 2.8 g
cholesterol	: 47 mg
iron	: ★
vitamin B$_2$	: ★

Kelong Treasures

The merits of fish are many. Eaten as an alternative to red meat, it results in less saturated fat and calorie intake. Moreover, the special omega-3 fat found in fish may be beneficial to health. Fish is easily digested; it is also softer than red meat and therefore easier for young children who cannot chew very well. Prawns are best not given to children below 1½ years as they may trigger allergies in allergy-prone children, but do introduce seafood gradually into the diets of older toddlers so they do not miss out on the wide variety available here. ●●●●

Quantities are for two adults and two children unless otherwise stated.

Oriental fish envelope

2 pieces (250 g) white fish fillet (e.g. *kurau* or *garoupa*, snapper)

½ medium carrot, sliced in thin rounds

½ medium onion, cut in rings

3 pieces Chinese mushroom, softened and sliced

6 thin slices green pepper

1 stalk spring onion, cut in 4-cm pieces

2 slices ginger

½ tsp *Hua Tiao* (Chinese wine)

dash of salt and pepper

squeeze of lime or lemon juice

½ tsp unsaturated oil

Marinate the fish fillets with seasoning for 15 minutes or more. Brush with oil, place each on a piece of aluminium foil and arrange the vegetables on top. Wrap in the foil to seal and bake in a preheated oven (200°C) for 10–15 minutes until cooked. Open and squeeze the lime or lemon juice over the fish just before serving. Serve with rice or potato and a vegetable dish of your choice.

Portion analysis	
energy	: 67 kcals
protein	: 11 g
fat	: 1 g
fibre	: 0.7 g
cholesterol	: 34 mg
vitamin A	: ★★

Grilled sesame fish fingers

200 g white fish fillet (e.g. *kurau* or red snapper), cut into strips the size of two fingers

1 egg

2 Ch sp sesame seeds

½ cup breadcrumbs*

dash of salt and pepper

Lightly season the fish strips with salt and pepper. Next, brush or dip the fish in beaten egg and toss in the breadcrumbs and sesame seed mixture. Place on greased aluminium foil or wire rack and grill or cook in the oven until golden brown on both sides. Alternatively, shallow fry in a little oil until crispy and cooked inside. Serve with a twist of lime or lemon, or tomato sauce (see recipe on page 140).

Fish fingers are quick and nourishing as a snack or for breakfast. Frozen packet varieties are often expensive. Make extra, wrap individually in cling film and freeze in a box.

* Make your own breadcrumbs by drying some wholemeal or white bread in a very slow oven (140°C) then breaking into small pieces and whizzing in the blender until fine.

Portion analysis	
energy	: 109 kcals
protein	: 15 g
fat	: 3 g
fibre	: 0.7 g
cholesterol	: 97 mg

20 medium prawns, shelled (keeping tail intact) and deveined
120 g white fish fillet, cut in 3-mm thick slices
1 small segment lotus root, sliced in thin rounds
1 smal brinjal, sliced in thin rounds
1 medium green pepper, cut into big squares
unsaturated oil for frying

For the batter:
1 cup sifted plain flour
1 medium egg
about ¾ cup cold water
(Double the amount if more is needed.)

Accompanying sauce:
tempura dipping sauce
2 Ch sp finely grated white radish
1 Ch sp finely grated ginger

Tempura fish and prawns with vegetables

Prepare the fish, prawns and vegetables. The batter should be made just before use to prevent it from turning gluey. Stir the egg and mix with refrigerated cold water to make up one cup. Make a well in the sifted flour and gradually add in the egg mixture, mixing lightly but not beating it. Do not keep the batter close to any source of heat as it should remain cold. Dip the prawns and fish in the batter and deep fry in heated oil. Do not overcrowd the wok to prevent sticking. Do likewise for the vegetables. Drain and soak off the excess oil with absorbent paper. Try to serve the tempura immediately. Rice and bean curd or miso soup are the usual accompaniments.

Dipping sauce for the tempura is available from most supermarkets. Many other varieties of vegetables can be cooked tempura-style: carrots, cauliflower, sweet potato, etc.

Although high in fat due to the frying, if offered once-in-a-while, tempura makes a welcome change in our home cooking.

Portion analysis	
energy	: 387 kcals
protein	: 18 g
fat	: 8 g
fibre	: 4.6 g
cholesterol	: 133 mg
vitamin A	: ★
vitamin B	: ★
vitamin C	: ★★
iron	: ★

400 g white fish cutlet
   (e.g. *ikan parang*)
2 egg whites
2 Ch sp milk
1 tsp ginger juice
½ tsp cornflour
1 Ch sp chopped spring
   onion
salt and pepper to taste
water to mix

Easy homestyle fish balls

With a metal spoon, scrape the flesh from the skin of the fish along the bone lines. Take care not to include any bones. Pound the fish in a mortar until the meat is fine. Mix the ginger juice and chopped spring onions in a little water to further extract the flavour. Squeeze and strain the liquid. Add the milk to this. Mix the egg white and seasoning with the scraped fish. When well-mixed, add in the milk and stir the mixture in one direction in a big bowl. Adjust the water content if necessary. If you are using your hands, you can use repeated light throwing and kneading movements until the mixture is sticky but "springy".

Scoop or form into balls and soak in slightly salted cold water until ready for use. A time-saving way is to place the fish meat and the other ingredients in a blender instead of a mortar and mix together. Take out the meat, knead a little and form into balls. Soak as before.

This is a nutritious home-made alternative to the fish and flour mixture often sold in the markets. Fishballs are a favourite food among young children and can be used with versatility in soups or with noodles. The fish paste can be used as fillings for *yong tau foo*. For variety, use an equal mixture of minced prawn and fish flesh. Similarly, finely chopped lean beef or pork can be made into beef or pork balls.

Portion analysis	
energy	: 80 kcals
protein	: 16 g
fat	: 1 g
fibre	: 0 g
cholesterol	: 50 mg
niacin	: ★

Tuna potato pie

Tuna potato pie

2 cans light or dark tuna meat (canned in water), drained
½ medium onion, finely chopped
1 small carrot, diced and blanched
½ cup green peas, blanched
4 medium potatoes, boiled and mashed with a little milk
1 cup white sauce (see recipe on page 142)
2 cups water
2 Ch sp grated cheese
½ Ch sp unsaturated oil
salt and pepper to taste

Lightly fry the onion and carrots in the oil until soft. Make the white sauce. Mix the onions, carrots, tuna and peas into the sauce. Season. Place the mixture in a pie dish or individual dishes. Spread the mashed potatoes to cover the top. Make patterns on the mashed potato with a fork and sprinkle the grated cheese on top. Bake in a pre-heated medium oven (180°C) until the potato is nicely browned.

For the younger children, the tuna can be flaked or pureed and mixed with a little cheese or yoghurt. Place in a small pie bowl or foil patty case, cover with a layer of pureed or grated carrot, followed by peas and mashed potatoes. Bake in apre-heated medium oven (180°C). This makes an attractive and colourfully layered pie.

Portion analysis	
energy	: 223 kcals
protein	: 15 g
fat	: 5 g
fibre	: 3.1 mg
cholesterol	: 78 mg
vitamin A	: ★ ★
niacin	: ★ ★

Grilled sea bass

1 medium (300 g) sea bass
1 medium lemon, sliced
2 tsp lemon juice
½ Ch sp oyster sauce
¼ tsp honey
dash of ground black or white pepper

When you buy the fish from the fishmonger, ask for the fish to be gutted and sliced open from the belly, with the centre bone removed but leaving the scales on. (The scales are left on to prevent the skin from sticking to the tray or foil.) When cleaned and ready for use, open up the fish, flesh facing upwards. Rub with pepper and honey and squeeze 1–2 tsp lemon juice over. Then spread the oyster sauce over the top, cover with the thin lemon slices and grill (preheat the grill) for 10 minutes or until the fish is slightly brown.

This is a simple and tasty way of cooking fish. However, do not over-use the oyster sauce as it is high in sodium. Be sure to buy one which is of a good grade and does not have any preservatives.

Portion analysis	
energy	: 59 kcals
protein	: 13 g
fat	: 0.3 g
fibre	: 0 g
cholesterol	: 34 mg

Prawn and bean curd delight

200 g medium prawns,
    shelled and deveined
150 g bean curd,
    parboiled, drained
    and diced
1 medium tomato, skinned,
    seeded and cubed
1 Ch sp finely chopped
    spring onion
1 clove garlic, finely
    chopped
1 tsp finely chopped
    ginger
½ cup chicken stock
1 tsp cornflour, dissolved
    in a little water
1 tsp *Hua Tiao* (Chinese
    wine)

Seasoning for prawn:
dash of salt, pepper and
    sugar
¼ tsp sesame oil
½ Ch sp unsaturated oil

Prepare prawns and marinate with the seasoning. Heat the oil in the pan, stir-fry the garlic and ginger, add in the wine, then the stock and cornflour. When the stock boils and thickens, add the prawns, bean curd, tomato and spring onion. Boil for a further 1–2 minutes and adjust the seasoning to taste. Remove and serve with rice.

Portion analysis	
energy	: 95 kcals
protein	: 12 g
fat	: 4 g
fibre	: 0.5 g
cholesterol	: 100 mg

- 1 medium fish
  (e.g. red snapper, sea
  bass, *garoupa*, white
  pomfret), gutted and
  cleaned
- ½ medium tomato,
  sliced in rounds
- 2-3 pieces Chinese
  mushroom, softened
  and shredded
- 2-3 slices ginger
- salt and pepper to taste
- 1 piece preserved sour
  plum (optional)
- ½ cup chicken bone
  stock (or soaked
  mushroom water)
- 1 clove garlic, thinly
  sliced
- ½ tsp fried shallot oil
- ½ tsp light soya sauce
- 1 Ch sp chopped spring
  onion
- 1 Ch sp coriander
  leaves, for garnishing

Teochew style steamed fish

Slit the back of the fish where it is thickest. Season lightly with salt and pepper. Place the fish on a dish and cover with the shredded mushroom, ginger, tomato and preserved sour plum (if used). Cover and steam over boiling water for about 8–10 minutes, depending on the size of the fish. Add in the hot stock mixture and sprinkle chopped spring onion over the fish. Cover and steam for another 1–2 minutes, garnish with the coriander leaves and serve with rice.

Variation:

Line a plate with a small bowlful of soaked *bee hoon*, and add ¼ cup vegetable stock or chicken bone stock. Place the fish over the *bee hoon* and steam as before.

Portion analysis	
energy	: 50 kcals
protein	: 10 g
fat	: 0.5 g
fibre	: 0
cholesterol	: 27 mg

1 egg, lightly beaten
2 Ch sp milk
1 Ch sp finely grated
  cheese (e.g. cheddar)
⅓ slice ham, chopped
½ tomato, chopped
½ onion, chopped
3 button mushrooms,
  sliced
2 tsp unsaturated oil
salt and pepper to taste

Petite savoury omelette
(makes 1 portion)

Heat 1 tsp unsaturated oil in a small non-stick pan and sauté the onion, mushroom and ham briefly. Remove from the pan. Mix the egg with the milk and pepper. In a small non-stick omelette pan, heat the remaining oil and pour in half of the egg mixture, stirring quickly with a fork. Let it set slightly, then add half of the tomato and the rest of the ingredients over one half of the omelette. Sprinkle some grated cheese on top, cook briefly and fold over the other half. Repeat for the remainder egg and filling. Serve immediately. Omelettes are very versatile and many filling combinations are possible. They take very little preparation and are particularly handy for breakfast, a quick lunch or part of a main meal with rice.

Tip: If you do not have a small pan, use an old tin (e.g. a round luncheon meat tin) which is open at both ends. Place it on the frying pan and pour the egg into the middle. Remove it when the egg is sufficiently cooked to stop spreading.

Portion analysis	
energy	: 283 kcals
protein	: 16 g
fat	: 22 g
fibre	: 1.2 mg
cholesterol	: 246 mg
calcium	: ★
iron	: ★

Stuffed egg rolls

3 medium eggs, beaten
2 Ch sp milk
100 g minced meat
   (pork, chicken or beef)
1 Ch sp finely chopped
   onion
1 Ch sp diced carrot,
   boiled
1 Ch sp sweetcorn
   kernels
1 Ch sp peas, boiled
   briefly
½ tsp mild curry powder
salt and pepper to taste
1 tsp cornflour, dissolved
   in 2 Ch sp water
   or stock
1 Ch sp unsaturated oil

Heat ¾ Ch sp of the oil and fry the onion. Add in the curry powder, then the minced meat and the vegetables. Sauté, mixing well, pour in the cornflour mixture, add salt and pepper to taste and cook until almost dry. Remove the ingredients and set aside. Make egg pancakes by coating the pan with the remainder of the oil and pouring in a small ladleful of beaten egg to make a thin 10–12 cm round. Cook on both sides until slightly browned. Remove and fill each pancake with some of the mixed stuffing, roll up and serve.

This is a variation of the savoury omelette and pancake. A little cooked rice may be added to the minced meat and vegetables before rolling up the pancakes if desired.

Portion analysis	
energy	: 163 kcals
protein	: 11 g
fat	: 10 g
fibre	: 0.7 mg
cholesterol	: 187 mg
iron	: ★
vitamin A	: ★
vitamin B$_1$	: ★

Scotch egg

4 medium eggs,
   hardboiled and
   shelled
2 Ch sp minced lean
   chicken or pork
½ slice lean ham, finely
   chopped (optional)
1 Ch sp finely chopped
   onion
1 tsp cornflour
2 Ch sp breadcrumbs
   (see recipe for "Grilled
   sesame fish fingers" on
   page 170)
salt and pepper to taste
a little beaten egg, for
   coating
unsaturated oil for frying

Season the minced meat and mix with the ham, onion and cornflour. Divide into four portions and wrap each one around one egg. Coat with a little beaten egg, then roll in the breadcrumbs. Deep fry in oil, drain well and soak off the excess oil with absorbent paper. Cool slightly, slice in half and serve with an accompanying coleslaw or green salad.

Scotch eggs are fun and most suitable as picnic food or as a packed snack. Traditional recipes use sausage meat, but we have substituted it here with lean meat. However, due to the deep frying, scotch eggs are rather high in fat and thus best served only occasionally.

Portion analysis	
energy	: 164 kcals
protein	: 9 g
fat	: 11 g
fibre	: 2.4 mg
cholesterol	: 231 mg

Five-spice soya sauce egg

4 medium eggs, hard-boiled
1 Ch sp dark soya sauce
1 Ch sp light soya sauce
1 tsp five-spice (*ngoh hiang*) powder
2 tsp sugar
6–8 cloves garlic, crush slightly but keep skin intact
3–4 cups water

Remove the shells of the hard-boiled eggs carefully. Wash and dry the garlic, heat the pan gently and add the garlic, sugar and five-spice powder. When the sugar melts (do not burn by overheating the pan), add the soya sauce and water. Increase the heat and boil the liquid. Add in the eggs and simmer for an hour or so until the eggs are nicely browned on the outside. Slice and serve hot or cold, with porridge or with rice.

Soya sauce eggs are usually made together with soya sauce meat (pork or chicken) in the same liquid. Without pouring the sauce over the sliced egg, it is still fragrant but not as salty and thus suitable for children.

Portion analysis	
energy	: 74 kcals
protein	: 6 g
fat	: 5 g
fibre	: 0
cholesterol	: 255 mg

Wholemeal tuna quiche (makes 6 portions)

Pastry:
100 g wholemeal flour (blend if coarse)
140 g plain flour, sifted
120 g unsaturated margarine
dash of salt
a little cold water to mix

Filling:
3 eggs, beaten
½ cup skimmed milk
½ onion, chopped
2 Ch sp grated cheese
4 Ch sp tuna (canned in water)
2 tomatoes, sliced in rounds
2 tsp unsaturated oil
a little dried basil
dash of salt and pepper

Make the pastry by rubbing the margarine into the sifted plain and wholemeal flour mixture. When the mixture resembles breadcrumbs, add a little water and mix it into a dough. Roll out the dough on a floured board. Line a greased, medium quiche tin or pie dish with the dough and chill until ready to use.

Add the beaten egg to the milk and beat briefly to mix well. Brown the chopped onion in a little oil, mix in the tuna and seasoning and set aside to cool for a while. Spread the tuna mixture over the pastry and pour in the milk and egg mixture. Sprinkle grated cheese evenly over and cover with the sliced tomatoes. Place in a preheated medium oven (180°C) and bake for 45 minutes or until set and golden. Serve warm or cold with a green or mixed salad or vegetable soup.

Although quite high in fat, this dish is nutrient-rich and makes a tasty occasional snack. It is especially useful for picnics and outings or in a packed lunch box. It is also handy as a light lunch for the older toddler or young school-going child.

Portion analysis	
energy	: 398 kcals
protein	: 16 g
fat	: 23 g
fibre	: 2.6 mg
cholesterol	: 124 mg
iron	: ★
vitamin A	: ★★★
niacin	: ★

Meat Delights

M any mothers moan about their children who dislike or will not chew meats. This may be due, in part, to the over-protective practice of offering finely ground meat until a child is three or four years old. Offering soft and tender cooked meat after a child has mastered the art of chewing (which most do well even with six to eight teeth) will help the child accept meat pieces later on.

Lean meat, liver and poultry have a lot going for them nutritionally. They are the chief sources of quality protein, B vitamins, iron and zinc, and a moderate meat intake will ensure an adequate supply of these nutrients. Using lean cuts, removing poultry skin and cooking with less fat will lay a good foundation for your child's eating habits.

You can "stretch" meat protein by combining it with a plant protein source like beans, bean curd or lentils. This is not only healthy due to the lower fat, higher fibre content of most plant protein foods but will be economical too. You will be surprised at how versatile and tasty such combinations can be. Mild curry spices, herbs and vegetables will add flavour and help cut down the reliance on salty seasonings for taste. ●● ●

Quantities are for two adults and two children unless otherwise stated.

Baked lemon chicken

½ medium chicken, skin and fat removed
2 Ch sp plain flour
½ tsp paprika
1 tsp *Hua Tiao* Chinese wine
1 tsp light soya sauce
dash of salt and pepper to taste
1 tsp cornflour
2 leaves iceberg lettuce, shredded

Mix and use as sauce:
dash of sugar
1 tsp garlic, finely chopped
juice of one medium lemon

Cut the chicken into big pieces and season with wine, soya sauce, salt and pepper for ½ to 1 hour. Sift the paprika with the flour and coat the chicken pieces. Bake in a pre-heated oven (160°C) for half an hour. Sprinkle some of the unthickened lemon sauce over the chicken and return it to the oven for another 10 minutes or until the chicken is cooked. Serve this over shredded lettuce with rice or potato and vegetables of your choice. Thicken the remainder of the lemon sauce by heating it with the dissolved cornflour, and use it as a dip for the chicken.

Portion analysis	
energy	: 204 kcals
protein	: 26 g
fat	: 6.5 g
fibre	: 0.4 g
cholesterol	: 83 mg
niacin	: ★

Minced chicken patties

200 g minced lean chicken
½ medium onion, finely chopped
1 medium potato, boiled and mashed
1 Ch sp finely chopped leek (optional)
2 tsp light soya sauce
½ tsp *Hua Tiao* Chinese wine
a few drops ginger juice
dash of pepper and sugar
1 Ch sp unsaturated oil

Marinate the minced chicken with all the ingredients except the oil and shape into small flat patties. Heat the oil in a frying pan and fry the patties until they are cooked and lightly browned. Alternatively, spread the mixture in a heated pan to form a round thin layer. With a frying slice, cut the layer into quarters and, when the underside is done, turn the pieces over and sauté for a few more minutes. When done, you may like to cut them into triangles and serve them with vegetables. This dish is good for a snack lunch and can be eaten cold on a picnic.

Portion analysis	
energy	: 153 kcals
protein	: 15 g
fat	: 7 g
fibre	: 0.5 g
cholesterol	: 47 mg
niacin	: ★

200 g chicken breast
    meat, diced
1 small carrot, diced and
    blanched
½ medium green
    pepper
½ medium onion
½ can (100 g) button
    mushrooms, diced
2-3 water chestnuts
2-3 slices ginger
1 Ch sp chopped spring
    onion (optional)
1 Ch sp unsaturated oil
    for cooking
1 tsp *Hua Tiao* Chinese
    wine
2–3 leaves fresh lettuce

Seasoning for meat:
2 tsp light soya sauce
2 tsp cornflour
1 tsp unsaturated oil

Sauce:
2 tsp oyster sauce (good
    grade)
dash of pepper, sesame
    oil, and sugar
⅓ cup chicken bone
    stock or water
1 tsp cornflour, to thicken
    the stock

Chicken surprises

Season the meat. Heat the oil in a frying pan and add wine. Fry the ginger and diced vegetables till heated through. Add the chicken meat and fry until the colour changes. Pour the sauce over the mixture and simmer for 3 minutes. Sprinkle the chopped spring onion (if used) and remove from the heat. Serve by wrapping a Chinese spoonful of the mixture in a small piece of lettuce leaf.

This dish offers a good mix of fresh and cooked vegetables, and is also suitable as a light lunch, served with rice.

Vegetarian variation:
Substitute the chicken with shredded mock duck (*mian jin* or gluten).

Portion analysis	
energy	: 184 kcals
protein	: 16 g
fat	: 8 g
fibre	: 1.6 g
cholesterol	: 47 mg
vitamin A	: ★ ★
vitamin C	: ★
niacin	: ★

Mixed **satay**

100 g chicken meat, cut
  into bite-sized pieces
100 g lean beef, pork or
  mutton, sliced thinly in
  wide strips
2 sets chicken liver, cut
  into bite-sized pieces

5 small shallots
1 thumb-sized piece of
  turmeric (pounded
  and ground together)

1½ tsp coriander
1½ tsp cumin (roasted
  briefly in a heated
  pan and then ground
  to a powder)

1 stalk lemon grass,
  pounded with a little
  water to extract the
  juice
1 tsp sugar
½ tsp fresh lime juice
dash of salt and pepper
1½ Ch sp unsaturated oil

Vegetables (cut into
  bite-sized pieces):
• 3 tomatoes
• button mushrooms
• large baby corn
• green pepper

Mixed satay

Combine the ground shallots, the coriander mixture and the lemon grass extract with the sugar, salt and lime juice. Add in ½ Ch sp oil and use this mixture to marinate the meat for one to two hours. Skewer the vegetables and meats separately on wooden skewers and grill in the oven or over the traditional charcoal fire. Baste the meats and the vegetables with the remaining oil (add a little water to it) while grilling. To prevent toughening or burning of the meat, do not over-grill. Baste the vegetables with the oil and water mixture and grill briefly. Serve the satay and vegetables with rice (or more appropriately, *ketupat*), diced cucumber and onion, and the home-made peanut sauce (see recipe on page 226).

Satay is almost a "national" dish in the region and an Asian child who is not fond of satay is generally the exception rather than the rule. This homestyle version is less oily and the meat can be eaten with or without the satay sauce. The accompanying vegetable kebabs ensure a balanced meal. You can even serve fresh fruit on skewers to make it a complete meal-on-sticks.

Portion analysis	
energy	: 185 kcals
protein	: 16 g
fat	: 10 g
fibre	: 1.5 g
cholesterol	: 95 mg
iron	: ★
vitamin A	: ★★★
vitamin B$_1$	: ★
vitamin B$_2$	: ★
niacin	: ★

Easy pan pizza

200 g spaghetti sauce
  (see recipe for "Tasty
  spaghetti" on page 163)
180 g plain flour
30 g unsaturated
  margarine
½ cup skimmed milk
120 g grated cheese
  (cheddar or mozzarella)

Make the spaghetti sauce and set aside to cool. Rub the margarine into the flour, add milk gradually and work into a semi-soft dough. Knead until the dough is smooth, roll it out into a round to fit an 20–23-cm frying pan or non-stick pan. Cover the dough with the spaghetti sauce, sprinkle with the grated cheese and cook covered over moderate heat for 20 minutes or until the dough is cooked through and golden. This recipe offers an easy and fast no-yeast pizza, especially if the spaghetti sauce is prepared beforehand and kept frozen. It is delicious and good for a quick lunch or snack.

Portion analysis

energy	: 399 kcals
protein	: 17 g
fat	: 19 g
fibre	: 2.2 g
cholesterol	: 33 mg
calcium	: ★★
vitamin A	: ★★★
vitamin B$_2$	: ★

Homestyle meat and lentil burger (makes approximately 6 large patties)

200 g ground lean beef,
  mutton or pork
½ cup orange lentils,
  cooked
½ medium onion, finely
  chopped
1 medium potato, boiled
  and mashed
1 medium egg
dash of salt, mixed herbs
  and pepper
½ tsp cornflour, dissolved
  in a little water

Mix all the ingredients together and shape into round burger patties. Dust with a little flour and sauté in a little oil to brown (2 to 3 minutes each side). If the patties are not to be consumed immediately, cover them with cling film and freeze in a box. Remove the individual patties and fry or grill as desired, when needed. Serve with sesame seed bun or bread, and coleslaw (see recipe on page 212) for older children. The younger ones can have the patties with cooked vegetables.

Hamburgers have, in recent years, established a large following among Asian children. Making your own is easy and you have the added advantage of being able to cut down the fat content. With this recipe, the meat is tender and juicy. Serve it with soya bean milk or any other nutritious drink and you have a winner for a "don't know what to cook" lunch that often befalls a busy mum!

Analysis per patty

energy	: 150 kcals
protein	: 14 g
fat	: 5 g
fibre	: 1.3 g
cholesterol	: 86 mg
iron	: ★
vitamin B$_1$	: ★★
niacin	: ★

Easy pan pizza

Simple liver paté

2 large sets chicken liver, chopped
1½ Ch sp chopped onion
1 medium egg, hard-boiled and chopped (omit the egg yolk if desired)
dash of salt and pepper to taste
dash of mixed herbs

Cover the liver and onion in sufficient water and simmer for 20 minutes. Strain and keep stock aside. Mince the liver, onion and hard-boiled egg together in a blender or chopper until smooth. Add enough stock to bind. Adjust the seasoning and chill in the refrigerator. You can use paté as a spread on toast or crackers once in a while.

Variation: In place of the egg, use 1 Ch sp plain yoghurt and half an apple. Blend these with the chicken livers. Reduce the stock accordingly so that the paté will not be too runny.

Portion analysis	
energy	: 44 kcals
protein	: 4 g
fat	: 2 g
fibre	: 0 g
cholesterol	: 113 mg
iron	: ★
vitamin A	: ★★★
vitamin B$_2$	: ★

Chicken and liver envelopes

4 pcs chicken thigh, bone, skin and fat removed
2 sets chicken liver
2 stalks spring onion
1 medium onion, sliced in rings
a few pieces of carrot, cut into shapes
dash of pepper and salt to taste

Seasoning for meat:
½ Ch sp dark sauce
½ tsp oyster sauce
¼ tsp five spice powder
1 tsp *Hua Tiao* (Chinese wine)
1 tsp ginger juice

Cut the chicken into bite-sized pieces. Marinate the chicken and liver with the seasoning and onions for a few hours. Wrap one piece of chicken, a piece of liver, an onion ring, a couple of carrot slices and a short piece of spring onion in cut aluminium foil. Wrap as square envelopes, place on a tray and bake in a moderate pre-heated oven for 20–30 minutes or until the chicken is cooked.

Portion analysis	
energy	: 178 kcals
protein	: 25 g
fat	: 6 g
fibre	: 0.6 g
cholesterol	: 128 mg
iron	: ★
vitamin A	: ★★★
vitamin B$_2$	: ★★
niacin	: ★★

Grilled tandoori chicken

4 pcs (500 g) chicken drumstick, thigh or breast meat, skin and fat removed

3–4 cloves garlic, chopped

2 slices ginger, finely chopped

¾ cup plain yoghurt

1 Ch sp tomato paste

1 tsp sugar

dash of salt and pepper to taste

juice of one fresh lime (*limau nipis*)

dash of paprika or chilli powder

½ Ch sp unsaturated oil

Debone and cut the chicken into convenient sized pieces, prick with a fork and marinate with all the other ingredients, except the oil, for half a day or overnight in the refrigerator. Heat the oil, add in the chicken and the marinade, and cook briefly to dry up the marinade, turning to prevent burning. Lightly brush the chicken pieces with a little extra oil and a squeeze of lime juice. Grill for 5 to10 minutes in the oven or over charcoal. To retain juiciness and prevent burning, do not over-grill. Serve this dish with rice and vegetables or with *chapatis* and curry.

A well-liked Indian dish that is cosmopolitan in its appeal, this version is mild and without the usual added colouring. For young children, shred the meat and serve with some vegetables and pureed cottage cheese.

Variation: Use white fish fillet in place of the chicken. Omit the frying and grill directly after marinating.

Portion analysis	
energy	: 250 kcals
protein	: 33 g
fat	: 10 g
fibre	: 0
cholesterol	: 100 mg
iron	: ★
vitamin B$_2$	: ★★
niacin	: ★★

Curry dishes form a major part of the Asian diet especially among the Malays and the Indians. Although they are usually spicy and hot to stimulate our palate, milder forms of curry, adapted to suit the children in the family, can still be very tasty.

1 medium chicken, chopped and skin removed

3 medium tomatoes, sliced

2 large onions, sliced

½ large tin evaporated milk

1 Ch sp *korma* powder

2-cm piece ginger, lightly pounded

3 cloves garlic, pounded

2 3-cm pieces cinnamon

5 cloves

2 stalks fresh coriander leaves, cut into 2-cm lengths

1 Ch sp unsaturated oil

salt to taste

Optional:
one red chilli
one green chilli
  (quartered and seeds removed

Chicken korma
(makes 8 portions)

Fry the cinnamon and cloves in oil until the cinnamon turns dark brown. Add the ginger, garlic and onions and fry a further minute or so. Then add the chicken and salt and fry for a few minutes.

Dilute the evaporated milk with an equal volume of water and mix the *korma* powder in. Add the tomato and green chilli and pour this mixture over the chicken. Bring to the boil, cover and simmer until cooked. Add red chilli five minutes before the cooking is finished, and garnish with the fresh coriander leaves before serving.

To further reduce the fat in this dish use skimmed milk or low fat yoghurt instead of evaporated milk.

Portion analysis	
energy	: 210 kcals
protein	: 25 g
fat	: 10 g
fibre	: 1.1 g
cholesterol	: 81 mg
niacin	: ★

1 square soft bean curd,
   cut into 4-cm squares
250 g lean minced meat
2 Ch sp green peas
2–3 slices of ginger
½ medium onion,
   chopped
2 tsp mild curry powder,
   mixed with some
   water
1 tsp dark soya sauce
2 tsp cornflour, dissolved
   in some water
dash of salt to taste
1 Ch sp unsaturated oil
½ cup bone stock/water

Mild curry mince with bean curd

Dip the bean curd in hot water, drain and pat dry. Fry the onions and ginger in heated oil. When fragrant, add the curry paste, stir briefly and then add the minced meat and other ingredients. When the mixture turns brown, add the cornflour and stock, bring to the boil, and finally add the peas and the bean curd. Simmer gently for 5-10 minutes. This curry can be served with rice.

Portion analysis	
energy	: 186 kcals
protein	: 19 g
fat	: 11 g
fibre	: 0.9 g
cholesterol	: 43 mg
iron	: ★ ★
vitamin B₁	: ★ ★
niacin	: ★

1 square soft bean curd
250 g diced mixed
   vegetables
1 egg, beaten
seasoning, as above

Vegetarian variation:

Replace the minced meat with mixed vegetables; the frozen variety will do. Fry the vegetables and then add in the bean curd. Break the latter up and mix well with the vegetables and curry powder. Thicken with the cornflour and add the stock. Stir in the beaten egg, simmer briefly and serve.

Portion analysis	
energy	: 151 kcals
protein	: 9 g
fat	: 8 g
fibre	: 0.9 g
cholesterol	: 56 mg

350 g lean mutton, cubed
1 medium onion, chopped
2 medium tomatoes,
   sliced
3 cloves garlic, pounded
2-cm piece ginger,
   pounded
4 cloves
2 small sticks cinnamon
2 Ch sp mild curry powder
1 Ch sp plain yoghurt
1 Ch sp unsaturated oil
2 cups water
dash of salt

Mild mutton curry

Boil the mutton in water until tender. Keep the cooking liquid. Fry the cloves and cinnamon in the oil until they darken. Add the ginger, garlic and onions and continue frying for a minute or so. Add the curry powder and fry for another few minutes, adding a little warm water to prevent sticking. Add mutton, tomatoes and salt, mix well and pour in the mutton stock. Simmer until the gravy begins to thicken. Add in the yoghurt before serving.

Portion analysis	
energy	: 238 kcals
protein	: 16 g
fat	: 16 g
fibre	: 0.6 g
cholesterol	: 69 mg
iron	: ★ ★
vitamin A	: ★ ★ ★
niacin	: ★
vitamin C	: ★ ★

Fragrant chicken curry

½ medium chicken, chopped and skin removed
1 Ch sp mild curry powder, mixed with a little water
3–4 medium potatoes, peeled and quartered
2 Ch sp plain yoghurt*
1 cup warm water
2–3 slices ginger, pounded
6 cloves garlic, ground into fine paste
1 medium onion, chopped finely
2 medium tomatoes, cubed
5 cloves and 2 small sticks cinnamon
dash of salt
1 Ch sp unsaturated oil

Fry the cloves, cinnamon, onion, ginger and garlic in heated oil and then add in the curry paste. Stir until it is fragrant. Mix in the chicken pieces and potatoes. Add in the yoghurt, tomatoes and water, and bring to the boil gently. Adjust the liquid by adding more water if necessary, cover and simmer until the chicken pieces are tender. Serve with rice, bread or *chapati*.

* This is a healthier alternative to the traditional coconut milk, particularly if the low fat type is used.

Portion analysis

energy	: 282 kcals
protein	: 26 g
fat	: 10 g
fibre	: 2.2 g
cholesterol	: 72 mg
iron	: ★★★
niacin	: ★★
vitamin C	: ★★

Easy chapatis (makes 8)

200 g fine wholemeal flour or *atta* flour
¼–½ cup water to mix

Add the water gradually to the flour, mixing to form a firm dough. Knead until smooth. It should not feel wet. Cover with a damp cloth and set aside for an hour. Break off pingpong ball-sized pieces, sprinkle dry flour on the table and roll out the dough into thin rounds.

Place the *chapati* on a cast-iron griddle or hot plate to cook. Turn over when slightly browned and press down on it to release the air if the chapati puffs up. Remove when the second side is browned, and repeat with the other pieces.

Chapatis are an ideal accompaniment to curries and are healthy, being low in fat and high in fibre.

Analysis per *chapati*

energy	: 83 kcals
protein	: 3 g
fat	: 0.5 g
fibre	: 2.4 g
cholesterol	: 0

Healthy Vegetables

There are hundreds of common vegetables eaten throughout the world. They take the form of leaves, like cabbage and lettuce; roots, like carrot and turnips; fruit, like gourds and marrows; flowers, like broccoli; stalks such as celery; and seeds like peas and beans.

Besides their nutritive value, the variety of taste and texture is an important role of vegetables in the diet. With their varied and often bright colours, vegetables enhance the visual appearance of a meal. Vegetables are also used for their decorative qualities. Chopped parsley, celery and spring onions are common garnishes; so too are carrot and tomato slices.

Certain vegetables are regarded as practically essential for the flavour of dishes: no curry or stew would be complete without onions, and tomatoes feature as a flavour base for many sauces, curries and casseroles.

The ways of serving vegetables are endless, and imaginative cooks can use them to add to the attractiveness of dishes. So, parents, aim to make your child view vegetables not as "yukky" foods to be swallowed because they are good for him, but as interesting and tasty components of a meal in their own right.

Quantities are for two adults and two children unless otherwise stated.

50 g chicken meat,
  diced

50 g cauliflower, cut in
  bite-sized florets

100 g bean curd, sliced
  in rectangles

50 g canned button
  mushrooms, whole
  or halved

50 g snow peas

50 g carrot, sliced

½ cup chicken stock

2 tsp light soya sauce

1½ tsp *Hua Tiao*
  (Chinese wine)

1 tsp cornflour

2 cloves garlic, finely
  chopped

1 tsp finely chopped
  ginger

pepper and sugar to
  taste

1 Ch sp unsaturated oil

1 Ch sp coriander
  leaves, chopped
  (for garnishing)

Claypot mixed vegetables

Season the meat with half the soya sauce and wine. Parboil the bean curd and drain to dry. Set aside. Heat the oil, fry the garlic and ginger, add in the remaining wine and quickly sauté the cauliflower, snow peas and carrot. Add in the diced chicken, then the mushroom and bean curd, and stir gently for a few minutes. Pour in the stock and the remaining soya sauce, cover the claypot and simmer gently for 5 minutes. Thicken the sauce with the cornflour and adjust the seasoning. Serve garnished with the chopped coriander leaves.

Vegetarian variation:
Substitute with 50 g vegetarian mock duck (gluten).

Portion analysis	
energy	: 96 kcals
protein	: 7 g
fat	: 5 g
fibre	: 3.1 g
cholesterol	: 12 mg
vitamin A	: ★ ★
vitamin C	: ★

50 g minced meat (lean chicken or pork)

50 g prawns, shelled, deveined and chopped

1 piece (250 g) bean curd

2 water chestnuts, skinned and chopped

a few green peas, for garnishing

Seasoning for meat mixture:

1 tsp finely chopped spring onion

½ tsp *Hua Tiao* (Chinese wine)

1 tsp light soya sauce

pepper to taste

Optional:

1 tsp dark soya sauce

2–3 drops sesame oil

Steamed savoury bean curd

Mix the minced meat, prawns, water chestnut and spring onions with the seasoning. Cut the bean curd into 2-cm thick round or rectangular slices. Arrange on a plate and spread a heaped teaspoon of meat mixture on top of each. Decorate with one or two peas. Steam over high heat for 5 minutes. Add a dash of dark soya sauce and sesame oil (mixed with 1 Ch sp of the liquid that has collected on the plate) if desired. This is a tasty and simple favourite among bean curd lovers.

Portion analysis	
energy	: 80 kcals
protein	: 10 g
fat	: 4 g
fibre	: 0.5 g
cholesterol	: 34 mg

Broccoli with baby corn and liver

Broccoli with baby corn and liver

2 sets chicken liver, sliced

250 g broccoli, cut into bite-sized florets

60 g baby corn, sliced

2 cloves garlic, finely chopped

2 slices ginger, finely chopped

1 shallot, thinly sliced

1½ tsp light soya sauce

1 tsp *Hua Tiao* (Chinese wine)

½ cup chicken stock

1 Ch sp unsaturated oil

salt, pepper and sugar to taste

2 tsp cornflour

Season the liver with the soya sauce, pepper and 1 tsp cornflour. Heat half of the oil in the pan and fry the garlic and ginger. Add in the wine, followed by the liver. Sauté briefly, remove and set aside. Heat the remaining oil, fry the shallot, add the broccoli and corn, and season with the salt and pepper. Sauté till the broccoli turns bright green, then add in the stock and meat. Adjust the seasoning if necessary. Cover the pan and simmer for 3–5 minutes, then thicken the sauce with 1 tsp cornflour. Chicken meat can be used in place of the liver if preferred.

Portion analysis	
energy	: 94 kcals
protein	: 5 g
fat	: 5 g
fibre	: 3.1 g
cholesterol	: 57 mg
iron	: ★
vitamin A	: ★★★
vitamin B$_2$	: ★
vitamin C	: ★★★

Crispy soya patties (makes about 6 patties)

100 g ground soya (from cooked beans or residue when making soya bean milk (see recipe on page 262))

2 Ch sp rice flour

50 g minced meat

50 g prawns, shelled, deveined and chopped

1 medium egg

1 Ch sp chopped spring onion

1 tsp light soya sauce

¼ tsp *Hua Tiao* (Chinese wine)

salt and pepper to taste

1 tsp cornflour

a little flour, for coating

2 Ch sp unsaturated oil

Season the minced meat with the soya sauce, pepper and wine. Mix all the other ingredients, and add pepper and salt to taste. Form into small flat patties, coat with flour and fry in heated oil on both sides until golden and crispy. Drain on absorbent paper and serve with rice or as a snack. Make the patties flat to ensure thorough cooking of the beans.

Analysis per patty	
energy	: 129 kcals
protein	: 7 g
fat	: 7 g
fibre	: 0.5 g
cholesterol	: 60 mg

Stuffed hairy gourd

1 medium hairy gourd
100 g minced lean pork
8 medium prawns,
  shelled and deveined
1 Ch sp dried black
  fungus, softened
  (by soaking) and
  chopped
1 clove garlic, chopped
salt and pepper to taste
¾ cup chicken stock or
  water
½ Ch sp unsaturated oil

Seasoning for meat
  mixture:
1 tsp light soya sauce
½ tsp cornflour

Mix the chopped black fungus with the meat and seasoning. Cut the hairy gourd into 2–3 cm rings and scoop out the core with the seeds. Fill the centre of the gourd pieces with the minced meat mixture and pack tightly. Heat the oil, fry the chopped garlic, then sauté the gourd pieces until they are slightly brown on both sides. Arrange the gourd pieces in a claypot or casserole, then pour in the stock and simmer covered for 20 minutes or until the gourd pieces are soft. Add the seasoning to taste and you may thicken the sauce slightly with cornflour if desired.

Portion analysis	
energy	: 77 kcals
protein	: 8 g
fat	: 4 g
fibre	: 0.6 g
cholesterol	: 42 mg
vitamin C	: ★★★

Stuffed mushrooms

6–8 medium-sized dried
  mushrooms, softened
  in hot water
½ cup liquid obtained
  from soaking
  mushrooms
100 g meat mixture,
  seasoned as for the
  previous recipe
1 tsp cornflour
salt and pepper to taste

Squeeze out the liquid from the softened mushrooms and make a slit on the underside if the cap is fairly thick. Stuff it with the seasoned meat mixture. Arrange the mushrooms on a plate, stuffed side up, and steam over boiling water for 15 minutes. Thicken the mushroom liquid with the cornflour, add seasoning to taste, boil and pour over the mushrooms before serving.

Portion analysis	
energy	: 38 kcals
protein	: 5 g
fat	: 1 g
fibre	: 0.2 g
cholesterol	: 34 mg

Oriental chicken and mango salad

- 200 g chicken meat, cooked & shredded
- 50 g prawns, shelled, cooked, deveined & sliced
- ½ medium green pepper, seeded & thinly sliced
- 50 g mango, sliced or cubed
- 1 red chilli, seeded and thinly sliced (optional)
- 100 g (¼ large) lettuce, washed, drained & shredded
- 2 Ch sp peanuts, roasted & pounded slightly

- 3 cloves garlic, thinly sliced
- 3 small shallots, thinly sliced
- (fried till crisp and golden)

- 1½ Ch sp *limau kasturi* or lemon juice
- ½ tsp sugar
- dash of pepper
- 1 Ch sp coriander leaves, chopped

Prepare the meat and vegetables. In a bowl, mix the lime juice, sugar and pepper until well blended. Add in the chicken and prawn, a little of the fried garlic and shallot, then the green pepper, mango and chilli (if used). Toss lightly until all the ingredients are well mixed. Serve over a bed of shredded lettuce on a salad plate and garnish with the remaining garlic, shallot and the coriander leaves.

Portion analysis	
energy	: 185 kcals
protein	: 20 g
fat	: 9 g
fibre	: 2.6 g
cholesterol	: 72 mg
vitamin A	: ★
niacin	: ★
vitamin C	: ★★★

VEGETARIAN DISHES

Cauliflower florets with cheese sauce

200 g cauliflower (or broccoli), washed and cut into bite-sized florets
2 Ch sp grated cheese
salt and pepper to taste
dash of mixed herbs (optional)

For white sauce:
1 cup milk
1 Ch sp plain flour
1 Ch sp unsaturated margarine

Boil the cauliflower florets in just sufficient water to cook them but not till they are too soft. Make the white sauce with the milk, flour and fat, add in the grated cheese and stir to melt under low heat. Serve the vegetable with the sauce poured over. This is a tasty accompaniment to baked or grilled fish or meat.

Portion analysis	
energy	: 121 kcals
protein	: 6 g
fat	: 7 g
fibre	: 1.2 g
cholesterol	: 14 mg
calcium	: ★
vitamin C	: ★ ★ ★

Grilled tau kwa pok

2 large bean curd cakes (*tau kwa*)
3 Ch sp beansprouts, boiled briefly
3 Ch sp grated cucumber
2 Ch sp chopped pineapple
2 Ch sp shredded apple
2 Ch sp peanut sauce (see recipe on page 226)
dash of sugar (optional)

Shallow fry each *tau kwa* until it is browned on both sides. Drain away the excess oil on absorbent paper. Halve each piece of *tau kwa* diagonally. Mix the vegetables and fruit together with the peanut sauce. Scoop out the centre of each *tau kwa* triangle and fill with a Chinese spoonful of the mixture. Grill in the oven toaster for two minutes. Serve as a snack or as part of a meal.

Portion analysis	
energy	: 151 kcals
protein	: 15 g
fat	: 8 g
fibre	: 1.8 g
cholesterol	: 0
calcium	: ★
iron	: ★

150 g *tempeh*, cut in
  strips
1 medium green
  pepper, cubed
1 medium carrot, thinly
  sliced and parboiled
2 Ch sp whole kernel
  sweetcorn (canned or
  frozen)
2 Ch sp pineapple
  chunks (fresh or
  canned)
1 tsp finely chopped
  ginger
1 tsp cornflour
2 Ch sp unsaturated oil

Sauce:
½ cup water
1 large tomato, skinned
  and chopped
2 tsp vinegar
1 tsp honey

Sweet and sour tempeh with mixed vegetables

Heat the oil in the frying pan, fry the *tempeh* until it is golden brown, remove and set aside. Try to absorb as much oil from the fried *tempeh* by draining on absorbent paper. Add the vegetables to the pan and sauté until they are tender-crisp. Next add the pineapple and *tempeh*. Stir-fry all this briefly, pour in the sauce and thicken with the cornflour. Bring it to the boil. Serve this dish hot with rice.

Portion analysis	
energy	: 131 kcals
protein	: 8 g
fat	: 6 g
fibre	: 1.8 g
cholesterol	: 0
iron	: ★★
vitamin A	: ★★★
vitamin C	: ★★★

1 piece (300 g) bean
curd, parboiled,
drained and mashed
1 large potato, boiled
and mashed
1 medium carrot, sliced,
boiled, drained and
mashed
2 Ch sp peas, parboiled
1 medium egg
2 Ch sp finely chopped
onion
salt and pepper to taste
2 Ch sp sesame seeds
2 Ch sp flour, for coating
unsaturated oil for frying

Golden vegetable balls

In a bowl, stir or blend the mashed vegetables and egg together to form a well mixed paste. Add in the seasoning to taste. Shape the mixture into small balls and roll them in the flour and sesame seeds to coat. Fry them till they are golden and soak off the excess oil with absorbent paper before serving.

Portion analysis	
energy	: 211 kcals
protein	: 11 g
fat	: 11 g
fibre	: 3.5 g
cholesterol	: 56 mg
calcium	: ★
iron	: ★★
vitamin A	: ★★★

Variation:

Tasty vegetable toast

4 slices wholemeal
bread, crusts removed
100 g golden vegetable
ball mixture
2 Ch sp sesame seeds

Spread the vegetable mixture over the bread, sprinkle the sesame seeds on top and toast in the oven toaster until slightly browned. Serve hot.

Portion analysis	
energy	: 121 kcals
protein	: 4 g
fat	: 3 g
fibre	: 3.7 g
cholesterol	: 8 mg

Vegetarian wonton

5 pieces dried Chinese mushroom, softened in hot water and chopped
300 g five-spiced (ngoh hiang) bean curd cake (tau kwa), shredded
2 Ch sp dried lily flower, soaked and chopped
2 water chestnuts, skinned and chopped
1 Ch sp black fungus, soaked in water and chopped
1 Ch sp carrot, grated
2 small shallots, thinly shredded
1 tsp Hua Tiao (Chinese wine)
salt and pepper to taste
1 Ch sp unsaturated oil

Heat the oil and fry the shallot till fragrant. Add the wine, then the rest of the vegetables and the tau kwa. Add the seasoning to taste, sauté the mixture till it is dry and set aside to cool. Wrap a heaped teaspoonful of the vegetable mixture in a wonton skin and steam or boil briefly to cook the skin. Alternatively, you could fry the wonton until golden and crispy. This, however, is rather oily and should only be served occasionally.

Portion analysis	
energy	: 100 kcals
protein	: 10 g
fat	: 5 g
fibre	: 1.2 g
cholesterol	: 0
iron	: ★
vitamin A	: ★

Stuffed lady's fingers

200 g lady's fingers, slit lengthwise and seeded
150 g vegetarian wonton stuffing (see previous recipe)
1 tsp finely chopped ginger
1 tsp dark soya sauce
½ tsp Hua Tiao (Chinese wine)
¼ tsp sugar
½ tsp cornflour
½ cup liquid from the soaked mushroom and lily flower
salt and pepper to taste

Sauté the wonton vegetables as in the previous recipe. Fill each lady's finger with the vegetable stuffing. Arrange the lady's fingers on a plate and steam over high heat for 5 minutes. Fry the ginger in oil, add wine, then the liquid and seasoning. Thicken the sauce with cornflour and boil briefly. Pour the sauce over the steamed lady's fingers and serve. The lady's fingers can be sliced into bite-sized pieces after steaming for easier eating, but arrange them back in shape for better presentation.

Portion analysis	
energy	: 60 kcals
protein	: 5 g
fat	: 2 g
fibre	: 1.6 g
cholesterol	: 0

Gado-gado

2 medium eggs, hard-
boiled and quartered
lengthwise
2 medium potatoes,
boiled and sliced
100 g beansprouts, tails
plucked off and
boiled briefly
150 g cabbage,
parboiled and
shredded
150 g long beans, boiled
and cut into 5-cm
lengths
2 squares (300 g) bean
curd cake (*tau kwa*),
fried, drained and
sliced
1 cup peanut sauce
(see recipe on page
226)

Arrange the prepared vegetables on a plate, pour the peanut sauce over, toss to mix and serve as a salad dish or as a snack. Occasionally, you might like to garnish the top of this dish with some lightly crushed prawn crackers.

Portion analysis	
energy	: 315 kcals
protein	: 22 g
fat	: 16 g
fibre	: 6.1 g
cholesterol	: 112 mg
calcium	: ★
iron	: ★★
vitamin A	: ★
vitamin B$_1$	: ★★
niacin	: ★
vitamin C	: ★★★

Saffron potatoes

4 medium potatoes,
boiled, cooled and
diced
8 shallots, finely sliced
½ tsp mustard seeds
1 tsp turmeric powder
1 Ch sp unsaturated oil
salt to taste

Fry the mustard seeds in the oil until they "pop". Add the shallots and fry until they soften. Add the turmeric powder, salt and then the potatoes. Stir-fry until heated through.

Portion analysis	
energy	: 110 kcals
protein	: 2 g
fat	: 4 g
fibre	: 1.1 g
cholesterol	: 0

Spinach and bean curd quiche (makes 6 portions)

¾ cup plain flour, sifted
60 g unsaturated margarine
dash of salt
a little cold water to mix
250 g bean curd, mashed
2 medium eggs, beaten
½ onion, chopped
200 g spinach, boiled, drained and chopped
2 medium tomatoes, skinned and sliced into rounds
30 g fresh button mushrooms, sliced thinly
salt and pepper to taste
½ Ch sp unsaturated oil

Preheat the oven to 180°C. Mix the sifted flour and salt in a bowl and rub in the margarine with the fingertips until the mixture resembles fine breadcrumbs. Mix in a little water to bind the dough. Press gently for a firm dough and knead lightly on a floured board to form a ball. Roll out thinly and lift gently on to a pre-greased loose bottom quiche pan. Press the pastry lightly into shape, trim the edges and reinforce the lower edge with strips of pastry if needed. Keep the pastry refrigerated while preparing the vegetables. Fry the onion in heated oil, add in the mushroom slices and sauté briefly. Remove from the heat, stir in the mashed bean curd, then the beaten egg and mix well. Spread half the mixture on to the pastry, followed by a layer of chopped spinach. Cover with the remaining half of the mixture and top with tomato slices. Bake for about 45 minutes or until the mixture is set and puffed up, and the pastry is golden brown. Serve it hot with a salad for a light meal, or on its own as a snack.

Portion analysis	
energy	: 258 kcals
protein	: 9 g
fat	: 13 g
fibre	: 3.2 g
cholesterol	: 75 mg
iron	: ★
vitamin A	: ★★★
vitamin C	: ★★

Dhal curry

1 cup *dhal* (yellow split peas)
1 medium onion, sliced
1 large tomato, sliced
1 heaped tsp mild curry powder
8 shallots, sliced
1 green chilli, cut into quarters, with seeds removed
½ tsp mustard seeds
4 cups cold water
1 Ch sp unsaturated oil
dash of salt

Remove the stones and dirt from the *dhal*, then wash and place in a pot with four cups of cold water. Add the curry powder, shallots, tomato and salt. Boil until the mixture thickens, adding more water if necessary.

Heat the oil and fry the mustard seeds, sliced onions and chilli. When onions turn light brown, add mixture into the *dhal*.

Variation: Chop and lightly fry five lady's fingers and one large brinjal and add when the *dhal* is about three-quarters cooked. Add ½ tsp turmeric powder and ½ cup of tamarind juice to this version.

Portion analysis	
energy	: 258 kcals
protein	: 13 g
fat	: 4 g
fibre	: 7.7 g
cholesterol	: 0
iron	: ★★★
vitamin B$_1$	: ★

Mixed vegetable and fruit salad

- 1 medium apple, washed and sliced or diced
- 150 g silken bean curd, parboiled, drained and cubed
- 1 medium potato, boiled, and diced
- 1 medium carrot, diced and boiled
- ½ stalk celery, outer fibres removed and diced
- 4 leaves lettuce, washed, drained and shredded
- 1 Ch sp almonds, toasted and chopped
- ½ cup bean curd salad dressing (see recipe on page 225)
- dash of salt and pepper

Mixed vegetable and fruit salad

Prepare all the ingredients and place in a salad bowl. Toss the salad with the bean curd salad dressing and keep it chilled before serving. This is a refreshing accompaniment for burgers or sandwiches, or as a light snack or meal.

Portion analysis	
energy	: 115 kcals
protein	: 7 g
fat	: 5 g
fibre	: 2.5 g
cholesterol	: 0
calcium	: ★
iron	: ★
vitamin A	: ★ ★ ★
vitamin C	: ★ ★

Shredded coleslaw

200 g cabbage, washed, drained and grated or shredded
½ medium cucumber, skinned, seeded and shredded
1 medium carrot, grated
2 Ch sp low fat mayonnaise (see recipe on page 225)
salt, sugar and pepper to taste

Toss all the ingredients in a salad bowl to blend well. Chill in a refrigerator before serving. Use as a side vegetable dish for a light meal, e.g. with sandwiches, pies or burgers. Chopped red apple, pineapple or raisins make delicious additions to coleslaw.

Portion analysis

energy	: 56 kcals
protein	: 2 g
fat	: 2 g
fibre	: 2.2 g
cholesterol	: 19 mg
vitamin A	: ★★★
vitamin C	: ★★★

Spinach with pumpkin

300 g spinach, chopped
½ medium onion, chopped
¼ medium pumpkin, diced
2 cloves garlic
1 Ch sp unsaturated oil
1 cup water
salt to taste

Fry the onion and garlic in the oil for a minute or so, then add the spinach stems and pumpkin cubes. After a few more minutes, add the water and simmer, covered, until almost cooked. Add in the spinach leaves and stir until the water has almost evaporated off and the leaves are cooked. Add the seasoning.

This simple vegetable dish can be made into a soup by adding diluted coconut milk instead of the water and not allowing it to boil dry.

Portion analysis

energy	: 43 kcals
protein	: 3 g
fat	: 2 g
fibre	: 3.7 g
cholesterol	: 0
iron	: ★
vitamin A	: ★★★

Wholesome Soups

Soups and stocks are important components of any child's diet, for increasing fluid intake as well as boosting nutrient consumption. The basic stocks made from meat bones and vegetables can be used to cook rice porridge (congee) or can be added to pureed food to improve flavour and consistency. Stocks can also be used as a base for the thicker cream soups which, together with sandwiches, are ideal for a light meal. ● ○ ● ○

Meat bone and vegetable stock

Place pieces of uncooked bones (marrow bones if available) or bones removed from roast meat joints in a pot of boiling water. The bones of chicken, pork, beef or mutton may be used. Add in half an onion, a few leaves of cabbage, one stick of carrot, celery or radish. Cover the pot and simmer for over an hour with a few drops of wine to fully extract the flavour. Strain and use as desired. This stock can be frozen in cubes (using an ice tray). Empty the frozen soup cubes into a plastic bag, seal and label it, and store it in the freezer. The required amounts can then be removed and heated when necessary. This is especially useful when cooking in small quantities.

Vegetarian stock

Omit the bones and, instead, use more vegetables for better flavour.

Fish stock

Use larger pieces of bones and trimming from fish (better if some flesh can be included). Simmer with vegetables as in the meat stock. Strain and use.

A commonly consumed fish stock for Asia is that made from dried *ikan bilis* boiled together with some greens such as spinach or *heng chye*.

Strong fish stock: For stronger fish broth, poach or simmer whole fish or fish head with vegetables for half an hour or more until the flesh begins to flake off easily. Strain the stock and mash the fish meat until it is quite fine in texture. This may then be returned to the stock if desired. Add a few ginger slices, some spring onion or a few drops of lemon juice to remove the stronger fish smell. Milk can be used in place of part of the stock if a rich creamy soup is required.

Canned soup with bean curd

For the occasion when you have to resort to the use of canned or packet soups, it is wise to make them a little more diluted to reduce the saltiness. Add in cut pieces of soft bean curd or vegetables for variety and an extra helping of nutrients. Use a melon scoop and you have "bean curd balls".

The nutritional analysis for each recipe is based on a quarter of the recipe ingredients.

Cream vegetable soup

This is a rich soup made from pureed vegetables with added milk. The vegetables are usually sautéed in a little oil first for added flavour, but this is not essential.

Prepare and cut up the vegetables, sauté lightly in ½ Ch sp heated oil if desired, add in the stock and simmer for 20 minutes or until the vegetables are quite cooked. Skim off the fat, sieve or blend the vegetables, add the milk into the pureed stock, stir and gently bring to the boil. Add the seasoning and serve. The consistency can be adjusted with extra milk or stock.

(*Skimmed milk may be used in place of whole milk to cut down the fat content.) For nutritional analyses see Table 1 on page 216.

Carrot soup	500 g carrot
	1 medium onion
	1 stick celery (optional)
Spinach soup	500 g spinach
	1 small onion
Watercress soup	500 g watercress
	1 small onion
Lentil soup	½ cup orange lentils
	1 small onion
	1 small carrot
Tomato soup	600–800 g tomatoes
	1 medium onion
Green pea soup	300 g green peas (frozen variety)
	1 small onion
Celery soup	500 g imported celery (remove coarse outer fibres)
	1 medium onion

Table 1: Comparison of the Energy and Nutrient Content of Various Cream Vegetable Soups (using whole milk)

Soup	Energy (kcals)	Protein (g)	Fat (g)	Fibreª (g)	cholesterol (mg)
Watercress	78	6	3	4.5	8
Carrot	104	3	2	4.1	8
Spinach	78	4	2	8.2	8
Lentil	164	9	2	4.4	8
Tomato	96	5	3	3.2	8
Green pea	131	5	2	5.1	8
Celery	64	3	2	2.2	8

ª The fibre content is for vegetables before pureeing. The blending process will destroy some of the fibre. The actual figures will therefore be lower.

Soup	Calcium	Iron	Vitamin A	Vitamin B$_2$	Vitamin C
Watercress	*	**	***	*	***
Carrot			***		
Spinach	*	*	***	*	***
Lentil		*	***		
Tomato			**		***
Green pea			*		
Celery					

NB: In most cases, when the level of a nutrient does not meet the star rating, it can still, however, make a valuable contribution to our overall intake.

Bean curd fish soup

1 piece (300 g) soft bean curd, cut into cubes
250 g white fish fillet
100 g long Chinese cabbage, sliced
4-5 cups water or fish bone stock
1½ tsp *Hua Tiao* (Chinese wine)
2 tsp cornflour, dissolved in a little water
½ Ch sp unsaturated oil
1–2 cloves garlic, crushed
2 slices ginger
dash of salt, pepper and sugar
3–4 pieces carrot, cut in patterns
a little coriander leaves, chopped

Boil the cabbage in water or stock until cooked. Marinate the fish fillet with the wine and steam for approximately 3-5 minutes. Remove the fish from the heat and mash with a fork until it is fine. Heat the oil in the pan, add the garlic and ginger slices, then stir fry the fish briefly. Add in the bean curd, cabbage and stock and bring to the boil. Thicken the soup slightly with the cornflour mixture and season with a dash of salt, pepper and sugar. Serve hot, garnished with chopped coriander and carrot slices.

This soup is tasty, nutritious and easily digestible. It is rich in protein and calcium and is suitable for the very young to the very old.

Portion analysis	
energy	: 173 kcals
protein	: 15 g
fat	: 11 g
fibre	: 1.0 g
cholesterol	: 50 mg
calcium	: ★
iron	: ★

Wintermelon soup

¼ large wintermelon, pulp removed and diced
100 g chicken meat, diced
1 slice lean ham, diced
1 Ch sp canned button mushroom, diced
2 pieces Chinese mushroom, softened in hot water and diced
2 Ch sp lotus seeds, pre-cooked
5 cups chicken bone stock
1–2 slices ginger
dash of salt and pepper

Simmer all the ingredients together in the chicken stock until the meat is tender and tasty. A more novel way is to buy a whole wintermelon. Rinse it, place it on a bowl and boil it in a deep pot of water for 15 minutes. Drain away the water and cool the wintermelon in cold water. Slice off the top and scoop out the seedy centre pulp. Add in all the ingredients and some stock till the melon is three-quarters full, replace the top and steam for about an hour. Place the whole melon on a platter and serve.

Although this method requires more work, the results are worth it. The soup is delicious and has a delicate flavour. This wintermelon soup is believed to be "cooling" by the Chinese and is usually taken during a hot, dry spell.

Portion analysis	
energy	: 97 kcals
protein	: 10 g
fat	: 3 g
fibre	: 2.3 g
cholesterol	: 26 mg

Seaweed and minced meat soup

2 thin sheets round
    purple seaweed*,
100 g minced meat
    (pork or chicken)
1 medium egg, beaten
2 small shallots, thinly
    sliced
1 Ch sp chopped spring
    onion
1–2 slices ginger
dash of salt and pepper
1½ litres *ikan bilis* stock
    or bone stock

Seasoning for meat:
1 tsp light soya sauce
1 tsp cornflour
¼ tsp *Hua Tiao* (Chinese
    wine)

Sauté the sliced shallots in some oil until they turn golden brown. Drain and set this aside for use later. Season the minced meat and make into small meatballs if desired. Add the meat to boiling stock, add the seaweed and boil a further 10 minutes. Next, pour the beaten egg into the soup, stirring constantly. Adjust the seasoning to taste. Sprinkle the spring onion and fried shallot over the soup just before serving.

Alternatively, you could fry the minced meat and seaweed with the shallot in a little oil before adding them to the stock. This is a quick-to-fix and nutritious soup. It makes the seaweed more readily accepted by the young ones and is a good source of iodine, other minerals and fibre.

*The seaweed can be bought from most provision shops and leading supermarkets. Wash the seaweed over a strainer to remove sand particles.

Portion analysis	
energy	: 77 kcals
protein	: 7 g
fat	: 6 g
fibre	: 1.2 g
cholesterol	: 73 mg
iron	: ★
vitamin B₁	: ★

Vitamin soup

½ Chinese cabbage
    (*pek chye*) chopped
3 stalks *chye sim*, chopped
1 large carrot, sliced
10 baby corns, sliced
    in two
2 Ch sp snow peas or
    green peas
1 egg
chicken stock
2 tsp cornflour, dissolved
    in a little water
salt and pepper to taste

Boil the vegetables in the stock, allowing more time for the carrots and baby corn. Next, add the *chye sim* stalks and snow peas, and finally the *chye sim* leaves and the cabbage. When cooked, break in the egg and stir briefly just before serving. Thicken with the cornflour if desired, simmering for another 2 minutes.

Almost any combination of vegetables can be cooked in a simple soup of this sort. Chop the leafy greens shortly before adding to the soup and do not overcook to retain maximum vitamin C content.

Portion analysis	
energy	: 62 kcals
protein	: 4 g
fat	: 2 g
fibre	: 6.2 g
cholesterol	: 56 mg
iron	: ★
vitamin A	: ★★★

Soyabean milk and sweetcorn soup

2 cups unsweetened
   soyabean milk
   (see recipe on page
   262)
1 cup chicken stock
   or water
1 can (480 g) cream-
   style sweetcorn
1 slice lean ham, finely
   chopped
   or 30 g chicken meat,
   minced or chopped
1 Ch sp coriander
   leaves, finely chopped
salt and pepper to taste

Boil the chicken stock, add in the sweetcorn, meat and soyabean milk. Simmer briefly while stirring. Add in the coriander leaves and seasoning, and serve.

For those unfamiliar with soyabean milk other than as the sweetened drink, it is surprisingly versatile and can be suitably incorporated into soups, adding flavour and boosting the nutritional value of the soups.

Portion analysis	
energy	: 148 kcals
protein	: 8 g
fat	: 3 g
fibre	: 2.2 g
cholesterol	: 7 mg
iron	: ★

Liver and kei chi leaf soup

100 g liver (e.g.pig's),
   thinly sliced
5–6 stalks medlar leaves
   (kei chi leaves) use
   only the leaves
1 Ch sp medlar berries
   (kei chi)*, washed
4–5 cups water of
   chicken bone stock

Seasoning for liver:
1 tsp light soya sauce
½ tsp cornflour
dash of pepper

Lightly marinate the liver slices in the seasoning. Boil the water or bone stock in a pot, add in the kei chi and simmer for about 10–15 minutes to impart flavour. When ready to serve, add in the washed and drained greens, boil briefly for 3–5 minutes, add the liver slices and serve as soon as the liver is cooked. Do not overcook liver as it will toughen.

This soup is easy to make and yet nutritious, with a good supply of protein, iron and vitamin A as the ingredients are rich sources of these nutrients. (Incidentally, the Chinese believe that kei chi is good for the eyes. This is quite valid since it is a relatively good source of vitamin A.) The brief cooking also ensures the retention of most vitamins and minerals.

* Available in supermarkets or Chinese medicine shops.

Portion analysis	
energy	: 43 kcals
protein	: 6 g
fat	: 1 g
fibre	: 0.7 g
cholesterol	: 65 mg
iron	: ★★
vitamin A	: ★★★
vitamin B$_2$	: ★★
niacin	: ★

Soto ayam

½ medium chicken,
skinned and visible fat
trimmed off
2 slices ginger
2-cm square *galangal*
(*lengkuas*)
2-cm piece turmeric
6–7 pieces candlenut
(*buah keras*)
1 stalk lemon grass
8 small shallots
3 cloves garlic
1 stalk leek
100 g beansprouts,
tails removed and
parboiled
2 medium potatoes,
boiled and diced
1 small bundle
(20 g) glass vermicelli
(*tang hoon*), boiled
½ Ch sp unsaturated oil
6–8 cups hot water

Lightly pound the lemon grass, ginger and *galangal*. Set this aside. Blend the turmeric, candlenut, shallots and garlic until fine. Fry the two lots of ingredients together in a little oil until fragrant, then add in the hot water. When this comes to the boil, put in the chicken and leek and simmer for 20 minutes. Remove the chicken, allow it to cool and then shred the meat. Replace the bones in the soup for further simmering. Skim off the fat, strain all the solids and season the soup with a dash of salt when ready to serve. The soup should be served with diced potatoes, chicken shreds, boiled beansprouts and a little boiled glass vermicelli. Sprinkle the top of the soup with some fried shallot and add a squeeze of lime juice to each bowl of soup. Serve with rice to complete the meal.

Portion analysis	
energy	: 172 kcals
protein	: 16 g
fat	: 5 g
fibre	: 1.4 g
cholesterol	: 47 mg
niacin	: ★

Saucy Secrets

S auces and dressings literally "dress up" a dish. For children, the value of sauces lies in adding extra nutrients as well as moistening otherwise dry foods. Traditional sauces are usually rich and many people use them too liberally. This can add a substantial amount of calories, fat and sodium to a dish. The sauces included in this section are modified versions of the more common sauces accompanying some familiar Western and Asian fare. The basic white sauce (see recipe on page 142) is a useful and nutritious base for many of our suggested weaning foods; it can also be adapted for family meals. Yoghurt- and fruit-based sauces add a refreshing touch to salads, while the good old peanut sauce ensures the best for your home-made satay. Go beyond these examples and create your own magic sauces using healthy and fresh ingredients. With these secrets up your sleeve, you can say goodbye to all the worries about artificial ingredients and preservatives that are present in many commercial sauces. ● ○ ○

Quantities are for two adults and two children unless otherwise stated.

Sweet 'n' sour sauce
(makes about 2 cups)

4 large tomatoes,
  skinned* chopped
  finely
3 cloves garlic, pounded
2 slices ginger
¾ cup water
1½ Ch sp tomato ketchup
2 tsp light soya sauce
½ Ch sp vinegar
2 tsp sugar
salt and pepper to taste
½ Ch sp unsaturated oil
1 red chilli, seeded and
  pounded (optional)
2 heaped tsp cornflour,
  mixed with 2 Ch sp
  water

* Dip the tomatoes in
  boiling water first to
  facilitate peeling.

Fry the garlic, ginger and chilli (if used) in oil. Add water and tomatoes and cook until the tomatoes turn into a soft pulp. Add the other ingredients, bring to the boil and thicken with cornflour.

Analysis per 1 Ch sp	
energy	: 10 kcals
protein	: 0.2 g
fat	: 0.3 g
fibre	: 0.2 g
cholesterol	: 0

Simple tomato sauce
(makes about 1 cup)

2 Ch sp finely chopped
  onion
4 medium red tomatoes,
  boiled, skinned and
  chopped
1 Ch sp tomato paste
½ cup water
½ Ch sp unsaturated oil
salt and pepper to taste

Heat the oil and fry the onion until it is soft. Add the chopped tomatoes, water and paste and bring to the boil till slightly thick. After seasoning the sauce to taste, remove it and blend it in a blender. Keep it refrigerated in an airtight container if it is not to be used immediately.

Analysis per 1 Ch sp	
energy	: 15 kcals
protein	: 1 g
fat	: 1 g
fibre	: 0.5 g
cholesterol	: 0

Vegetarian bean curd salad dressing (makes about 1½ cups)

To be mixed together:
250 g bean curd
150 g plain yoghurt or
   2 Ch sp skimmed milk
   powder
½ Ch sp lime or lemon
   juice
100 ml water

dash of chopped
   dried basil or parsley
   (optional)
1 tsp honey
1–2 drops vanilla
   essence

Blend all the ingredients in a blender until smooth. Chill and serve as a nutritious and refreshing dressing, e.g. with potato, fruit and vegetable salads, as well as with burgers and sandwiches. This dressing can be kept in the refrigerator for 2–3 days.

Analysis per 1 Ch sp	
energy	: 17 kcals
protein	: 2 g
fat	: 1 g
fibre	: 0.1 g
cholesterol	: 0

Healthy low fat mayonnaise (makes about 1 cup)

2 Ch sp plain flour
1 medium egg
150 ml skimmed milk
1 Ch sp unsaturated oil
1 Ch sp lemon or
   lime juice
dash of salt and pepper
dash of mustard powder
   (optional)

Whisk the milk and flour in a double boiler over low heat. Add in the egg, salt, pepper and mustard (if used). Stir the mixture continuously over slightly simmering water until the sauce thickens and is smooth. Remove from the heat and quickly stir in the lemon juice and oil to blend well. Cool, then chill in the refrigerator; making sure that the mayonnaise is stored in a tightly covered container. This mayonnaise has less than half the calories of regular mayonnaise. Use it with salad or in making sandwiches such as those with a tuna (canned in water) filling. It will keep well in the refrigerator but is best used within a week. Alternatively, you can also buy reduced calorie mayonnaise which is now available in the supermarkets.

Analysis per 1 Ch sp	
energy	: 40 kcals
protein	: 2 g
fat	: 2 g
fibre	: 0.1 g
cholesterol	: 23 mg

Easy peanut satay sauce
(makes about 2 cups)

250 g fresh peanuts,
discard the spoiled
or mouldy ones

Grind in blender:
1x1 cm piece *galangal*
(*lengkuas*), sliced
4 shallots
3 dried chillies, seeded
2 cloves garlic
2 pieces candlenut
(*buah keras*)

1 stalk lemon grass,
pounded
1¾ cup tamarind water
(use 2 tsp tamarind)
1 Ch sp lemon or lime
juice
1 Ch sp sugar
½ Ch sp unsaturated oil
salt to taste

Roast, then skin and grind the peanuts. Heat the oil in the pan, add the blended ingredients, stir and fry till fragrant. Add the tamarind water, sugar and salt and boil for 10 minutes. Add the roasted ground peanuts and lemon juice and stir until the sauce thickens. Serve with satay or *gado gado*. Reduce or omit the chillies if it is to be taken by children. With the availability of the food processor, preparation of the satay sauce ingredients is no longer tedious. Therefore, substituting fresh peanuts with peanut butter is not necessary, and will only give a second grade sauce. The sauce can be kept refrigerated for a few days in an airtight container.

Analysis per 1 Ch sp	
energy	: 50 kcals
protein	: 2 g
fat	: 3 g
fibre	: 0.6 g
cholesterol	: 0

Sweetcorn sauce
(makes about 1 cup)

4 Ch sp cream-style
corn
½ cup skimmed milk
1 Ch sp plain flour
1 Ch sp chopped onion
½ Ch sp unsaturated
margarine

Lightly fry the chopped onion in heated margarine, add the flour and make into a *roux*. Blend in the milk, stir and lightly boil until it thickens and becomes smooth. Add in the sweetcorn and serve. This is a tasty variation of the basic white sauce.

For a wholesome and quick meal, add chopped cooked chicken meat and serve over rice. Alternatively, spread on bread and toast lightly.

Analysis per 1 Ch sp	
energy	: 30 kcals
protein	: 3 g
fat	: 1 g
fibre	: 0.1 g
cholesterol	: 8 mg

1 kg plain yoghurt
(home-made or
commercial)
¼ tsp salt (optional)

Fresh yoghurt cheese

Mix the salt with the yoghurt and pour over a large strainer or sieve lined with muslin, which is sitting on a container. Cover and leave the yoghurt to drain in the refrigerator for 1–2 days. The whey* will be collected in the container, leaving a soft cheese in the muslin. Remove the whey at regular intervals so that the cheese will not be sitting in moisture, thus preventing it from holding its shape. Use as a soft cheese and serve with bread or biscuits, etc. The cheese can be kept by storing in a clean container. (Pour a little oil, preferably olive oil, to seal and preserve.) For variation, use a melon scoop to form into balls, roll over biscuit crumbs or roasted sesame seeds and keep in the freezer compartment for a short time to harden.

*The collected whey can be used in sauces, stocks or as cooking liquid.

½ cucumber, seeded
and grated
½ cup plain yoghurt
1 Ch sp finely chopped
onion
1 medium tomato,
skinned, seeded and
shredded
1 tsp thinly shredded
fresh chilli (remove the
seeds)
dash of mint, chopped

Yoghurt chutney
(makes about ¾ cup)

Squeeze and drain the cucumber and onion to remove the excess moisture. Mix all the ingredients and season with a dash of salt if desired. This is an excellent accompaniment for curries.

Analysis per 1 Ch sp	
energy	: 17 kcals
protein	: 2 g
fat	: 0.3 g
fibre	: 0.5 g
cholesterol	: 2 mg

3 Ch sp tomato paste
1 Ch sp plain yoghurt
1 tsp honey
2 tsp lemon or lime juice
dash of salt and pepper
dash of paprika

Tomato yoghurt sauce
(makes about ⅓ cup)

Stir and mix all the ingredients until well blended. Substitute for commercial tomato ketchup and use with fish fingers, etc.

Analysis per 1 Ch sp	
energy	: 28 kcals
protein	: 2 g
fat	: 0.1 g
fibre	: 0
cholesterol	: 0

Home-made skimmed milk yoghurt

Yoghurt is an excellent food for both children and adults. For the many Asians who cannot take well to milk, yoghurt is the ideal alternative as the lactose in the milk has been converted to lactic acid, making it easier to digest. It is also a valuable source of calcium and the B vitamins.

Analysis per ½ cup (125 g)	
energy	: 88 kcals
protein	: 8 g
fat	: 2 g
fibre	: 0
cholesterol	: 12 mg
calcium	: ★★
vitamin B$_2$	: ★

In our part of the world, the temperature is just right for making yoghurt at home, without the need to use any fancy gadgets. A clean stainless steel or porcelain bowl and some patience are all that is needed. The proportions for one cup of yoghurt are:

2 heaped Ch sp skimmed milk powder

1 cup warm water

1 Ch sp starter (existing plain yoghurt)

Take the starter out of the refrigerator and leave it to reach room temperature. Dissolve the milk powder in warm water (body temperature; it should not feel hot when dropped on the back of the hand). Mix the yoghurt with a little milk and then mix it into the rest of the milk evenly. Cover and leave to set undisturbed for 10–12 hours. The inside of an oven is a good place to leave it. You can make the yoghurt just before going to bed for it to work overnight. When set, it is like a soft curd (like *tau huay*). Place the yoghurt in the refrigerator or have it fresh for breakfast. If you leave it outside for too long after the curd is formed, the yoghurt may get too sour. Always leave some aside as a starter for the next batch. The starter can be kept frozen in cubes (1 Ch sp each) for when next needed. If a thicker curd is preferred, more milk powder can be used during reconstituting.

The soft consistency of the yoghurt is just beautiful for children and the home-made variety is not as sour as the commercial ones. It can be taken plain or with fruit, or used in cooking. Plain yoghurt, flavoured with lemon juice, chopped herbs, curry powder, fruit, etc, can be used as a dressing over salads.

Fruit sauce

Mashed, grated or pureed fruit heated with a dash of sugar (if required) makes a wonderful tasty dessert sauce. Apple, mango, pineapple, etc, will go well with pancakes, scones, and cold meat sandwiches too. Thicken the sauce with a little dissolved cornflour before heating if the consistency of the fruit puree is too thin.

30 g sesame seeds
1 Ch sp miso paste (fermented soyabean paste)
1 Ch sp *mirin* (Japanese sweet cooking wine)
½ Ch sp soya sauce (Japanese or local light)
1 Ch sp rice vinegar
2 tsp sugar
2 Ch sp bone stock or water
1 tsp unsaturated oil
dash of chilli powder (optional)

Sesame steamboat sauce (makes about ⅓ cup)

Toast or lightly fry the sesame seeds and grind in a mortar while still hot. Coat a small frying pan with the oil and lightly heat the miso paste till fragrant. Add the stock and other seasoning ingredients, boil briefly and turn off the heat. Mix in the sesame seeds until well blended. Cool and serve as a sauce for steamboat meat.

It is also delicious when used as an accompaniment for chilled bean curd. Cut the silken bean curd into 5-cm rectangles or rounds, dip briefly into boiling water, remove, drain and cool in the refrigerator if desired. Serve with the sauce and garnish with a little chopped spring onion.

Analysis per 1 Ch sp	
energy	: 81 kcals
protein	: 2 g
fat	: 5 g
fibre	: 1.9 g
cholesterol	: 0

Sweet Dreams

The size of most fruit counters in our markets is ever expanding, with mouth-watering local fruit and an increasing variety of imported ones. These should be given to children regularly so that eating fruit every day becomes a habit that will accompany them into adulthood. There are, however, occasions when some sweet desserts can be offered as a special treat. Taken in moderation and not on a regular basis, they will be a welcome change. Many of these desserts can be fruit-based and can also be made with healthier ingredients. *Kuihs* and desserts made with coconut milk should be minimised or adapted. ● ● ○ ●

Quantities are for two adults and two children unless otherwise stated.

Tropical fruit pudding (makes 8 small portions)

1 cup fresh fruit flesh (e.g. mango, honeydew, kiwi, banana, etc)
½ cup evaporated milk, kept chilled
1 cup skimmed milk
1 egg, beaten
4 tsp gelatine
1 rounded Ch sp sugar
1 tsp lemon (or lime) juice

Puree two-thirds of the fruit. Cut the rest into small pieces and add the lemon juice to prevent browning. Dissolve the gelatine in some hot water. Heat the skimmed milk with sugar. Stir in the beaten egg, and continue stirring over a low heat until the mixture thickens slightly (do not boil). Add in the melted gelatine, then cool slightly. Whip the evaporated milk with a beater and mix in all the ingredients. Line the bottom of the mould with cut fruit pieces. Pour in the fruit mixture and chill it in the refrigerator to set. Turn out the pudding on to a plate and serve.

Portion analysis	
energy	: 60 kcals
protein	: 3 g
fat	: 2 g
fibre	: 0.3 g
cholesterol	: 34 mg
vitamin A	: ★
vitamin C	: ★★★

Chilled lemon cheesecake (makes 10 portions)

8 pieces digestive biscuits, crushed finely
50 g unsaturated margarine
3 tsp gelatine, dissolved in 2 Ch sp water
2 medium eggs, separated
200 g cream cheese (e.g. Philadelphia)
150 g low fat cottage cheese
100 ml evaporated milk, chilled
2 Ch sp castor sugar
30 ml lemon juice
1 tsp grated lemon rind
2 kiwi fruits, sliced into thin rounds

Mix the crushed biscuits with the margarine until well mixed. Press the mixture into the base of a loose-bottomed cheesecake tin (springform pan). Stir the gelatine in water and heat to melt it. Stir in the lemon juice and egg yolk and keep warm in a hot water bath. Blend the cream cheese and cottage cheese in a mixer with a tablespoon or so of the evaporated milk until smooth. Whisk the egg whites until soft peaks form. Whip the chilled evaporated milk until thickened (use a chilled mixing bowl for easy whipping). Add the gelatine mixture into the cheese, add the whipped milk and, lastly, fold in the egg white evenly. Pour into the tin and chill in the refrigerator till set. Serve plain or decorated with sliced kiwi fruit. This is a light, nutritious and delicious cheesecake, a real treat on special occasions.

Variation:

For orange cheesecake, simply substitute the lemon juice with orange juice. Add a squeeze of lime juice for extra zing. For cheesecake with a hint of spice, add a quarter teaspoon of powdered ginger or mixed spice to the crushed biscuits.

Portion analysis	
energy	: 190 kcals
protein	: 10 g
fat	: 10 g
fibre	: 2.0 g
cholesterol	: 53 mg
vitamin C	: ★★★

Melon and mixed fruit jelly

½ medium-sized ripe honeydew or rock melon
½ cup diced mixed fruit (e.g. kiwi fruit and mango)
¼ cup fresh orange juice
1½ tsp plain *agar agar* powder

Scoop out the seeds of the halved melon to have a reasonably-sized hollow (remove a little of the flesh if necessary and add to the fruit mixture). Mix the *agar agar* powder in a little orange juice and heat it to dissolve the powder. You will need to stir this constantly. Add the mixture to the rest of the juice. Use the cut fruit to fill the hole in the melon half, then pour the orange mixture over this. Sit the melon in the refrigerator to let it set. When chilled, slice in wedges and serve. Other fruit such as papaya can also be similarly used in place of the melon.

Portion analysis	
energy	: 126 kcals
protein	: 1 g
fat	: 0.2 g
fibre	: 3.3 g
cholesterol	: 0
vitamin A	: ★★★
vitamin C	: ★★★

Red bean soup (makes 8 small portions)

¾ cup red beans
1 Ch sp uncooked rice (unmilled preferably)
2 pieces dried tangerine peel
or peeled rind of half an orange
100 g rock sugar
1½–2 litres water

Wash and soak the red beans for an hour or two. Boil with the rice and the tangerine peel until the beans are soft and the soup thick. Remove the peel and add the sugar. Simmer till the latter dissolves. Serve hot or cold or in paste (blend in processor) form. Green beans and black glutinous rice can also be cooked likewise for variation. Cook an extra portion of red bean soup and freeze as red bean lollies or ice cream (see recipe on page 265) which is a firm local favourite.

Portion analysis	
energy	: 140 kcals
protein	: 6 g
fat	: 0.3 g
fibre	: 4.5 g
cholesterol	: 0
iron	: ★
vitamin B$_1$	: ★

Variations:

1) Use green bean and pearl sago in place of red bean and rice. Preboil the sago in water before adding to the green bean. Omit the tangerine peel.

2) *Bubor kacang* is made similarly, except that in place of some water, coconut milk is added to give the *lemak* flavour that is so typical of our local favorites. By substituting half the water with skimmed milk and the rest with thin coconut milk (second squeeze), the *bubor kacang* can be made healthier.

20 g dry white cloud
  fungus
10 small quail's eggs
100 g rock sugar
8–10 dry red dates
1 Ch sp sweet almonds
  (South Chinese
  almond)

"Clouds" and quail's egg dessert (makes 8 small portions)

Soak the white cloud fungus in water until softened and expanded (about half to one hour). Wash and discard the yellow hard base if present. Boil the quail's eggs gently until hard-boiled, soak in cold water and remove the shells when cooled. Wash and remove the seeds from the red dates. Boil the white fungus in 1½ cups water with the red dates until semi-soft (or soft if desired). Add the quail's eggs and rock sugar and simmer further until the sugar dissolves. Serve hot or cold.

White cloud fungus is a treasured Chinese delicacy and is a relatively good source of calcium and other minerals. It is now widely available and cheap and most children love it as a dessert.

Alternatively, boil the ingredients with chicken or bone stock (omit sugar) and to transform it into a tasty savoury soup.

Variation:
White cloud fungus with papaya dessert
Use 300 g papaya (firm and not too ripe), cubed, in place of the quail's eggs and simmer together with the white cloud fungus. Omit the red dates.

Portion analysis	
energy	: 89 kcals
protein	: 2 g
fat	: 3 g
fibre	: 0.8 g
cholesterol	: 50 mg

Wholemeal bread pudding (makes 8 portions)

4 slices wholemeal bread
1½ tsp unsaturated margarine
2 Ch sp mixed raisins and sultanas, chopped
1½ Ch sp brown sugar
2 medium eggs
1 cup milk

Lightly spread margarine on the bread and quarter into triangles or squares. Line one layer of bread, margarined side down, over the bottom of a glass pie dish or individual small bowls. Sprinkle the dried fruit over and cover with the rest of the bread, margarined side upward. Mix half of the sugar with the egg and beat lightly with a fork. Heat the milk (do not boil), and stir into egg mixture to melt the sugar. Strain the milk mixture over the bread and leave to soak for 10–15 minutes. Sprinkle with the rest of the sugar and bake in a medium (180°C) oven for 20–30 minutes or until the pudding is nicely set and golden brown on top. Serve hot.

Bread pudding is very British in origin but universal in its appeal. It is a good disguise or alternative for giving milk and egg and a change from the usual egg custard.

Portion analysis	
energy	: 220 kcals
protein	: 5 g
fat	: 4 g
fibre	: 3.5 g
cholesterol	: 60 mg
iron	: ★

Mixed fruit salad bowl

2 cups mixed seasonal fruit, diced for example:
½ medium ripe mango
1 kiwi fruit
1 slice papaya
1 small banana
1 small red apple (with skin)
squeeze of lemon juice

Diced mixed fruit in any combination are perennial favourites and a nice change from the one fruit that is usually taken after meals. Add a squeeze of lemon juice over the cut fruit to prevent browning. Chill and serve plain or with yoghurt. Pay attention to the colour combination for added attractiveness and the children will enjoy the bite-sized pieces even more.

Variation:
Fruit _kebabs_
Cut the fruit in thicker shapes (e.g. using small cutters) or small rounds and skewer a few assorted pieces on to satay sticks. Chill and serve by themselves or with ice cream or sorbets on hot days.

Portion analysis	
energy	: 61 kcals
protein	: 1 g
fat	: 0.1 g
fibre	: 2.5 g
cholesterol	: 0
vitamin C	: ★★★

Gingko nut, barley and **fu-chok** soup

2–3 Ch sp dry pearl barley

100 g (about 40) precooked lotus seeds or 50 g dry lotus seeds

100 g (about 40) precooked *gingko* nuts or 70 g dry *gingko* nuts with their shells

1 dry sheet *fu-chok*, rope-like bean curd skin, shredded

1 medium egg (optional)

100 g rock sugar

Gingko nut, barley and fu-chok soup (makes 8 small portions)

If using fresh *gingko* nuts, shell them and remove the centre seedgerm. Soak in hot water, then peel off the brown sheath. Soak and boil the dry lotus seeds for 5 minutes, cool and remove the centre seedgerm if present. Wash and boil the barley in water together with the precooked or prepared dry gingko nuts and lotus seeds. Add in the shredded *fu-chok*. Simmer the mixture until all the ingredients are soft, add in the rock sugar and simmer further until the sugar dissolves. Stir in the beaten egg as for egg drop soup. Serve hot or chilled as a snack or dessert.

A favourite Chinese dessert, this soup has a fair supply of calcium and iron. Among the Cantonese, there is a belief that pregnant women who take this dessert often give birth to a fair and fine complexioned baby! (We are making no promises, though!)

Portion analysis	
energy	: 124 kcals
protein	: 7 g
fat	: 3 g
fibre	: 1.1 g
cholesterol	: 56 mg

Amma's green bean payasum (makes 8 small portions)

¾ cup green (mung) beans, without skins
1½ Ch sp sago (small)
handful dried wheat vermicelli
½ cup dark brown palm sugar (*gula melaka*)
½ tin (200 g) condensed milk
handful raisins or sultanas
handful cashew nuts, split lengthwise in half
½ Ch sp unsaturated oil

Roast the green beans over a low heat until light brown. Boil with sufficient water until cooked. Remove half the green beans from the pot and liquidise in blender. Return to the pot and add sago, vermicelli and brown sugar. Bring to the boil and simmer on low heat until the vermicelli and sago are cooked. Fry the cashew nuts and raisins in the oil until the nuts are light brown, and add with the condensed milk to the *payasum*.

The *payasum* thickens as it cools, and water should be added to bring it to the desired consistency before serving. This is an Indian dessert that is rich but delicious. Serve it as occasional dessert for variety.

Portion analysis	
energy	: 296 kcals
protein	: 10 g
fat	: 6 g
fibre	: 7.6 g
cholesterol	: 8 mg
iron	: ★★
vitamin B₁	: ★

Yoghurt jelly

150 ml plain yoghurt
1 cup skimmed milk
1 cup cut fruit, pureed (e.g. mango, papaya)
1 Ch sp sugar
2 tsp plain *agar agar* powder
1 tsp lemon or lime juice

Warm the milk, *agar agar* and sugar to dissolve the latter. Set aside to cool. Mix the pureed fruit with the yoghurt and stir into the cooled milk to mix well. Pour into a jelly mould or small individual jelly cups. Chill in the refrigerator until it sets. You can serve the jelly by itself or with cut fresh fruit.

Portion analysis	
energy	: 113 kcals
protein	: 5 g
fat	: 1 g
fibre	: 1.0 g
cholesterol	: 5 mg
calcium	: ★
vitamin A	: ★★
vitamin C	: ★★★

Teatime Munch

Children, especially the younger ones, can only eat small amounts of food at each meal. Nutritious snacks at mid-morning and afternoon will help in topping up the nutrients their growing bodies need. To maximise nutrition and minimise excess calories, their snacks planning is important. It will also reduce the "grab what's handy" habit that often ends with candy, salty chips, *keropok* and soft drinks, etc.

Here we have given some examples of nutritious munches you can prepare. Many of them can be used as breakfast food too. Let your little ones help in fixing their own snacks sometimes. This can be both fun and educational. For further ideas on providing healthy snacks, see Chapters 5 and 6. ●●○○

Quantities are for two adults and two children unless otherwise stated.

Steamed savoury sponge cake (makes 8 small portions)

1½ cups flour
100 g sugar
5 medium eggs
100 g lean minced meat
  (e.g. pork or chicken)
4 small shallots, thinly
  sliced
1 tsp dark soya sauce
½ Ch sp unsaturated oil
dash of pepper

Fry the shallots in the heated oil until golden, drain and remove. Fry the minced meat in the remaining oil with the soya sauce and pepper. Beat the eggs with sugar until frothy, then add in the sifted flour gradually, stirring to form a smooth paste. Cut a ring of greaseproof paper the size of the sponge tin ring (10-inch) and place over the bottom. Pour half of the sponge mixture into the tin, and steam over boiling water and strong heat for 8 minutes. Remove the tin from the water and sprinkle half of the shallot and meat over the sponge to form a thin layer. Pour the rest of the sponge mixture on top and sprinkle the rest of the shallot and meat on top. Steam for another 8 minutes, cool, slice and serve warm or cold.

The combination of meat and sponge cake may seem strange, but once you have tried it you will find that it never fails to delight.

Portion analysis	
energy	: 204 kcals
protein	: 9 g
fat	: 6 g
fibre	: 0.8 g
cholesterol	: 149 mg

Steamed yam kuih (makes 10 portions)

400 g yam, skinned and
  diced
15 g dried prawns, washed
100 g lean pork or chicken
150 g rice pour
½ Ch sp unsaturated oil
salt to taste
3 cups water
1 Ch sp sesame seeds

Seasoning for meat:
1½ tsp light soya sauce
dash of pepper
3 cups water
½ Ch sp sesame seeds

For garnishing:
a little fried shallot
1 stalk coriander leaves

Season the meat. Mix the flour with 1 cup water. Fry the prawn and pork in heated oil, add the yam and adjust the seasoning. Add in the remaining two cups of water and simmer till the yam is soft. Add the dissolved flour and stir till thick. Transfer to a cake tin or a pie dish. Steam for about 20–30 minutes. Sprinkle the sesame seeds over and garnish with fried shallot and coriander leaves.

This version of a local favourite is low in fat yet tasty and nutritious. A good savoury choice that is different from the usual sweeter cakes.

Portion analysis	
energy	: 120 kcals
protein	: 5 g
fat	: 2 g
fibre	: 1.4 g
cholesterol	: 12 mg

Mum's cake (makes 12 portions)

100 g unsaturated margarine
⅓ cup sugar
1½ cups plain flour, sifted
3 eggs
2 Ch sp milk
2 heaped tsp baking powder

Beat up all the ingredients except the baking powder for 3 minutes. Sieve in the baking powder and beat well again. Spoon the mixture into two cake tins or bun cases and bake at 190°C for 35 minutes (for the cakes) or 20 minutes (for the buns).

This cake can be sandwiched with a little cream (make from 45 g unsaturated margarine beaten with 75 g icing sugar) but is also delicious plain. Alternatively, spread with a thin layer of fruit jam and sprinkle dessicated coconut on top.

Variation: For chocolate cake, substitute 2 Ch sp flour with 3 Ch sp cocoa powder.

Portion analysis	
energy	: 170 kcals
protein	: 3 g
fat	: 8 g
fibre	: 0.5 g
cholesterol	: 56 mg
vitamin A	: ★

Choux pastry shells (makes about 20 pieces)

120 g plain flour, sifted
60 g unsaturated margarine
4 medium eggs, beaten
150 ml milk (or water)
¼ tsp salt

Heat the milk or water with the margarine till it is just about to boil. Stir in the flour and keep stirring until the mixture forms a soft ball of dough which does not stick to the sides of the saucepan. Remove from the heat and beat in the eggs gradually. Spoon or pipe into rounds (2–3 cm) or finger shapes (5-cm long) on to a baking sheet. Bake in a preheated 180°C oven for about 15 minutes or until well risen and golden. Remove from the baking sheet, cool slightly and slit open through the middle of the shells. Once cool, use as desired with the filling of your choice.

Choux pastry as eclairs or cream puffs are favourites among children. The shells can also be used for savoury fillings, e.g. cheese and egg, or salad. These provide interesting alternatives for bread sandwiches. For novelty, make tiny shells for use on special occasions. They can be kept refrigerated in a box for a few days until needed.

Analysis per shell	
energy	: 62 kcals
protein	: 2 g
fat	: 4 g
fibre	: 0.2 g
cholesterol	: 45 mg

Golden sultana pancakes (makes about 10)

¾ cup skimmed milk
1 cup plain flour
½ tsp unsaturated oil
1 Ch sp raisins, plumbed (soaked in a little water)
1 egg, beaten
1 Ch sp sugar
1 tsp baking powder
1 Ch sp unsaturated oil for frying

Sift the baking powder with the flour, then add in the sugar. Mix the beaten egg with the milk and mix into the flour gradually to form the batter. Continue stirring gently to remove all the lumps. Add the raisins and oil and mix well. Leave to rest for an hour if time permits. Heat and brush the centre of the pan with a little oil. Pour one Chinese spoon of the batter mixture over and lightly brown on both sides until cooked through.

Serve with sliced or pureed fruit, fruit yoghurt, jam or lemon juice. The pancakes can also be eaten plain.

These pancakes freeze well and are delicious when lightly toasted. Without sugar and sultanas, they are suitable as savoury pancakes, e.g. with flaked tuna in white sauce. For children, using shaped rings or small mould pans when making these pancakes will provide more visual effects and ensure greater interest in eating them.

The skimmed milk used produces lighter pancakes and the small amount of oil makes them more tender.

Analysis per pancake	
energy	: 88 kcals
protein	: 2 g
fat	: 2 g
fibre	: 0.5 g
cholesterol	: 23 mg

Easy crepes (makes 8)

1 cup plain flour (or ½ plain, ½ wholemeal), sifted
1 cup skimmed milk, warmed
2 medium eggs, beaten
1 small orange, washed and grated for the rind (optional)
1 Ch sp unsaturated oil for coating pan

Infuse the orange rind with the warm milk. Cool it, then add in the beaten egg and beat well. Gradually mix into the flour and stir until the texture is smooth and without lumps. Let it stand for 30 minutes or refrigerate it overnight if it is to be used the next morning. Heat the pan and coat it with a little oil, pour a thin layer of batter over (using a small ladle) and slightly brown both sides of the crepe. Serve by filling each crepe with mashed fruit and sauce or savoury fillings (e.g. tuna fish in white sauce) and folding or rolling it over.

Analysis per crepe	
energy	: 100 kcals
protein	: 4 g
fat	: 3 g
fibre	: 0.5 g
cholesterol	: 57 mg

½ cup plain flour, sifted
1¼ cups rolled oats
120 g unsaturated
  margarine
45 g castor sugar
¼ tsp baking powder
pinch of bicarbonate of
  soda

Flaky oatmeal cookies
(makes about 20 small cookies)

Cream the margarine and sugar until light and fluffy. Work in all the dry ingredients gradually until a dough is formed. Roll out on a floured board* to about 0.5 cm thick and cut into rounds. Bake on a greased baking tray at 190°C for about 20 minutes or until golden. Cool on a wire rack and sprinkle with castor sugar if desired.

* Rolling in some crushed cornflakes makes the cookies deliciously crunchy.

Analysis per cookie	
energy	: 90 kcals
protein	: 1 g
fat	: 5 g
fibre	: 0.6 g
cholesterol	: 0

Carrot bran muffins
(makes about 12)

½ cup rolled oats, blended till texture is fine
1 cup bran cereal (bran flakes, cheerios or raisin bran), blended in liquidiser (makes ½ cup)
1¼ cups plain flour, sifted
1 cup skimmed milk
¾ cup carrot, grated
1 tsp grated orange rind
3 Ch sp unsaturated oil
⅓ cup brown sugar
1 medium egg, beaten (you may use only the white)
1 tsp baking powder
1 tsp bicarbonate of soda

Preheat the oven to 200°C. Grease a dozen muffin cups or use paper baking cups. Sift the flour with the baking powder, combine with the oats and cereal and mix well. Add the remaining ingredients and mix until all the dry ingredients are moistened. Fill the muffin cups to almost full and bake for 20 minutes or until the muffins are golden brown. Cool slightly and serve warm. These muffins are tasty, nutritious and suitable for a snack or breakfast.

Analysis per muffin

energy	: 169 kcals
protein	: 3 g
fat	: 6 g
fibre	: 1.6 g
cholesterol	: 19 mg

Wholemeal scones
(makes about 12 slices)

120 g wholemeal flour
120 g self-raising flour
2 heaped tsp baking powder
45 g unsaturated margarine
½ cup milk to mix
2 Ch sp raisins (optional)
3 Ch sp castor sugar

Sift the flour with the baking powder. Rub in the margarine until it resembles breadcrumbs. Add the sugar and raisins (if used), then add the milk slowly until the mixture holds together but is not sticky. Roll out on a floured board to about 1.5 cm thick and cut into rounds with a fluted cutter. Place the scones on a greased tray and brush the top with beaten egg or milk. Bake at 190°C for 15 minutes. Cool on a wire rack.

Analysis per scone

energy	: 128 kcals
protein	: 3 g
fat	: 4 g
fibre	: 1.5 g
cholesterol	: 1 mg

4 small ripe bananas,
  peeled and mashed
  with a fork
2 Ch sp milk
1½ cups plain flour and
  ½ cup wholemeal
  flour
2 heaped tsp baking
  powder
2 eggs
5 prunes, pitted
90 g unsaturated
  margarine
90 g castor sugar
1 tsp grated rind of
  orange

Banana and prune bread (makes about 12 slices)

Sift together the plain flour and baking powder. Cream the margarine and sugar in a mixer until light and fluffy. Lightly beat the eggs, add to the milk and gradually add this into the creamed margarine, beating well to combine. Add the mashed and chopped fruit and rind. Lastly, beat in the sifted flour and baking powder mixture until smooth. Pour into a lightly greased loaf tin and bake in a preheated moderate oven (180°C) for 1 hour and 10 minutes or until the bread is done (it should shrink from the sides of the tin). Cool, turn out and serve in slices.

This fragrant banana bread is always a favourite among children. The added prunes enhance its nutritive value and flavour. It is a tasty snack or breakfast treat. It is also delicious when lightly toasted.

Variation:

Banana and walnut bread

Substitute the prunes with half a cup of broken or pounded walnuts. Place a few pieces on top of the dough before baking, for decoration.

Analysis per slice	
energy	: 182 kcals
protein	: 3 g
fat	: 7 g
fibre	: 1.9 g
cholesterol	: 38 mg
vitamin A	: ★

Sandwich Ideas

Any food concoction, hot or cold, that goes between two or more slices of bread, a roll or even chapati can be termed a sandwich. This can claim to be the most international meal ever invented, open to the ingenuity of anyone who chooses to make it. It is named in honour of the fourth Earl of Sandwich, Sir John Montagu, who popularised it during the 18th century. As a result of their versatility, sandwiches rank tops among any child's list of favourite foods, especially if he is free to pile in what he likes! They are a good quick-fix meal for mothers who are faced with the prospect of another meal to prepare for the children. With the right fillings, sandwiches can be just as nutritious as any hot meal and provide good alternatives for breakfast, snacks or a light lunch. Cut them into appealing shapes and you can tempt any finicky fledgling into opening his mouth.

Mix and match—wholemeal and white bread mixed with your choice of fillings and cut into rectangles, triangles, fingers or shapes (using large cutters).

Pinwheels—one or two thin slices of bread (mixed bread for an interesting colour combination) with fillings that bind. Instead of sandwiching, roll the bread up and wrap with polythene wrap for a while to retain the shape. Unwrap and cut into round slices.

Club deluxe—three or more thin slices of bread with different fillings or combinations of fillings between each layer, the size of the mouth being the only limit! These can be cut into thin vertical slices, like *kuih lapis*.

Sandwich fillings:

Unless specified, the quantities given are enough to make into four sandwiches, using eight slices of bread. For a very young child, half a sandwich will be enough for a light afternoon snack, while a more substantial snack will require one portion.

Seafood

Cooked or tinned flaked fish can be used, e.g. sardine, tuna, mackerel, etc. If prawns are used, you may like to chop them up. Mix with some sauce and dressings, sliced vegetables or beans.

Mashed sardine, egg and beans

8 slices wholemeal bread
120 g sardines in tomato sauce
1 hard-boiled egg
2 lettuce leaves, shredded
2 Ch sp baked beans (canned in tomato sauce)
1 Ch sp chopped onion
squeeze of lemon or lime juice

Mash the sardines and egg and mix with the beans, onions and lemon juice. Spread it over a layer of shredded lettuce between two slices of toast or bread. Shape or roll if desired.

Portion analysis	
energy	: 195 kcals
protein	: 13 g
fat	: 4 g
fibre	: 5.3 g
cholesterol	: 86 mg
calcium	: ★
iron	: ★
niacin	: ★

Tuna with coleslaw

8 slices wholemeal bread
½ small can tuna (packed in water), drained
3 Ch sp shredded coleslaw (see recipe on page 212)

Flake or mash the drained tuna, and mix with the coleslaw. Spread between bread or roll.

Alternatively, mix the tuna with finely chopped ¼ onion and ½ apple. Add a squeeze of lemon juice and dressing of your choice.

Portion analysis	
energy	: 156 kcals
protein	: 10 g
fat	: 1 g
fibre	: 4.5 g
cholesterol	: 9 mg

Cheese

Grated cheese, or a mixture of cottage and cream cheese can be used, together with fish, egg or meat, or mixed with some vegetables or fruit.

---

8 slices wholemeal
   bread meat
½ cup finely shredded
   roast or boiled
   chicken meat
3 Ch sp cottage cheese,
   pressed through a sieve
   or 3 Ch sp finely grated
   cheddar cheese
2 Ch sp shredded
   cucumber
dash of salt

Cottage cheese and chicken

Mix all the ingredients and spread between bread. You can roll this sandwich into a pinwheel if you like. Slice to serve.

Portion analysis	
energy	: 189 kcals
protein	: 15 g
fat	: 3 g
fibre	: 4.2 g
cholesterol	: 30 mg

---

8 slices wholemeal bread
½ cup home-style
   yoghurt cheese
   (see recipe on page
   228) or 3 Ch sp cottage
   cheese
1 apple, thinly sliced
1 Ch sp chopped kiwi fruit
½ small banana, chopped

Cheese and fruit

Mix all ingredients together and spread over the bread.

Portion analysis	
energy	: 155 kcals
protein	: 7 g
fat	: 1 g
fibre	: 5.2 g
cholesterol	: 2 mg
vitamin C	: ★

Liver

Liver paté or paste is an excellent sandwich filling. It goes well with fruit, cheese and shredded vegetables.

Liver/tomato

Mix all ingredients together and spread over the bread.

8 slices wholemeal bread
80 g liver paté (see recipe on page 192)
1 Ch sp chopped celery
1 Ch sp chopped tomato

Portion analysis	
energy	: 147 kcals
protein	: 7 g
fat	: 2 g
fibre	: 4.3 g
cholesterol	: 64 mg
iron	: ★
vitamin A	: ★ ★ ★

Egg

Eggs seem to be everywhere as far as sandwiches go. You can use them in combination with almost anything. The eggs may be boiled, scrambled or fried omelette style.

Egg and cheese

Mash the boiled eggs together with the cheese. Use a little mayonnaise or yoghurt to bind the mixture together. Spread on the bread. Alternatively, you beat the eggs and fry with tomato, ham and some grated cheese. This can be scrambled or done as an omelette.

8 slices wholemeal bread
2 boiled eggs
2 Ch sp grated cheese
1 Ch sp plain yoghurt
dash of salt and pepper to taste

Portion analysis	
energy	: 177 kcals
protein	: 9 g
fat	: 5 g
fibre	: 4.2 g
cholesterol	: 115 mg

Meat

Ham, chicken, beef or pork are the usual fare. Slice the meats thinly and cover with pickles or a sauce to moisten them. Some sliced or shredded vegetable and fruit can be used too.

Curry chicken

Mild curries blend beautifully with bread or rolls. Shred ½ cup curried chicken meat (see recipe on page 196), moisten with a little curry sauce and spread on to the bread with vegetables such as cucumber, tomato or lettuce.

| 8 slices wholemeal bread |
| 100 g thinly sliced roast pork or ham |
| 3 Ch sp apple sauce |
| 1 Ch sp chopped pineapple |
| 2 tsp unsaturated margarine, spread thinly on the bread |

Pork or ham with apple sauce

Place the meat slices over the bread, spread the sauce and fruit over and cover with another meat slice.

Portion analysis	
energy	: 184 kcals
protein	: 9 g
fat	: 4 g
fibre	: 4.7 g
cholesterol	: 8 mg
vitamin B$_1$	: ★

Sweet fillings

Jam, *kaya*, peanut butter with marmalade, etc, are but a few possibilities. With added fruit (e.g. bananas and prunes) or nuts, these fillings are acceptable occasional snacks and make for added variety.

| 1 slice of wholemeal or raisin bread |
| 1 banana, sliced in half |
| ½ tsp marmalade |

Banana wheel (for one person)

Spread a little marmalade on the bread. Place the banana on the bread and roll it up.

Variation:

Peanut butter and marmalade wheels

Spread a thin layer of smooth peanut butter then a layer of marmalade over a slice of bread (remove the crust). Roll it up tightly into mini pinwheel rolls (with the help of polythene wrap if necessary) and slice into rings.

Portion analysis	
energy	: 117 kcals
protein	: 2 g
fat	: 0.3 g
fibre	: 3.8 g
cholesterol	: 0
vitamin C	: ★

Toast topping treats

Wheaty sesame toast

4 slices wholemeal bread

20 g unsaturated margarine

1 tsp sesame seeds

2 cloves garlic, skinned and pounded

dash of mixed dried herbs

Mix the sesame seeds and the garlic paste with the margarine until well blended. Spread thinly over bread and toast in a moderate oven 160°C for 20 minutes or until golden brown. Cut into fingers and serve warm as a snack or with soup.

Portion analysis	
energy	: 105 kcals
protein	: 2 g
fat	: 5 g
fibre	: 2.3 g
cholesterol	: 0 mg

Cheesy bean toasties

4 slices wholemeal bread

8 Ch sp baked beans (canned in tomato sauce)

1 Ch sp grated cheddar cheese

dash of mixed dried herbs (optional)

Lightly toast the bread, spread the baked beans over one side and sprinkle mixed herbs, if used. Cover this with grated cheese and return to the oven toaster or grill. Remove the toast when the cheese melts and is slightly brown. Take care not to over-brown the underside of the bread. Cut into triangles or fingers annd serve immediately.

Portion analysis	
energy	: 102 kcals
protein	: 5 g
fat	: 1 g
fibre	: 5.4 g
cholesterol	: 2 mg

Quick pizza toast

4 slices thick wholemeal bread (or pita bread or wholemeal rolls)

2 Ch sp tomato paste

1 Ch sp thinly sliced green pepper

2 Ch sp thinly sliced button mushrooms

1 large tomato, skinned and sliced

2 Ch sp grated cheese (cheddar or mozzarella)

dash of pepper and mixed herbs

Spread the tomato paste on one side of the bread. Arrange the vegetables on to the paste and cover all this with the cheese and condiments. Grill until the cheese melts, taking care not to burn the bread. Cut into quarters or bite-sized pieces for younger children.

Portion analysis	
energy	: 100 kcals
protein	: 5 g
fat	: 2 g
fibre	: 2.6 g
cholesterol	: 4 mg
vitamin A	: ★
vitamin C	: ★★

Beef with avocado

4 slices wholemeal
    bread, toasted
100 g thinly sliced roast
    beef
½ avocado, thinly sliced
1 large tomato, thinly
    sliced
2 tsp unsaturated
    margarine, spread
    thinly on the bread

Place the beef and avocado slices over the bread and place the tomato slices over them.

Portion analysis	
energy	: 150 kcals
protein	: 9 g
fat	: 6 g
fibre	: 2.8 g
cholesterol	: 18 mg

Orange and raisin French toast

2 medium eggs, beaten
1 orange, squeeze for the
    juice and grate rind
1 tsp raisins, plumbed
    and chopped
4 slices wholemeal bread
1 tsp honey

Mix the orange juice, rind, honey and chopped raisins. Stir into the beaten egg to blend well. Soak each slice of bread in the orange mixture until the liquid is absorbed into the bread. Toast on greased trays, until both sides are golden and crisp. Alternatively, fry in a little oil until both sides are nicely browned. Serve hot, cut into fingers or shapes for the children.

Portion analysis	
energy	: 118 kcals
protein	: 5 g
fat	: 3 g
fibre	: 2.2 g
cholesterol	: 112 mg

Liver and orange (for open sandwich)

4 slices wholemeal
    bread, toasted
60 g liver paté (see
    recipe on page 192)
1 orange, skinned and
    thinly sliced

Spread the paté over toast or bread, top with thin orange slices, and serve as an open sandwich.

Portion analysis	
energy	: 76 kcals
protein	: 4 g
fat	: 1 g
fibre	: 2.1 g
cholesterol	: 48 mg
vitamin A	: ★★★

Cheese and chicken fingers

4 slices wholemeal bread
2 Ch sp plain yoghurt
½ cup minced or
    shredded cooked
    chicken meat
2 Ch sp grated cheese
dash of mixed herbs

Mix the chicken with the yoghurt and herbs. Spread over the wholemeal bread and sprinkle the grated cheese on top. Grill until the cheese melts and is bubbling. Do not over-brown or burn the toast. Cut into fingers and serve.

Portion analysis	
energy	: 145 kcals
protein	: 13 g
fat	: 4 g
fibre	: 2.1 g
cholesterol	: 33 mg

Cooling Down

Being in the tropics, we tend to need and consume more liquids. Physically active children, especially, need to replenish their extra fluid losses due to perspiration. Water is undoubtedly the best thirst quencher. Nourishing drinks, however, can be useful ways of disguising and getting nutrients into your stubborn little darling's body. They are definitely better alternatives than most of the sugar-filled commercial soft drinks that are alarmingly carving out a large market among our young. With a blender, you can whip up a tasty self-creation of a milk- or fruit-based drink. Nothing tastes better than a home-made ice cream or lolly on a hot sunny afternoon. Serve a slice or two local style, with bread, and you will have a lovely, substantial snack. ●●○●

Quantities are for two adults and two children unless otherwise stated.

Mixed fruit juices

water melon/tomato juice

starfruit/apple juice

orange/carrot juice

pineapple/starfruit juice

If you have a juicer, these are just a few of the fruit juice concoctions that can be enjoyed by the whole family. Otherwise, most drink stalls in hawker centres or shops offer them. Choose these rather than the commercial soft drinks, and request that no sugar or syrup be added.

With just a blender, you can easily make mango, papaya, watermelon, or tomato juice. Oranges can be squeezed manually on a citrus squeezer.

½ cup fresh fruit puree, e.g. papaya

1 cup skimmed milk

2–3 crushed ice cubes

Milky way
(makes about 2 cups)

Puree the flesh of local fresh fruit with a little water or milk in the blender. If dried fruit (e.g. prunes) is used, soak and simmer in just sufficient water, adding a dash of sugar if using the unsweetened variety, until it turns pulpy. Cool it. Blend the fruit with the cold milk and crushed ice and serve immediately.

This is a refreshing and nutritious after-activity drink or weekend breakfast treat.

Analysis per cup	
energy	: 73 kcals
protein	: 4 g
fat	: 0.2 g
fibre	: 1.7 g
cholesterol	: 2 mg
calcium	: ★
vitamin A	: ★
vitamin C	: ★ ★ ★

---

1 cup plain yoghurt

3 cups chilled water

dash of sugar (optional)

pinch of ground nutmeg (optional)

Lassi
(makes about 4 cups)

Blend the yoghurt until it is smooth and gradually add in the chilled water to blend until the desired consistency. Add a pinch of sugar and/or nutmeg if desired.

Analysis per cup	
energy	: 58 kcals
protein	: 5 g
fat	: 1 g
fibre	: 0
cholesterol	: 7 mg
calcium	: ★

Fruity bean curd ice cream (makes about 10 scoops)

200 g silken bean curd
1⅓ cups pureed fruit
3 Ch sp sugar
1 cup skimmed milk
1 tsp lemon juice

Warm the milk with the sugar, stir to mix well but do not boil. Blend with the bean curd, pureed fruit and lemon juice until smooth and creamy. Freeze as for other ice creams.

The versatile usage of bean curd has gained wide recognition. Incorporating it into ice cream has solved many a problem for vegetarian ice cream lovers. By using skimmed milk and omitting egg, you have a delicious low fat and low cholesterol dessert for the health-conscious.

Variation:
For strict vegetarians, substitute the milk with soyabean milk.

Analysis per scoop

energy	: 68 kcals
protein	: 3 g
fat	: 1 g
fibre	: 0.5 g
cholesterol	: 0.5 mg
vitamin A	: ★
vitamin C	: ★★

Sugar cane/water chestnut juice (makes 8 cups)

5 pieces of 20-cm long sugar cane
10–15 water chestnuts
rock sugar to taste
8 cups water

Wash and clean the water chestnuts, and cut in half with the skin intact. Crush slightly if desired. Clean the sugar cane and pound slightly with a pestle. Boil and simmer together in the water for one hour. Add a little rock sugar if you like the drink to be sweeter.

This is a refreshing drink that can be served either hot or cold. The Chinese believe it to be especially good on hot, humid days and for those who have sore throats and fevers.

Yoghurt sparkle (makes 2 cups)

½ cup plain yoghurt
½ cup fresh orange juice
½ cup fruit puree, e.g. mango
2–3 crushed ice cubes

Blend all the ingredients together and add extra juice or milk if desired. Use fruit juice ice cubes (if previously prepared) for an extra touch.

Analysis per cup

energy	: 130 kcals
protein	: 5 g
fat	: 1 g
fibre	: 1.1 g
cholesterol	: 7 mg
calcium	: ★
vitamin A	: ★★★
vitamin C	: ★★★

Assorted ice kacang

1 cup cooked red
  beans
½ cup sweetcorn
  (whole kernel, canned
  or frozen)
12 *attap* seeds*
½ cup chopped *chin
  chow* (black seaweed
  jelly)
¼ cup evaporated milk
4 Ch sp blackcurrant
  syrup
4 cups shaved ice

If you have an ice shaver, home-made *ice kacang* will offer a delightful thirst quencher. You can involve your little ones in mixing their own concoctions. Apportion the ingredients in dessert bowls or plates and pile finely shaved ice over them. Next, pour a little blackcurrant syrup and some evaporated milk over the top of the ice shavings. The snow mountain will now be ready for the "treasure" digging!

*These are the seeds of the nipah palm.

Portion analysis	
energy	: 122 kcals
protein	: 4 g
fat	: 1 g
fibre	: 3.4 g
cholesterol	: 5 mg
vitamin C	: ★★★

Fresh fruit ice cream (makes about 10 scoops)

1 cup flesh of ripe
  seasonal fruit
  (e.g. mango)
3 Ch sp sugar
1 cup milk
1 medium egg
½ tsp gelatine (optional)
1 tsp lemon juice
rind of 1 lemon

Blend the fruit in a blender. Warm the milk with the sugar and stir in the beaten egg. Continue to heat over a low fire (do not boil) until the milk is slightly thickened. You may need to strain the mixture if some of the egg curdles. Add the lemon juice, milk and dissolved gelatine (if used) to the fruit puree and mix well. Pour into an ice cream maker to beat and then freeze the mixture. Alternatively, pour the mixture into a shallow container, cover with cling film or a lid and freeze. When half set, remove and stir or beat (repeat this routine one more time if time permits) to reduce crystal formation. Return to the freezer. A wide variety of local fruit make wonderful and delicious ice creams, e.g. banana, pineapple, mango, durian, etc. Serve with fresh chopped fruit or as an ice cream sandwich with wholemeal bread. Ice cream puffs (with choux pastry shells, see recipe on page 243) are equally tasty and fun for the children.

Analysis per scoop	
energy	: 65 kcals
protein	: 1 g
fat	: 1 g
fibre	: 0.4 g
cholesterol	: 26 mg
vitamin A	: ★
vitamin C	: ★

Soyabean milk
(makes about 2 litres)

1 cup dry soyabeans

8 cups water

120 g rock sugar (omit for plain or savoury)

3–4 pieces pandan leaves

2–3 drops unsaturated oil (optional)

Soak the soyabean for half a day or overnight. Blend the beans in 4 cups of fresh water, strain and squeeze through fine muslin. Blend the pulp again with the remaining 4 cups of water and strain again. Boil the collected milk with rock sugar and pandan leaves over low heat. Add a few drops of oil and stir occasionally to prevent sticking and frothing. Strain again after boiling if you want to ensure smoothness (but unnecessary if well strained before boiling). Serve hot or chilled.

It is surprisingly easy to make this refreshing and nutritious drink at home. Soyabean milk is a good source of protein and other nutrients and is most suitable for those who are sensitive to milk. It cannot, however, replace milk in terms of calcium supply, especially that which is commercially packaged or which you buy from the drink stalls, because it is too dilute. Hot soyabean milk with *yu char kuay* is an all-time favourite. Well chilled, it is an unbeatable thirst quencher on hot, humid days.

The strained soya pulp can be kept frozen (if not to be used immediately) and used for making patties (see recipe on page 201) later. Make this versatile drink often to benefit your whole family!

Analysis per cup

energy	: 145 kcals
protein	: 7 g
fat	: 4 g
fibre	: 0.9 g
cholesterol	: 0
iron	: ★

Juicy bean curd shake
(makes 3 cups)

1 cup silken bean curd, crumbled and chilled

1½ cups fruit juice, e.g. orange

2–3 plain or fruit juice ice cubes

Blend the crumbled bean curd with the rest of the ingredients until smooth. Serve immediately.

Analysis per cup

energy	: 115 kcals
protein	: 7 g
fat	: 3 g
fibre	: 0.3 g
cholesterol	: 0
iron	: ★
vitamin C	: ★★★

Yoghurt fruit freeze
(makes about 10 scoops)

1 cup plain yoghurt

1 cup pureed fruit, e.g. papaya

½ cup diced fruit

2 tsp gelatine

2 Ch sp sugar

1 Ch sp lemon juice

Dissolve the gelatine and sugar in a little water and lemon juice. Mix the yoghurt with the gelatine mixture and refrigerate in a shallow dish until slightly thickened (30-45 minutes). Remove from the refrigerator and whip with the pureed fruit in a blender. Add the diced fruit and pour into a container for freezing (2-3 hours). Let the mixture stand for 5-10 minutes at room temperature before serving. Alternatively, use an ice cream maker, if available, or freeze the mixture in popsicle or lolly sticks for the children.

Frozen yoghurt has gained popularity recently but is not widely available yet. Make this refreshing and nourishing family dessert at home to familiarise your children with yoghurt if they are not used to it. Any ripe fruit or fruit combination can be used.

Analysis per scoop	
energy	: 52 kcals
protein	: 2 g
fat	: 0.4 g
fibre	: 0.7 g
cholesterol	: 1 mg
vitamin C	: ★ ★ ★

Lemon barley drink
(makes 6 cups)

½ cup barley

juice of ½ lemon or 2 small limes

rock sugar to taste or 10 pieces of preserved sugared winter melon

Wash and boil the barley in 6 cups of water together with the sugar or winter melon pieces for 20 minutes. For a thicker drink, simmer for 30-45 minutes. Add in the lemon or lime juice just before serving if desired.

Barley is thought to be beneficial for various ailments according to Asian beliefs, but it is used most commonly for thirst quenching.

South-sea **sorbets** (water ices)

½ cup papaya (or
   pineapple, banana,
   etc)
1½ cups fresh orange
   juice
2 Ch sp sugar
½ cup water
2 egg whites (optional)

South-sea sorbets (water ices)
(makes about 10 scoops)

Boil the sugar with the water briefly to make the syrup (add orange peel if you like the extra flavour), then cool. Puree the fruit together with the orange juice and mix in the syrup. Freeze the mixture for 2–3 hours until it is half frozen. Shortly before it is time to re-whip the mixture, whisk the egg whites till soft peaks form.

Remove the semi-frozen sorbet from the freezer and whip it. Fold the whisked egg white into the sorbet and freeze again. If used, the egg whites will make the sorbets lighter and finer. Serve when the sorbet is softly frozen. If the sorbets are frozen hard, thaw slightly in the refrigerator, then scrape into dessert cups to serve.

Sorbets or water ices (fruit juice, sugar and water) were actually made by the Chinese as early as the 8th century, well before the time of Marco Polo who introduced them to Italy and the rest of Europe. Natural fruit sorbets are superior home substitutes for children who love commercial ice sticks which are usually high on colouring and flavouring and little else.

Analysis per scoop	
energy	: 44 kcals
protein	: 0.6 g
fat	: 0
fibre	: 0.3 g
cholesterol	: 0
vitamin C	: ★★★

Red bean lollies
(makes about 10 lollies)

Use 1½ cups cooked red bean pureed into a thick paste, in place of the fruit and lemon juice and rind in the previous recipe. If the presence of whole beans is desired, blend only 1 cup of the cooked beans. Sieve the pureed beans through a fine strainer to remove the grit. Mix with milk and egg, etc, as for the previous recipe, and finally add in the ½ cup of the remaining unblended red beans. You can freeze this ice cream in a tub or as lollies. Red bean lollies are a favourite among local children. Sweetcorn and attap seeds are other possible delicious variations.

Analysis per lolly	
energy	: 93 kcals
protein	: 3 g
fat	: 1 g
fibre	: 1.4 g
cholesterol	: 26 mg

References

We have not listed every scientific reference consulted during the writing of this book, but the following list comprises our key references and includes books which the reader might find useful as sources of further information.

Nutrition Basics

Candlish, J.K., Gourley, L. and Lee H.P. (1987), Dietary Fibre and its Components in some Southeast Asian Foods. *Asia Pacific Comm. Biochem.* 1:13-17.

Food and Agricultural Organization/US Department of Health, Education and Welfare (1972), Food Composition Table for use in East Asia. Rome: FAO.

Food Composition Table, (1985), 8th ed. People's Health and Hygiene Publication, Beijing, People's Republic of China.

Goodhart, R.S. and Shils, M.E. (1980), *Modern Nutrition in Health and disease.* Lea & Febiger, Philadelphia.

Health Promotion Board, Singapore (2007), Recommended Daily Dietary Allowances for Normal Healthy Persons in Singapore

McCance R. E., Widdowson E.M., Holland B. and Great Britain Ministry of Agriculture, Fisheries and Food (MAFF) (1991), *The Composition of Foods.* The Royal Society of Chemistry and MAFF.

Pennington, J.A.T. and Church, H.N. (1985), Bowes and Church's *Food Values of Portions Commonly Used,* 14th ed. J.P. Lippincott Company, Philadelphia.

Siong, T.E. (1985), Nutrient Composition of Malaysian Foods: A preliminary table (first update). *ASEAN Sub-committee on Protein,* Kuala Lumpur.

Suitor, C.W. and Crawley, M.F. (1984), *Principles and Application in Health Promotion,* 2nd ed. J.P. Lippincott Co., Philadelphia.

US Food and Nutrition Board (1980), Recommended Dietary Allowances. National Academy of Sciences, Washington.

Nutrition in Pregnancy

International Food Information Council. "Everything you need to know about caffeine". July 1998.

Malhotra, A. and Sawers, R.S. (1986), Dietary Supplementation in Pregnancy. *Brit. Med. J.,* 293:465-466.

Owen, A.Y. and Frankle, R.T. (1986), Chapter 9: Maternal Nutrition, in *Nutrition in the Community,* 2nd ed. Times Mirror/ Mosby, St Louis.

Stoppard, M. (1985), *Pregnancy and Birth Book.* Dorling Kindersley Ltd., London.

Suter, C.B. and Ott, D.B. (1984), Maternal and Infant Recommendations: A review. *J. Amer. Diet. Assoc.,* 84:572-573.

Department of Health, UK (2009). Vitamin D, an essential nutrient for all. Crown Copyright, London.

Health Promotion Board, Singapore (2013). Online article: "Pregnancy and diet", 16th May 2013.

Milk—Baby's First Food

Chee, S. (1989), Survey of the Success in Breastfeeding, *The Professional Nurse,* 16(4):19-20.

Chong YS, Liang Y, Tan T, Gazzard G, Stone RA, Saw SM. (2005), Association between breastfeeding and likelihood of myopia in children. J. Amer. Assoc., 293 (2): 3001-3002.

Chung, S.Y. (1979), Breastfeeding behaviour in women attending a Maternal and Child Health Clinic in Singapore, M.Sc. thesis. Dept. of Social Medicine and Public Health, National University of Singapore.

Counsilman, J.J. and Viegas, O. (1985), A Review of Recent Patterns of Infant Feeding in Singapore. *Trop. Biomed.,* 2:161-165.

Cunningham, A.S. (1979), Morbidity in Breastfed and Artificially Fed Infants, II. *J. Paediatr.,* 95:685.

Dodge, J.A. (1983), ed., *Topics in Paediatric Nutrition.* Pitman, London.

Food Safety Authority of Ireland (1999). Recommendations for a national infant feeding policy.

Helsing, E. and Savage Icing, F. (1983), *Breastfeeding in Practice: A Manual for Health Workers,* 2nd ed. Oxford Medical Publications, Oxford.

Krame MS and Kakuma R. (2002). The optimal duration of exclusive breastfeeding: a systematic review. Cochrane Library.

Lonnerdal, B. (1986), Effects of Maternal Dietary Intake on Human Milk Composition. *J, Nutr,* 116:499-513.

Millis, J. (1955) Some Aspects of Breastfeeding in Singapore. *Med. J. Malaya,* 10:157-161.

Minchin, M. (1985) *Breastfeeding Matters.* Alma Publications and George Allen & Unwin, Sydney.

Ritchley, S.J. and Taper, L.J. (1983), *Maternal and Child Nutrition.* Harper and Row, New York.

Savage King, F (1985), *Helping Mothers to Breastfeed.* African Medical and Research Foundation, Nairobi.

Singapore Breastfeeding Mothers' Group (1988), *Practical Hints on Breastfeeding,* 2nd revised ed., Singapore.

Worthington-Roberts, B.S., Vermeersch, J. and Williams, S.R. (1981), *Nutrition in Pregnancy and Lactation,* 2nd ed. C.V. Mosby Company, St. Louis.

Yong, A. (1986) Physical, Health, Behavioural, Environments and Dietary Influences on Breastfeeding Behaviour, B.Sc. Thesis. National University of Singapore, Singapore.

Weaning

Cameron, M. and Hofvander, Y. (1983), *Manual on Feeding Infants and Young Children.* Oxford University Press, Oxford.

McLaren, D.S. (1982) ed., *Textbook of Paediatric Nutrition.* Churchill Livingstone, Edinburgh.

Satter, E. (1984), Developmental Guidelines for Feeding Infants and Young Children. *Food and Nutrition News,* 56(4).

Turkewitz, D. and Bastian, C. (1986), Infant and Child Nutrition: Controversies and Recommendations. *Postgraduate Medicine,* 79(2):151-164

Feeding Your Toddler and Pre-schooler

McWilliams, M. (1980), *Nutrition for the Growing Years,* 3rd ed. John Wiley and Sons, New York.

Somogyi, J.C. and Haenzel, H. (1982), eds., *Nutrition in Early Childhood and its Effects in Later Life.* Karger, Basel.

Food and the School-going Child

Neumann, C.G. (1977), Obesity in the Preschool and School-age Child. *Pediatric Clinic of North America,* 24(1):117-122.

Pipes, P.L. (1985), *Nutrition in Infancy and Childhood,* 3rd ed. Times Mirror/Mosby College Publications, St. Louis.

Taitz, L.S. (1983), *The Obese Child.* Blackwell Scientific Publications, Oxford.

Diet in Special Circumstances

Cant, A.J. (1985), Food Allergy in Childhood. *Hum. Nutr. Appl. Nutr.,* 39A:277-293.

Francis, D.E.M. (1987), *Diets for Sick Children.* Blackwell Scientific Publications, Oxford.

Goldman, A.S. and Douglas, C.H. (1977), Clinical Aspects of food Sensitivity: Diagnosis and Management of Cow's Mik Sensitivity. *Pediatric Clinic of North America,* 24(1):133-139.

Hausman, P. (1987), *The Right Dose - How to Take Vitamins and Minerals Safely.* The Rochale Press, Emmaus, Pennsylvania.

MacFarlane, J.A. (1980), *Child Health* (Asian Edition Pocket Consultant). Grant McIntyre, London.

Wong, H.B. (1980), *Care for Your Child.* People's Association and Singapore Paediatric Society, Singapore.

Wood, C:B.S. (1986), How Common is Food Allergy? *Acta Paediatr. Scand. Suppl.* 323:76-83.

Traditional Food Beliefs and Vegetarianism

A Collection of Traditional Dietary Therapies, (1983), People's Health and Hygiene Publication, Beijing, People's Republic of China.

Elliot, R. (1986), *The Vegetarian Mother and Baby Book.* Pantheon Books, New York.

Koo, L.C. (1982), *Nourishment of Life: Health in Chinese Society.* The Commercial Press Ltd., Hong Kong.

Laderman, C. (1984), Food Ideology and Eating Behaviour: Contributions from Malay Studies. *Soc. Sci. Med.* 19(5):547-559.

Ling, S. (1975), Diet, Growth and Cultural Food Habits in Chinese American Infants. *Amer. J. Chinese Med.* 3(2):125-132.

Ling, Y.W. (1976), Theoretical Foundation of Chinese Medicine: a Modern Interpretation. *Amer. J. Chinese Med.* 4(4):355-372.

Manderson, L. (1984), "These are Modern Times": Infant Feeding Practice in Peninsular Malaysia. *Soc. Sci. Med* 18(1):47-57.

Medicinal Porridge in Traditional Therapy, (1983), People's Health and Hygiene Publication, Beijing, People's Republic of China.

Sonnenberg, M.A., Zolber, K. and Register, U.D. (1981), *The Vegetarian Diet – Food for Us All.* American Dietetic Association, Chicago.

Wu, D.H. (1979), *Traditional Concepts of Food and Medicine in Singapore.* Occasional paper No. 5, Institute of Southeast Asian Studies, Singapore.

Index to Recipes

Index